ISBN 978-1-331-99391-9
PIBN 10264624

English
Français
Deutsche
Italiano
Español
Português

www.forgottenbooks.com

Mythology Photography **Fiction**
Fishing Christianity **Art** Cooking
Essays Buddhism Freemasonry
Medicine **Biology** Music **Ancient**
Egypt Evolution Carpentry Physics
Dance Geology **Mathematics** Fitness
Shakespeare **Folklore** Yoga Marketing
Confidence Immortality Biographies
Poetry **Psychology** Witchcraft
Electronics Chemistry History **Law**
Accounting **Philosophy** Anthropology
Alchemy Drama Quantum Mechanics
Atheism Sexual Health **Ancient History**
Entrepreneurship Languages Sport
Paleontology Needlework Islam
Metaphysics Investment Archaeology
Parenting Statistics Criminology
Motivational

TO

THE RIGHT HONOURABLE

𝔐𝔞𝔯𝔶,

COUNTESS HARCOURT,

WHOSE TASTE AND BENEVOLENCE

HAS

EMBELLISHED AND BENEFITED

𝔐𝔞𝔩𝔳𝔢𝔯𝔫,

AND UNDER WHOSE PATRONAGE AND ASSISTANCE

THE AUTHOR WAS ENCOURAGED TO PROCEED
IN ITS HISTORY,

𝔗𝔥𝔦𝔰 𝔅𝔬𝔬𝔨

IS BY PERMISSION DEDICATED,

BY HER MOST OBEDIENT AND OBLIGED SERVANT,

J. CHAMBERS.

PATRONS OF THE WORK.

Large Paper Copies.

HIS ROYAL HIGHNESS THE DUKE OF GLOUCESTER

HER ROYAL HIGHNESS THE DUCHESS OF GLOUCESTER

HER ROYAL HIGHNESS THE PRINCESS AUGUSTA

HER ROYAL HIGHNESS THE PRINCESS CHARLOTTE OF WALES

HIS SERENE HIGHNESS LEOPOLD GEORGE CHRISTIAN FREDERICK, DUKE OF SAXONY, PRINCE OF SAXE COBOURG SAALFELD.

The Rt. Hon. Gen. Earl Harcourt

The Right Hon. the Countess Harcourt

The Right Hon. Baroness Lyttelton

The Rt. Hon. Earl Bathurst

The Right Hon. the Countess Bathurst

The Rt. Hon. Lord Beauchamp

The Right Hon. the Countess Beauchamp

The Right Hon. the Countess Effingham

The Hon. Mrs. E. Yorke

The Hon. Mrs. T. Yorke

The Very Rev. the Dean of Worcester

The Rev. James Meakin, Prebendary of Worcester

The Rev. Dr. Collinson, ditto

The Rev. J. F. S. St. John, do.

The Rev. R. Kilvert, ditto

The Rev. Charles Jenkinson, ditto

The Rev. W. Stillingfleet, do.

Lady Smith

Sir Edward Donny, Bart.

Sir Roger Gresley, Bart.

Sir Christ. Robinson, Knt.

Edwd. Foley, Esq. Stoke Park

Dr. Wall, Oxford

Dr. Wilson Philip

Dr. Woodyatt

Dr. Prattenton, Bewdley

Rev. Richard Grape

Rev. Thos. Bedford

Henry Clifton, Esq.

Samuel Crane, Esq.

James Shuttleworth, Esq.

Mrs. Tighe, Malvern

Rev. H. B. Domvile, Leigh

Col. Newport, Hanley Court

Richard Griffiths, Esq. Thorngrove

Mrs. Griffiths, Barton Court

Rev. F. Ford

Rev. H. Card, Malvern

Capt. Horton, Powick

M. Benson, Esq.

Major Bund, Wick

John Phillips, Esq. Hanbury Hall

John Richards, Esq.

Richard Hurd, Esq.

Wm. Gordon, Esq.

P. Bunny, Esq. Well-house

W. Tyndall, Esq.

——— Taylor, Esq.

Rev. W. Tilt

Wm. Wall, Esq.

Edward Barrett, Esq. Hope End

—— Lewis, Esq. Hanley

A. Lechmere, Esq.

Rev. J. R. Ingram

Wm. Sandford, Esq.

E. Isaac, Esq.

Rev. John Pierce Haekin, Coddington Parsonage, Ledbury

Rev. S. D. Pechell

A. Edge, Esq. Essex-street, Strand

E. Spilsbury, Esq.

Mr. Downes, Malvern.

Small Paper Copies.

Mrs. Fernyhough

Rev. Digby Smith

—— Maccabe, Esq.

John Sayer, Esq.

Rev. Thos. Price

G. Lawson, Esq.

Rev. Wm. Morgan

John Clifton, Esq.

Henry Wakeman

Wm. Carey, Esq.

Rev. W. Stafford

Rev. T. H. Shirley

Mr. W. Williams

Rev. S. Sheen

Mr. George Hill, Attorney

A. B.

Messrs. Flight Barr and Barr

Mr. James Ross

The Kempsey Library

Longman and Co. 25 copies

Mawman, 12 ditto.

✱ For the motto attached to the title, I am indebted to Dr. Woodyatt, of Worcester, who being introduced to Mr. Burke, thought proper to mention something in reference to the sublime and beautiful, and pointing to the Herefordshire beacon, asked his opinion of it, which Mr. Burke gave as we have stated, stretching out his hands at the same time to exemplify their shape. This took place at the Rev. James Birt's, M. A. Canon Residentary of Hereford Cathedral, Master of St. Catherine's Hospital, in Ledbury, and Vicar of Lydney, county of Gloucester, under the mulberry tree in his garden, in the year 1800—the year before Mr. Birt died.

MALVERN.

CHAPTER I.

Its Etymology, Geography, and Ancient State.

GREAT MALVERN,

In the county of Worcester, is situate in the lower division of the hundred of Pershore, and deanery of Powick, bounded on the east by Hanley Castle, on the west by Mathon, in Worcestershire, and Caldwall, in Herefordshire, on the south by little Malvern, and on the north by Leigh.

The village of Great Malvern is most delightfully situated on the eastern declivity of the hill, distant, 8 miles from Worcester, 22 from Cheltenham, 120 from London, 8 from Ledbury, and 9 from Upton.

It consists of about 50 houses, chiefly neat buildings, to which are attached gardens and plantations of fruit, trees, shrubs, and evergreens. Here the

B

aspect of the hill is particularly striking, its bold ascent and huge rocks, that rise through the surface, have certainly a grand effect. The route from Worcester to Malvern, lies through the villages of Powick and Newland.

The name of Malvern is probably derived from the British word *Moel* signifying bald, and *Wern* alders, importing a bald hill, with alders at the bottom, or rather, from Moel, which, in British, signifies a mountain.

Malvern is most frequented by visitors from Cheltenham, and other contiguous places, few of whom remain long: notwithstanding a residence at this salubrious spot is so much more salutary to the invalid's recovery than the less pure air of a more crouded atmosphere.

Before the conquest, Malvern was a wilderness thick set with trees, in the midst of which, some monks who aspired to greater perfection, retired from the priory of Worcester, and became hermits. This enthusiasm spread so fast, that their number soon increased to 300, when forming themselves into a society, they agreed to live according to the order of St. Benedict, and elected Alwin, one of their countrymen, to be superior. Thus was this monastery founded in the 18th year of William the Conqueror, in the year 1083, with the consent and approbation of St. Wolstan, Bishop of Worcester. It was dedicated to the Virgin Mary, and some say to St. Michael. In the registry of Godffrey Giffard, who was elected Bishop 1268, (f 157 a) is an account of the foundation of the priory.

In the additions to Dugdale's Monasticon, is an extract from the pleas taken before the King at York, in the Michaelmas Term, 11 Ed. II. rot. 28; wherein the prior says, that some time before the conquest, there was a congregation of hermits at Malvern; that soon after, the abbot of Westminster, with consent of Urso d'Abitot, placed there a prior and monks, and gave them the manors of Newland, Wortesfeld, and Poiwyk: Osbert Fitzpontz gave them the manor of Longeneye: Guy Fitz Holgod gave them 2 hides of land, and Roger de Chaundos the town of Hatfeld, which donation Henry I, son of William the Conqueror, confirmed, and gave them likewise 10l. worth of land, with its appurtenances, in Badenhale, Malverne, Northwod, and Fulford, to hold free from all services.

Tanner says—that Great Malvern was a place of great antiquity, for here in the wild forest, was an hermitage, or some kind of religious house, for seculars, before the conquest, endowed by the gift of Edward the Confessor, as it is stated, more than once, in the second charter of King Henry I, recorded in the Monast. Anglic. vol. 1, p. 366. About 1083, Adelwine,* the chief of this place, who,

* Or Alwin, had been made a monk by Walstan, the Bishop of Worcester, who dissuaded him from going a pilgrimage to Jerusalem, as he had intended, with assurances that the place of Malvern, which he had chosen for his habitation, would be wonderfully favoured by God,

in the Annales Wigorniensis, is expressly called
the founder, and said to have lived till A. D. 1140,
was persuaded by St. Wolstan, Bishop of Worcester, to turn Benedictine monk, upon which, he immediately set about procuring benefactions for the
building, and maintaining a prior of that order,
contradicting most fully, the assertion of Bishop
Thomas, who says Urso D'Abetot was founder before the conquest. That it was founded by Urso
D'Abetot before the conquest, as the learned and
curious author of the antiquities of this place asserts, upon the authority of the plea roll in Monast.
vol. 1I, p. 876, may be justly doubted, first, because
of the entire silence of both charters of King Henry
I, in which, the preceding benefactions are particularly recited; secondly, the name seems very un-
like a Saxon name, and most probably this Urso
was a Norman, and came over with King William
the Conqueror, who made him Sheriff of Worcestershire, and gave him several estates which belonged
to the Saxon, before the conquest. But to return.

Among the benefactors to the priory of Malvern,
was William the Conqueror; but the greatest benefactor to this order of Benedictines, was Henry
I. who gave them one rood of land at Badenhale,
and the land of Achissey, for which the farmers
paid 2s. rent, two hides of land, the one in Worces-

which Alwin, in some measure, saw fulfilled, living to have 30 monks of
the order of St. Benedict under him, who were all plentifully supplied by
the neighbouring people, who thought themselves happy in assisting them.

tershire, the other in Staffordshire, with the lands of Wordesfield and Limberg, also the churches of Tantarabaton, Lacton, and many other particulars to be seen there. The charter of King Henry confirms all former grants made to the church, and adds, of his own, the town of Longen, in Gloucester, &c. this is dated anno. 1127; Quat and Fuleford, in Staffordshire, Hathfield in Herefordshire, and other lands. Gislebert, abbot of Westminster, with consent of his convent, assigned to them several manors and estates, for that purpose, at a yearly rent, according to the Lincoln taxation, of 24*l.* 13*s.* 4*d.* whereupon this monastery was looked upon as a cell, or at least subordinate to Westminster Abbey.—The abbot of Westminster, always claiming the patronage, and, upon that account, approved and confirmed the election of the prior, and at length got this priory wholly exempt from the jurisdiction of the Bishop of Worcester: but yet this prior and convent acted in the management of their estates, &c. as an independent corporation.

Gilbert de Clare, Earl of Gloucester, Lord of the Forest, contributed largely to the revenues of this house. Osborne and Richard Fitzpontz, or De Pontibus, were likewise considerable benefactors, other contributors in later ages, especially to the building of the church and house, may be known from the curious painted windows, of which only broken remains are now to be seen, but which were perfèct in Mr. Abingdon's time, from whose papers we shall hereafter give an account of them.

Wolston, prior of Worcester, with consent of his convent, gave to the church of Great Malvern, sundry lands in Powick, Braunceford, and Leigh.

The church of Powyke was appropriated to the priory of Great Malvern by Walter de Maydeston, about the year 1314, and the vicarage instituted in the year following. William Lynn, Bishop of Worcester, in the year 1368, confirmed to the priory the church of St. Thomas the Martyr, of Malvern, the church of Powick; and the church of Longeney.

The church of Upton Snodsbury was appropriated to the priory of Great Malvern by Henry Wakfield, about the year 1392. The prior and convent were likewise lords of Knightwick, which manor they assigned over to Godfrey Giffard, Bishop of Worcester, with consent of King Edward, son of Henry. This conveyance was made by order of King Edward, in order to terminate a dispute which had long and violently subsisted between Richard Ware, Abbot of Westminster, and Godfrey Giffard, concerning the subordination of the priory of Malvern. The litigation was at length settled thus :—that the Bishop should have Knightwick, and that the priory should be subordinate to Westminster. The dispute seems to have begun in the reign of Henry II. when both the Abbot of Westminster and Bishop of Worcester claimed the jurisdiction of the priory, the right of appointing priors, of visiting and receiving procurations. The monks, wishing to be exempt from the power of their diocesan, and subject to Westminster, persuaded the abbot to institute one Walter, whom they had chosen for prior. At this, the Bishop being offended, suspended the prior, and recovered his jurisdiction, about the year 1165. Anno. 1279, William de Ledeburgh was elected prior, approved by the Abbot of Westminster, and instituted by the Bishop. He, being a man of an irregular course of life, was admonished by the Bishop; but not reforming his morals, a regular visitation was held, and he was deprived, being charged with many atrocious crimes. William de Wykeman was elected in his room, which the Abbot of Westminster resented, and the whole dispute was revived with great violence, both the Bishop and the Abbot appearing to be men of high spirit, and very tenacious of their rights; however, they were both appeased at the expence of the priory of Great Malvern, the Bishop having Knightwick given to him and his successors; and the jurisdiction of Malvern, together with the profits dependent thereon, being given to the Abbot of Westminster.

Before the church of Powyke had been appropriated to the priory of Great Malvern, they had the manor of Canterbauhhan, and the parish church of Laugh Mayn, in the diocese of St. David, together with a prebend in the said church, the manor of Foleford, in the diocese of Litchfield and Coventry, and the parish church of Pichetote, (Pichcot) in Lincoln diocese; all which had been taken from them, so that they could hardly support their number of monks, which was twenty-six, together with thirty poor people, whom they constantly maintained.

William Burdet, A. D. 1159, gave to God and St. Mary, of Malverne, and to the monks, serving God there, all the land he had, called Aucot, with the mill, and Schetinton, with all its appurtenances; there were to be two monks, the first year to serve the church, the next year two more were to be added. The prior of Malverne was to appoint the prior of this place, with the advice of the Abbot of Westminster, but neither of them to diminish the substance of the place.

Avicot, in Warwickshire, was a cell to Malvern, where were four monks. Brockbury, likewise, in the parish of Colwall, in Herefordshire, was a cell, and contained two monks. At the time of the dissolution of religious houses, in the reign of Henry VIII. their revenues amounted to 308*l*. 1s. 5¼d. according to Dugdale; but according to Speed, it was 375*l*. 0s. 6d. ob. It consisted chiefly in the following articles: the manors of Newland, Wortefeld, and Powyk, in the county of Worcester; Northwode, in Shropshire; the town of Hatfield, and lands in Baldenhale, Malvern, Brannesford, and Lye: tythes at Arehesfonte, in the diocese of Salisbury, of the yearly value of 40s. The priory of Malvern had likewise the appropriate churches of Longeney, Powyke, and Malvern ; the patronage of the churches of Hanleye, in the deanery of Powyke, of Upton Snodsbury, in the deanery of Pershore, and of Eastlech, in the deanery of Fayrford, in the county of Gloucester.

This priory was granted 36th Henry VIII, to *William Pinnocke*, who alienated it to *John Knotesford*, serjeant at arms, whose daughter Anne married *William Savage*, of the family of Savage, of Rock Savage, in the county of Chester, from whom, by inheritance, it came to *Thomas Savage*, Esq. of Elmley Castle, in the county of Worcester : his descendant (by a female) *Thomas Byrche Savage*, Esq. sold the demesne to *James Oliver*, of the city of Worcester, about the year 1774, the scite of the old priory being sold a few years before.

The gateway of the priory is all that now remains, except the church which the parish purchased of John Knottesford, and of which a particular description will be given. The old parish church was dedicated to *St. Thomas the Apostle*, and stood not far from the present church, at the N. W. corner of the church yard. It was in length 90 feet, in breadth 36, and had one small chapel to the South.

PRIORS OF GREAT MALVERN.
Alwinus tempore Willelmi Conquestoris.
Walcherus*, ob. 1st Oct.......................1135
Rogerus, 5 Henry II. 1159

* Inscriptis super tumulum. William of Malmsbury says that whoever did not believe the words of Walcher did an injury to Religion.

Walterus, ...1165
Walterus, ...1191
Willielmus Normannus, ...1222
Thomas, ob. 1242

Johannes de Wigornia, 1242, presentatus per Abbatem Westm, in vigilia beati Johannis Baptiste, anno gratie 1242: resignavit die Lune proxima post festum beati Luce Evangeliste, 1259.

Thomas de Brudone,..............................1259
Frater Will'us de Ledebury, ...1279
Ricardus de Estone, ob. 3 nou Martii, ...1300
Hugo, circa 1314
Frater Johannes Malvern, ...1435
Johannes Benet, ...1449
Ricardus Dene, ...1462
Ricardus Bone, (see the windows of the church)
Ricardus Frewen,
Maculiaus Ledbury, 2nd Feb. 1503
Frater Thomas Kegworth, 20th Jan. 1511

Richard Whitborne, alias Bedyll, the last prior, had a pension of 66l. 13s. 4d. assigned him at the dissolution.

In the year 1553, an enquiry was made what religious were then alive who received pensions, and the following are noticed :—

	£.	s.	d.
Richard Suckley,	6	0	0
William Humbersley,	6	13	4
William Bennet,	6	13	4
Richard Pole,	6	0	0
Thomas Powyke,	6	0	0
Reginald Waverton,	6	0	0
Christopher Aldwyn al, Moore,	6	0	0

At the dissolution of the religious houses, Bishop Latimer petitioned that two or three might be spared in each county, in particular that of Great Malvern might be suffered to remain, and that its revenues should be applied to the purpose of education ; but this was overruled by the cupidity of Henry VIII, or his counsellors. Queen Elizabeth, in her 31st year, granted to Richard Brathwayte, and Roger Bromley, and their heirs, all the tythes of lambs, pigs, calves, eggs, hemp, flax, and the oblations of the parish, and of the chapel of St. Leonard, on condition of their paying 8l. yearly, to the vicar, and 8s. 2d. to the Archdeacon of Worcester, in respect of a synodal and procuration issuing out of the said tythes. Harl. Mis.

The manor of Great Malvern anciently belonged to the Crown; in the reign of Edward I. it was given, together with the chase adjacent, the. castle of Hanley, and other lands, to Gilbert de Clare, Earl of Gloucester, on his marriage with Joan D'Acres, his daughter. A great dispute arose between this Earl of Gloucester *, and the Bishop of Hereford, concerning the bounds of the chase, to ascertain which, a great ditch, now called the Duke of Gloucester's ditch, was dug at the top of the hill, which ditch is still visible. Afterwards the Earl had a dispute with Godfrey Giffard, to end which, it was agreed that he and his wife Joan, and their heirs, should annually pay to the Bishop and his

* Called Red Beard.

successors, at their manor of Kemsey, two brace of good does at different times of the year; during the vacancy of the see they were to be paid to the Dean and Chapter. Gilbert, the only son of Gilbert and Joan abovementioned, being killed at Banockburn, in Scotland, and leaving no issue, Eleanor, wife of Hugh le Despencer, succeeded her brother; and from the family of the Spencers, after the third generation, it came, by a female, to Richard de Beauchamp, Earl of Warwick, in the time of Henry V. whose daughter Anne, heir to Henry Duke of Warwick, her brother, was married to Richard Nevill, Earl of Warwick and Salisbury; and by Isabel, their daughter, wife to George, Duke of Clarence, it descended to Edward, the unfortunate and last male branch of the Plantagenets; who being beheaded, it reverted again to the crown, and was, by Queen Elizabeth, granted to Sir Thomas Bromley, Knight, Chancellor of England, in whose family it continued for several generations; until John Bromley, of Horseheath, in the county of Cambridge, Esq. married Mercy, eldest daughter of William Bromley, Esq. of Holt Castle, in the county of Worcester, and left it to his son, Henry Bromley, afterwards created Lord Mountfort; who, about the year 1740, sold this manor, together with Holt Castle, to Thomas Lord Foley, in which family it still continues. As to the chase, which chase is said to contain, in Worcestershire, 7115 acres, besides 241 acres called the prior's land—in Herefordshire, 619 acres—in Gloucestershire, 103 acres—Charles I. in the year 1630, granted one third part of it to Richard Heath, and Sir Cornelius Vermyden, Knight, and the other two thirds to the neighbouring parishes who had a right of commoning. This division occasioned great disturbances, the King and Council, by letters patent, dated May 12, 1631, declared it free from the forest laws, which disafforestation was confirmed by act of Parliament, 16th Charles II. for which account we refer our readers to the article MALVERN FOREST. About a quarter of a mile below the village of Great Malvern is a light and very pleasant Chalybeate Spring. See Spring.

Near a mile from Great Malvern lies the chapel of Newland, dedicated to St. Leonard; it was formerly a grange or farm, belonging to the priory of Great Malvern : it belonged afterwards to the *Walwyns* and the *Dickens's*.

In the 5th of Elizabeth, Great Malvern contained 105 families, and the chapelry of Newland 13 ; according to the return made to Bishop North, A. D. 1776, it contained 120, while, at the same period, it paid to the land tax, at 4s. in the pound, 266*l*. 10s. and to the poor, 150*l*. From the information politely sent me by Mr. Card, the Vicar of Great Malvern, I find that in 1816 the poor rates amounted to the sum of 700*l*. the land tax 76*l*. 7s. exclusive of Mr. Foley's land-tax, which is redeemed, and that Great Malvern contains about 1,200 souls.

The Severn, which runs by the city of Worcester, with a rapid current, receives the Temde, Teme, Tame, or Tam, (a river that runs swift) which has its rise in Radnorshire, and enters Worcestershire a little above Tenbury, and receiving other little streams, until it comes to Powick-bridge, where it receives the Lawern, and falls into the Severn at a place called Teme-mouth. Hence the Severn runs to Kemsey, and before it reaches that place, receives a rill from Powick, and a little brook from the hills, by Lye Sinton and Branceford Lye, below Pixham's ferry. Another brook which comes round by Madersfield, the seat of the Lygons, falls into it; then it washes Stoke, and before it reaches Upton, the brook that comes from Malvern hill by Blackmore Park, the seat of the Horny-holds, mixes its waters with it, just by Severn-end, and the seat of the Lechmeres, in the parish of Hanley: below the bridge of Upton, the waters which come from Malvern chase, from the Berrow, and from Pendock, one branch of which comes by Welland, and another by Longden, run into it; and below this, it receives from the east, a rill out of Ripple Lake, and then passes on to Bushley, and going out of Worcestershire, at Tewkesbury, it then receives the Avon.

The following old song, in praise of Malvern, had not, before Dr. M. Wall published it, been circu-lated in Worcester, except in M. S. There are many circumstances, hereafter alluded to, which seem to establish the common opinion of its antiquity. If this opinion be well founded, (upon which subject perhaps popular tradition is stronger than any other argument) the song may be considered as one of the earliest records of the medicinal virtue and purity of these waters. On this account, Dr. M. Wall, thinking it immediately connected with his father's treatise, had determined to insert it in his essay so long ago as when he began to compile the materials of his publication. In the mean time it gained a place in a new work, entitled the Antiquarian Repertory, but without any light thrown upon its author, and is inserted without any preface, notwithstanding the known deepness of investigation of the editor of that work. In Worcestershire it has the reputation of great antiquity. In the copy which Dr. M. Wall transcribed some years ago, it was said to have been written soon after the year 1600, which is probably not far from the exact date, if we may judge from the style and the allusions to the deer in the chase; the adjoining woods, &c.

Mr. Barrett affirms that these lines were composed by the parish clerk, about the year 1590, from which time, he says it remained in M. S. till 1778, when it was published in Nash's history of Worcestershire; "it is, however, I believe," he continues "not very generally known, at what time it was first written."

1

As I did walk alone
  Late in an evening;
I heard the voice of one
  Most sweetly singing;
Which did delight me much,
Because the song was such,
And ended with a touch,
                O praise the Lord.

2

The God of sea and land
  That rules above us,
Stays his avenging hand,
  'Cause he doth love us;
And doth his blessings send,
Altho' we do offend;
Then let us all amend,
                And praise the Lord.

3

Great Malvern on a rock,
  Thou standest surely;
Doe not thyself forget,
  Living securely:
Thou hast of blessings store,
No country town hath more,
Do not forget therefore,
                To praise the Lord.

4

Thou hast a famous church
  And rarely builded:
No country town hath such—
  Most men have yielded,
For pillars stout and strong,
And windows large and long:
Remember in thy song
                To praise the Lord.

5

There is God's service read
  With rev'rence duely :
There is his word preached,
  Learned and truely ;
And every sabbath day,
Singing of psalms they say,
It's sure the only way
          To praise the Lord.

6

The sun in glory great,
  When first it riseth,
Doth bless thy happy seat,
  And thee adviseth,
That then its time to pray,
That God may bless thy way,
And keepe thee all the day,
          To praise the Lord.

7

That thy prospect is good,
  None can deny thee ;
Thou hast great store of wood
  Growing hard by thee :
Which is a blessing great
To roast and boil thy meat ;
And thee in cold to heat :
          O praise the Lord.

8

Preserve it I advise,
  Whilst that thou hast it ;
Spare not in any wise,
  But do not waste it :

D

Least thou repent too late,
Remember Hanley's fate, *
In time shut up thy gate,
        And praise the Lord.

9

A chase for royal deer
  Round doth beset thee ;
Too many doo I fear
  For aught they get thee ;
Yet tho' they eat away,
Thy corn, thy grass, and hay,
Doe not forget, I say,
        To praise the Lord.

10

That noble chase doth give
  Thy beasts their feeding ;
Where they in summer live
  With little heeding :
Thy sheep and swine there go,
So doth thy horse also,
Till winter brings in snow :
        Then praise the Lord.

11

Turn up thine eyes on highe,
  There fairly standing,
See Malverne's highest hill,
  All hills commanding ;

* Hanley Castle, coming by marriage to Richard the Great, Earl of Warwick and Salisbury, who was attainted of high treason, lost his life, and his estates were forfeited to the crown.

They all confess at will,
Their sovereign Malvern hill,
Let it be mighty still!

           O praise the Lord.

12`

When western winds do rock
  Both town and country,
Thy hill doth break the shock,
  They cannot hurt thee ;
When waters great abound,
And many a country's drown'd,
Thou standest safe and sound ;

           O praise the Lord.

13`

Out of that famous hill
  There daily springeth
A' water, passing still,
  Which always bringeth
Great comfort to all them
That are diseased men,
And makes them well again,

           To praise the Lord.

14·

Hast thou a wound to heal,
  The which doth grieve thee ?
Come then unto this well,
  It will relieve thee ;
Noli me tangeres,
And other maladies,
Have here their remedies,

           Prais'd be the Lord.

15

To drink thy waters, store
  Lie in thy bushes, *
Many with ulcers sore,
  Many with bruises ;
Who succour find from ill,
By money given still,
Thanks to the christian will :
                    O praise the Lord.

16

A thousand bottles there,
  Were filled weekly,
And many costrils rare,
  For stomachs sickly ;
Some of them into Kent,
Some were to London sent,
Others to Berwick went,
                    O praise the Lord.

* Though modern visitors do not now lie in bushes, yet so crouded was Malvern one season, that a lady of rank and fashion, with her equipage and servants, were actually obliged to be sent to the Workhouse. It is now the custom, during the season, to let out this house to visitors, and the money gained this way is applied to the funds for maintaining the poor.

CHAPTER II.

MALVERN HILLS.

Antiquity, Extent, and Geographical Situation.

THE earliest mention which we can find made of these hills, is in the poem called *The Vision of Pierce Plowman*, in which the monastic orders are ridiculed, and the visions are represented as appearing to him while asleep on one of the Malvern hills.

> " In a somer season when set was the sonne,
> And on a May morning, on Malverne hilles."

Robert Langland, the reputed author, is said to have been born at Mortimer's Cleobury, in Shropshire, and to have been a secular priest and fellow of Oriel Coll. Ox. In Nash's Worcester Corrections, p. 52, is a passage from Steven's Monasticon, according to which, the author is said to have been " John Malvern, a Benedictine monk, of Worcester; he flourished in 1342, and wrote a continuation of Polychronicon." Johannes Malvernius Wigorniensis, was, as we learn from A. Wood, fellow of the above-mentioned college.

Again, at a less remote period, the Malvern hills are mentioned by Leland, who died in 1552. " I marked" says he " that when at Worcester the high crests of Malverne hilles to be to the sight neare to

Worcester, but it is six miles to Greate Malverne priory." The Malvern hills are situate in the south western part of Worcester, the boundary which divides the counties of Worcester and Hereford passes along the western side.

It appears that the Malvern *hills* have been long distinguished by that title, but according to the rules of geography they will not properly bear that appellation; yet, from their size and form, they may be denominated the Alps of England.

The strata in these elevated tracts are arranged in a perpendicular direction, which is the discriminate mark or characteristic of a *mountain*, always attended to by those who have treated scientifically of that branch of knowledge. These eminences are situate in the several counties of Worcester, Gloucester, and Hereford; environed on the east by an expansive plain, and on the west by an uneven, but fertile tract of country. They are about 8 miles S. W. from Worcester, 20, E. from Hereford, and 14 N. W. from Gloucester. Their geographical situation is in about 52 degrees of north latitude, and 115 miles N. W. or 3 degrees longitude west, from the meridian of London. The hills extend in one chain about 9 miles in length, from north to south, nearly in a strait line, viz. from Leigh Sinton, in the county of Worcester, to Broomsberrow, in the county of Gloucester; the former being the most northern, and the latter the most southern extremity. Their breadth is very.

unequal, varying from 1 to 2 miles and upwards.
When viewed from a little distance on the eastern
side, we see that there is a gradual rise from south
to north, and that there are 3 hills which form the
principal features, as they stand considerably above
the general outline: the highest of these is in the
centre of the whole range, and is known by
the name of the Herefordshire beacon. The two
other prominent hills are situate nearly close together, at the northern extremity; of these, that which
is farthest south, is called the Worcestershire beacon,
and is the highest of the two, the other the north
hill. Mr. Barrett, however, in his "Description of
Malvern", tells us that the Herefordshire beacon
was *formerly* computed to be the highest point of the
hills, but continues he, " by an accurate mensura-
tion, the Worcestershire beacon is found to be
somewhat the highest; the former being about
1260, and the latter about 3000 feet, perpendicular height, from the surface of the adjacent level of
the plain." In Rees's Cyclopædia, article Malvern,
the compiler, or rather Nash, from whom it is extracted, says " the Herefordshire beacon is 1280 feet
in height, while the Worcestershire beacon is 1313
feet above the surface of the Severn, and that they
are 4 miles distant from each other." In the table of
altitudes taken in the course of the ordinance survey of England, and published by that board, the
height of the Malvern hills is stated, particularly
the Herefordshire beacon, to be 1444 feet. "I am in-

formed," says Mr. Horner, in his Mineralogy of the
Malvern hills, "by Lieutenant-Colonel Mudge, that
the particular hill to which this measurement refers,
is the Herefordshire beacon. "I had not," continues
Mr. H. "an opportunity of ascertaining the height of
the Herefordshire beacon above the adjacent plain.
I obtained, however, that of the Worcestershire
beacon, and of the north hill; the instrument I
made use of was Sir Henry Englefield's portable
barometer, and the following are the results of my
observations: my lowest station was at the north
eastern extremity of the common, called the Link,
from which point there is almost a dead level to the
banks of the Severn.

"The Worcestershire beacon, by the mean of
   3 observations, ... 1238 feet
The north hill, by the mean of 2 observations,   1151
The road before the door of the Crown Hotel,
   in Great Malvern, to be 273 feet above
   that plain, or 333 feet above the line of
   the Severn, by mean of 3 observations,   273."

As the right bank of the Severn, at the termination of the plain, from which these measurements
are calculated, is between 60 and 70 feet in perpendicular height; this, added to the above elevation of
the Worcestershire beacon, very nearly corresponds
with the statement in Nash's history of Worcestershire. On the eastern side, the hills rise at a considerable angle from a level plain that stretches to the
banks of the river Severn, a distance of between 3
and 4 miles. On the western side, the ascent is

more gradual, and the country for several miles to the westward, is formed by a succession of small hillocks, which are covered to their tops with coppice wood, the longitudinal bearings of these are in general parallel to that of the range. The Worcestershire beacon is nearly opposite the village of Great Malvern, and probably acquires its name with that of the Herefordshire *beacon*, from its being used as a signal post, when the adjacent country was the theatre of military achievements, and this idea is corroborated by the appearance of an ancient camp, still visible on the latter prominence. King, in his Monumenta Antiqua, p. 147, says, "there are a vast number of strong intrenchments in all parts of this island, situate chiefly on the tops of natural hills, and which can be attributed to none of the various people who have ever dwelt in the adjacent country, except to the ancient Britons, although indeed, the subsequent conquerors, Romans, Saxons, and Danes, and even the Normans, have, on certain emergencies, made use of them on account of their great original strength ; and although, erroneous and hasty conjectures, and even the crude reports of the country, have often called them Roman, Danish, or Saxon, yet can they only be attributed to the ancient Britons. One of the most important and considerable of these fortified places, is situate on a spot that could not fail to be an object of the utmost attention to the original inhabitants of these territories, which after-

E

wards were deemed, distinctly, England and Wales. This is the Herefordshire beacon, commanding that which was the only pass through the Malvern ridge of hills, and which is indeed very nearly so to the present hour. The Worcestershire and Hereford-shire beacons appear much higher than in fact they really are; they are celebrated as being the promi-nences, from which it is conjectured, a view of that desperate battle was beheld, which took place on Tewkesbury plain, where the great Earl of Warwick was defeated. "Now Malvern mountains," says Hume, " veil the wearied sun, and yet the conflict rages;" and father Daniel asserts, that at the conclu-sion of this celebrated battle, there happened such a dreadful storm of thunder and lightning, and such a thick darkness in the air, as were more terrible to the rebel party than the death of their chief.

Comparative height of the Malvern hills, with other principal mountains.

	English feet.
The height of Mount Ophir in Sumatra, above the level of the sea, is................	13,842
Chimberazo, the highest of the Andes..........	20,633
Peak of Teneriffe, ...	13,265
Mont Blanc, in Savoy,............................	15,662
Mount Ætna,...	10,954

Malvern hill, therefore, in round numbers, is not above a tenth-part as high as the peak of Teneriffe, and not above a seventeenth-part as high as the Andes, and notwithstanding, according to Dr. Booker, in his notes to his poem of "Malvern," " a distance of about 40 miles intervenes between me and my residence, these hills are very discernible by the unassisted eye, rising in general, like a cluster of dark clouds towards the west. Sometimes when the atmospheric medium is clear, not only the irregularities and colour of the surfaces are visible, but even the scattered habitations of the village."

The Malvern hills are the means of preserving a salubrious air to the countries beneath them, by condensing the mists in summer; but they also intercept too soon the rays of the setting sun in winter. Mr. Baxter is the only antiquary that brings Malvern within the southern limits of the Ordovices; or that part of North Wales, which contains the counties of Montgomery, Merioneth, Canarvon, Denbigh, and Flint.

Malvern, from her hills, is indeed rich in prospects: if a distant view delight you, you may here see the counties of Monmouth, Hereford, Radnor, Brecknock, Salop, Worcester, Gloucester, Stafford, Warwick, &c. the three cathedrals of Gloucester, Worcester, and Hereford, the Bristol channel, the rivers Severn, Avon, and Teme, and many market towns, and with the assistance of a glass, nearly a hundred churches; encircled by a majestic range of mountains, you behold the Wrekin and the Clee hills, in Shropshire, peering over Ludlow; also the black mountains of Brecknockshire, the hills of Monmouthshire, Abergavenny, and Ledbury mount, and ranging towards Birmingham, the Lickey hills also; with a telescope from

Malvern, you may perceive the venerable pile of Dudley Castle, including, in the whole, the following places :

Objects seen on the Worcester side of the Malvern Hills.

1	Dudley Castle	13	Croome
2	Clent Hills	14	Pershore
3	Frankley Beeches	15	Ridgeway Hill
4	Lickey Hill	16	Edge Hill
5	Worcester	17	Rouse Lench
6	Madresfield	18	Bredon Hill
7	Dripshill	19	Tewkesbury
8	The Rhyd	20	Gloucester
9	Blackmore Park	21	Cheltenham
10	Hanley	22	Cotswold Hills
11	Upton	23	Broadway Hills
12	Kempsey		

Objects which may be seen on the Herefordshire side.

42	Hills in Radnorshire	36	Abberly Hill
25	The Clee Hills, in Shropshire	37	Brockhampton, the Seat of J. Barnebey, Esq.
26	The Wrekin, in ditto	38	Ankerdine Hill, near Whitborne
27	The Black Mountain, bordering upon Brecon	39	Broadwas Terrace
28	The Sugar Loaf, in Monmouthshire	40	Stoke Edith, the Seat of E. Foley, Esq.
29	The Blorenge, on ditto	41	Hope-end, the Seat of E. M. Barrett, Esq.
30	Garnons, the Seat of Sir J. G. Cotterill, Bart.	42	Eastnor Castle, the Seat of Lord Somers
31	Hereford	43	Ledbury Mount
32	The Kymyn Hill	44	Penyard Woods, near Ross
33	Wall Hill Camp, near Thornbury		
34	Egdon Hill and Tedstone Delamere	45	May Hill, near Newent
35	Clifton Firs	46	King Road or Bristol Channel

Would you enjoy a nearer view? The pear trees of Worcestershire, when in blossom, "furnish a scene," says an old chronicler, "as the world beside cannot equal." On the western side, the apple trees of Herefordshire, with their purple hues, make an agreeable variety: the beautiful little hills and the rich woods, the salubrity and pureness of the air, combine to make Malvern, during the summer months, as desirable a situation as any in England.

The mountainous situation of Malvern has suggested to several persons, that it would afford good pasture to goats, and that this healthful spot might be resorted to, not only on account of the waters, but for the use of the goat whey. Many advantages would attend such an establishment, especially as the places frequented for that purpose, are situated at one corner of the island, at so great a distance from most parts of the kingdom, that many invalids, who might receive great benefit from the milk, are discouraged from taking so long a journey. Sir John Pringle, at one time, suggested to Dr. Wall some hints on this subject, and some directions relative to the use of goat's whey, but we believe the scheme was never put into execution. " We seldom want victuals, said a poor cottager to the compiler of a tour to Malvern, but we never want a Doctor: perhaps the cottager spoke truth, yet notwithstanding the general purity of the water, there are petrifying springs on the west side of the hills, which being used for culinary purposes, sometimes, it is said, occasion wens or strumous swellings of the maxillary glands."

There is a very extensive and beautiful view from the top of the Malvern Hills, and the different appearance of the two·sides present a very remarkable contrast; on the one hand, the widely extended plain of Worcestershire, stretching for many miles to the eastward, the continued level of which, is only here and there interrupted by small woody eminences, rising in detached spots; on the other hand, a constant succession of rising ground, which is terminated by the distant Welch mountains.

The eastern side does not present the same continued slope that extends on the western, from the summit to the base, but is very much broken by narrow vallies, or water courses, that run at right angles to the direction of the range : besides these, there are some vallies of more considerable extent, two of them are at the northern extremity, the one separating the Worcestershire beacon from the north hill, the other dividing it from what is termed the end hill, where the Herefordshire beacon falls back to the westward. In this part occurs a wide, and in some places, a thickly wooded valley, at the bottom of which is situate the retired village of Little Malvern. All these vallies run from west to east, and gradually widen as they descend: there are none parallel to the direction of the chain.

CHAPTER III.

GREAT MALVERN CHURCH.

Ancient State.

THE Litchfield manuscript * informs us, says an anonymous author, that the situation of Malvern was so much admired by Henry VII, his Queen, and their two Sons, Prince Arthur, and Prince

---

* " Letters on Malvern," lately published, mention the " Litchfield M.S." and contain a short account taken from it respecting the windows, which we shall insert. An account nearly the same is in the Antiquarian and Topographical Cabinet, published in 1807, vol. 1, article Malvern Abbey. " And upon enquiring," says Mr. Rudd, author of the very interesting " Reflections, relative to the Malvern hills," respecting the Lichfield M.S. (which I have not observed to be noticed in either Nash or Thomas,") I have been referred by a friend to a journey through England, in familiar letters from a gentleman here to his friends abroad, vol. 2. p. 171. ed. 3. London printed for J. Pemberton, 1732; in which book mention is made of an " ancient M. S. of the priory of Great Malvern," seen at Lichfield, and much the same account is given from it, with something more of its contents. Besides saying that Henry VII. his Queen, and two Sons, Arthur and Henry, took much delight in Malvern, and exceedingly beautified the church window, the subject of which it briefly notices; it states that the priory was first founded by Henry III. and Edward his son. This certainly is an error, either of the author of the M. S. or of the traveller The statement is contrary to the authorities in Nash, Thomas, and Dugdale, some of them original documents. I learn from the same friend, continues Mr. Rudd, that this M. S. has been missing for many years Henry III. began to reign in

Henry, that they were induced to beautify the church with stained glass windows to a degree of magnificence that made it one of the proudest ornaments of the nation. These windows form a mirror, wherein we may see how to believe, to live, and to die. Among the great multiplicity of sacred subjects delineated, is one of a representation of the day of judgment, which is not inferior with respect to grandeur and boldness of design, to the paintings of Michael Angelo. An account of this stained glass was taken by Mr. Habington, in the reign of Charles I, which Dr. Thomas translated into Latin, and published in his description of this church. Vide an account of Great Malvern Priory, and of the tombs in the church, and arms and pictures in the windows, from the same M. S. in the volumes of Mr. Habington's collections, formerly in Jesus College Library, Oxon, &c. p. 98, from which, and an old M. S. account of Malvern in our possession, the following detail is copied :

1216. In Thomas's Antiq. Malv. Chart. Orig. p. 97, is mentioned by name, a prior of 1191, in the time of *Robert*, Bishop of Worcester. This date accords with Thomas's account of Bishops, p. 119, who refers to Ang. Sac. Disputes respecting the jurisdiction of this priory existed in the time of *Roger*, Bishop of Worcester. Thomas, Antiq. Mal. Chart. Orig. p. 95, (I suppose, says Mr. R.) some incorrectness in *one* of the *dates* of this Chronicle. Or Roger was elected Bishop 1163, and died 1179. Account of Bishop, p. 112, with a reference to Ang. Sac.; and by an original document in Dugdale's (Monast. vol. 1. account of Malvern Abbey, which begins p. 336,) a prior as well as " monachi", is mentioned as belonging to Great Malvern in 1159; besides this, we have the tomb-stone of Walcher, a prior, dated MCXXXV.

The upper part of the great east window was divided in twelve compartments, in which were painted the twelve apostles: in the lower part were sixteen divisions, in which were described several transactions of our Saviour's life; such as line one, his riding on an Ass, celebrating the passover with his disciples, washing their feet, his agony, his being betrayed by Judas, brought bound before Pilate, sent to Herod, condemned; line two, cloathed with purple, scourged, bearing his cross, nailed to the cross, his death, his body taken down from the cross, his burial, the stone of the sepulchre sealed. This pane was broken and lost in the year 1749. Line three, he rose from the dead, the woman bringing spices, his appearance to Mary Magdalen; broken and confused in 1749. His appearance at the sea of Tiberius, to the disciple of Emaus, the descent of the Holy Ghost. The three southern panes were most of them broken in 1749.

In the upper part of the choir are six windows; in the first, from the east or the north side of the church, are certain images of Saints, with this inscription:

" Orate pro anima domini Johannis Malverne, qui istam fenestram fieri fecit. (He was prior in 1435).

In the second window are likewise representations of saints, and two monks praying, with this inscription :

" Orate pro animabus Johannis West, et Thome Lye, monachis hujus loci."

There are likewise two figures of knights with their shields; on one of them, three catherine wheels sable; on the other, a fesse indented argent, with this broken inscription:

" Thome Carter et Ricardi Oseven, et agnete uxoris ejus, et Thome......filli eorundem cujus munera in ista ecclesia......"

In the third window are the arms of Westminster Abbey, and two others ; Az. two Keys in Saltire one Or. the other, Arg. Az. on a chief indented Gu. two Gerbes Or. N. B. in this window is seen Aldwin, upon his knees, to have his patent signed by the King, to build this church; the King sends him to the Cardinal, who sends him back again to the King to sign it first, M. S. 1749.

On the south side of the choir, in the first window from the east, were represented the three Magi offering their gifts ; above the arms of Henry VII, and his son Prince Arthur.

In the lower part of the second window still remain Peter, Andrew, James and John; the arms of Lord Beauchamp, of Powick ; and on the left side, in a shield argent, a cross gules.

The saints in the upper part much broken and confused.

The third window is very much broken, having

only the arms of Lord Berkley and Lord Stafford.

In the north side of the nave are six windows, with six compartments in each ; in the first, on the west side, is represented Christ crucified, with St. John supporting the fainting Virgin, and the Centurion confessing Jesus to be the Christ; below, the three Marys, supported by St. Phillip, St. Simon, and St. Jude ; at bottom, two benefactors, and under them these words:

" Vos qui inspicitis animabus rememoretis P. Dene, nec non fratris Maculini."

The former was prior in 1462, and the latter in 1503. *

In the upper part of the second window were three angels and three saints; Laurence, George and Christopher ; at bottom, three benefactors and their wives kneeling, and on their mantles a shield with the arms of Crofte, party per pale per fesse indented Az. and Arg. in the first quarter, a lion passant guardant Or.

In the upper part of the third window were three angels and three saints; namely, Leodgarius, Elphegus and a third; at bottom, two benefactors praying, with the arms of Lyttelton and Stafford.

In the fourth were likewise three angels and three saints; Wannard, Martin and Nicholas; at bottom, two benefactors, with the arms of Besford and the Bracie ; the latter of whom owned Madresfield, in this neighbourhood.

* Here are to be seen the five wounds of our Saviour, at his Crucifixion, M. S.

In the fifth window were six saints; Paul, John the Evangelist, John the Baptist: at bottom, Mark, Giles and Leonard, with their names; and benefactors kneeling.

The sixth and last window represents in the upper part, St. Andrew, St. James, and St. Peter; at bottom, Ursula, Margaret and Catherine, and three benefactors with their wives, praying, with their names, Richard Halker, and his wife; Richard Toillewak, and his wife; and Richard Frewen, and his wife.

In the south side are likewise six windows of the same size and shape; in which are painted many histories of the old and new Testament : in the first, second, third, and fourth compartments, of the first window, are several histories from the creation to the expulsion of Adam out of Paradise.

In the fifth is John Alcock, Bishop of Worcester, sitting in a pontifical chair; before him these words :

"Pontificem dominum presento Johannem."

Behind him, his arms in a shield, argent a fess sable between three cock's heads erased, their combs and gills Gules, with this inscription :

"Orate pro bono statu religiosi viri Johannis Alcok episcopi Wigorn, cancellarii Angliæ."

In the four first compartments of the second window, were the history of Noah and the tower of Babel: in the fifth compartment, benefactors praying. In the four first compartments of the third window, were the history of Abraham, Lot, Isaac, Jacob and Esau; at bottom, benefactors praying. In the four first compartments of the fourth window, was the history of Joseph. The fifth window contained the history of Moses and the Israelites in Egypt, and the wilderness, and at bottom, benefactors as before. Of the sixth window nothing remained, in Dr. Thomas's time, but Aaron in his priest's dress, and Moses with his glorified face. In the great east window were fourteen compartments, representing the resurrection, and Christ coming to judge the world; the Virgin Mary and saints, in the seven lower compartments : benefactors to this window were, as appears by their arms, Richard III, and Anne his wife, daughter and coheir of Richard, Earl of Warwick and Salisbury. In the eastern window, of the north aisle, were three compartments; in the first was the Virgin Mary, in the second a priest saying mass, in the third St. John; under the Virgin two persons praying, having their arms there painted, S. across G. between four maid's heads, and quarterly one and four Az. a Sun Or. two and three S. three cranes, A. imp. V. on a Saltire ingrailed A. between four cross crosslets fitche Or. a fleur de lis, with this inscription :

" Orate pro animabus Ricardi Knight militis et Nycholai Devenyshe armigeri."

Under the priest these words:

" Orate pro animabus domini Johannis Prioris et Agnetis Leach."

Under St. John :

" Orate pro animabus Willielmi Harnis et Roberti Hille."

The great west window of the nave affords two shields in excellent preservation, one containing the arms and supporters of Richard III, the other of his Queen, both having coronets over them, which perhaps is the earliest instance of coronets borne over the arms of Princes and nobility, as at this day.

On the north side of the choir are three windows, each divided into four compartments ; in the first towards the east were four doctors of the western church, at the feet of each, the figure of William Braci, and in the upper part of his arms G. a fess O. in chief A: two spur rowels ; also quartering cheque O. and Az. and again A. frette, S. and again V. a bend O. between two cottizes G. also impaling and quartering Az. a cross indented O. and A. and Az. a cross A. In the lower division of this window are certain benefactors praying, and under them this inscription :

" Orate pro animabus Johannis Braci, Willielmi et Thome filiorum ejus :"

In the second, a man and his wife, with this inscription :

" Orate pro animabus Willielmi Braci et Isabelle uxoris ejus :"

In the third :

" Orate pro animabus Willielmi Braci et Johanne Uxoris ejus :"

In the fourth, a Knight kneeling, with the arms of Warren, and these words :

" O-ate......Willielmi de Braci et Agnetis uxoris ejus."

In the upper part of the second window several coats of arms cheque O. and Az. on a bend G. three lions passant guardant O. A. three Crescents S. Below G. two wings conjoined O. G. on a bend A. with a martlet for difference : Imp. A. three crescents S. and S. a spread eagle A. in a border ingrailed Az.

Also the first of these coats quartering the three preceding : below were several figures of benefactors, with these inscriptions :

" Orate pro animabus Henrici Clyfford, Senescalli de Longeney, et Elizabethe uxoris ejus, et Jacobi Clyfford armfilii eorundem et animabus parentum ae benefactorum eorundem."

The third window was adorned with the twelve prophets and the twelve apostles. In the eastern window, of the south aisle, were painted the arms of Beauchamp, and of Isabella, sister and heir of Richard Despencer, earl of Gloucester, owner of Malvern Chace. In the next window were several coats of arms : A. on a bend S. three spur rowels. O. O. a chevron erm. between three bull's heads S. paly of four A. and G. on a bend S. three spur rowels Or. In the fourth compartment a man with ten sons, and his wife, with ten daughters, with this inscription :

" Orate pro animabus Walteri Corbet et Johanne uxoris ejus."

Below, against the wall, lies a man armed,

holding in his right hand an axe, and in his left a round shield, supposed to represent John Corbet.

In the second window were, at top, two coats of arms, I. Barry of six O. and Az. in chief three palettes and a scutcheon of pretence A. the same with an impalement broken, helmeted and mantled. Two Az. a cross O. three G. a bend A. with an Annulet for difference, imp. the last, four A. two bends vair erm, G. and V. imp. A. on a cross S. a Leopard's head O. and in the dexter quarter frette G. underneath the figures of St. Lawrence, St. Nicholas, St. Stephen, and St. Giles, under these was a man and his wife praying:

" Willielmus Walwein and Jana uxor ejus." Also, " Christe nos adjuva," and, " per Lawrentii Nicholaeque...." Also, " Deus sit nobis propitius Stephani Egidiique precibus." And lower, " Omnes vos qui ituri estis istam per fenestellam pro animabus orate nostris ut det Deus..."

In the third and last window were four representations of saints, and some shields of arms, of which remains only quarterly, one per fess indented Az. and A. in the dexter quarter a lion Rampant O. two G. three lions Rampant A. three per pale G. and Az. three lions Rampant A. four broke, except in chief G. three Stag's heads O.*

In the south side of the nave of the church was a door which led to the cloisters: near this, in a little window, were the Braci's arms, and above it a monk kneeling, with various figures of an un-

---

* These arms are transcribed from Habington's M. S.

clean spirit: in the lower part a devil vomiting out an infant, which is received by other devils, and an angel praying for it. From hence to the west end are five little windows, of three compartments each: in the first an angel, an archangel, and a cherubim; in the second St. George, St. Sebastian, and St. Vincent; in the third St. Margaret ... and St. Wulstan; in the fourth St. Giles ... and St. Leonard, and under each of these is written:

" Orate pro anima Maculini, supprioris hujus loci."

In the fifth St. Katherine, St. Mary Magdalen, and St. Margaret, with these words:

" Orate pro anima Ricardi Freuen prioris hujus loci."

In the north aisle were painted in five windows, various histories from the new Testament: twelve stories in each window: in the first, the espousals of Joachim and Anne, an angel saying to Anne:

" Cum veneris ad partem auream virum tuum obvium habebis."

The angel appearing to Joachim: the rest broke: in the second, the angel appearing to the Virgin Mary, Mary saluting Elizabeth, Christ's birth, presentation in the Temple, the magi enquiring for him, and offering their gifts, and returning into their own country. The angel appearing to Joseph, Joseph and Mary flying into Egypt, murder of the innocents, Christ baptised by John. In the third, Christ turning water into wine, healing a paralytic, casting out a devil, tempted by the devil, placed on a pinnacle of the temple, carried to an high mountain, shewed the glories of the world, the pool of Bethesda; the rest are broken. In the fourth window, Christ walking upon the sea, casting out a devil, making clay, and opening the eyes of the blind, curing a fever, and the woman with the issue of blood; the rest broken. In the fifth window nothing remains but the crucifixion. From this aisle you go to Jesus Chapel, in which are two windows : in the large one to the north are twelve compartments, six above, and six below. In the upper are represented the Trinity crowning the Virgin, a chorus of angels and saints praising God on various instruments, Christ received into heaven, Michael fighting with the devil, Our Saviour bringing Adam and Eve out of hell ; the rest broken : below were the figures of Henry VII. armed and crowned with an imperial crown : on his upper garment, the arms of France and England : behind him Elizabeth, his Queen, with the same arms ; on her garment, behind her, Arthur, prince of Wales, likewise armed : behind him, Sir Reginald Bray, bearing, in a shield argent, a chevron between three eagle's legs erased sable : behind him John Savage, Esq. and Thomas Lovell, Esq. all kneeling, bearing palm branches lifted up to heaven, with this inscription :

" Orate pro bono statu nobilissimi et excellentissimi regis Henrici septimi et Elizabethe regine ac domini Arthuri principis filii eorundem, nec non predilectissime Consortis sue, et suorum trium militum." ·

This beautiful window was perfect in the year

1720, but soon after, a violent storm blew it down, and being very much broken, an ignorant glazier misplaced the pieces that were left. The last window to be described is the west window of this chapel, in the upper part of which were two coats of arms; one Erm. O. and Az. the other Erm. A. and Az. and under them the Trinity with the elevation of the host, and underneath the baptism of adults and infants; under this the Trinity repeated, and the Pope and these Cardinals, and these words:

" Parata sunt vobis loca in coelo."

In the middle compartment was the last supper, and in the third the town and church of Malverne with the chapel of St. Michael, situated on the side of the hill: in the southern angle of the window, an archer in the forest shooting a stag: underneath a prior and his monks, on one side of the prior his relations, on the other his monks, kneeling, with this inscription:

" Orate pro animabus domini Ricardi Bone prioris hujus loci et Maculini......Simonis, Nicholai, Agnetis, Willielmi, Mariane parentum eorundem."

The floor and walls of the choir were paved and decorated with square bricks, painted with the arms of Eugland, the Abbey of Westminster, Mortimer, earl of March; Bohun, earl of Hereford; Clare and Despencer, earls of Gloucester; Beauchamp, earl of Warwick, and baron of Powick: some of these quarries are dated 1453, others 36 H. VI. anno. r. H. Vl. xxxvi. Some few have the arms and scull of Wichenford, and others those of Stafford, of Grafton.

INSCRIPTIONS.

On the north side of the communion table is a flat stone, with this inscription round it, in capitals:

" Here lyethe the bodye of Peneleope, the wife of Robert Walweyn, of Neulande, gentleman, the daughter of Richard Ligon, of Madersfyelde, esquire, the sonne of William Ligon, esquire, sonne of Sir Richard Ligon, Knight, the sonne of Thomas Ligon, esquire, and Anne his wife, one of the daughters of the Lorde Beawchampe, her mother was Marye the daughter of Sir Thomas Russell, of Strensham, Knyghte. Obiit 13 Januarii 1596."

This stone formerly covered a raised monument, which stood where the communion table now is, on the wall; at her feet were these verses:

" Hic pia Penelope Walwini conditur uxor,
Jamdudum morbis languida, docta mori."

" Docta mori, vitæque breves transcendere metas
Nunc anima cœlum possidet, ante fide."

On the other three sides were thirty-five coats of arms: the principal were Walweyn impaling Ligon; some of the others were Godheard, Russell, Planges, Hodington, Cromeley, Somery, Albany, Haute, earl of Chester, Golafer, Cassy, Cookesey, Thurgrim, Cholmley, Askham, Rydal, Lygon, Bracy, Blanchminster, Giffard, Beauchamp, baron of Powick, D'Abetot, Hulgreve, Sir Gerard de Useslate, Lovetofte, Verdon, Greville.

On the south side of the choir, on a very curious alabaster tomb raised from the ground, is the figure of John Knotesford, Esq. armed, except his head and hands: on his right side lies his wife: at their feet this inscription:

" Here lieth the body of John Knotsesford, Esq. servant to King Henry the eyght, and Jane his wife, daughter to Sir Richard Knightley, Knight, who being first married to Mr. William Lumley, had issue John lord Lumley, and by Jonn Knotesford had issue five daughters and coheirs: he dyed in the yeare 1589 Novem. 23."

Over this inscription are his arms: Sable on a cross engrailed Argent an Annulet of the field, impaling; Or two palettes Gules. On the right side of the tomb, his daughters, Mary, the wife of Thomas Price, of Manaty, Esq. and Eleanor, wife of John Campion, Esq. on the left, Elizabeth, married to William Ridgley, of Ridgley, Esq. behind her Francis, married to Thomas Kirle, of Marcle, Esq. At her parent's head, kneels to a book on a pillar, Anne, their eldest daughter, who erected the monument, and was married to William Savage.

Near the south side of the south aisle, under the window, is a stone figure of a knight, completely armed, in his right hand a battle axe, and in his left a round target, having the appearance of great antiquity. We presume this is the one mentioned by Stukely.

He describes it as a carved stone image, by the south wall of the choir, of very rude and ancient workmanship. "It is a knight" he adds, " covered with a mail and his surcoat: in his right hand a halbert like a pickaxe, in his left a round target."

See Stukeley's Itiner. "This figure," says Gough, in his Sepulch. Monuments, "is in the oldest mail armour." An engraving of it may be seen in Carter's ancient Sculpture, vol. 2, p. 13.

Near the same place, on the ground, was a monument of white stone, about which was engraved this inscription :

"Edmundi hoc Harewell tumulo jam claudimur ossa
Quæ vita ad tempus post reditura fugit :
Sic et te fugiet quicunque inspexeris ista
Qod memorans pro me supplico funde preces.
vi Jan 1533"

Upon a flat stone is this inscription :

"Siste, hospes paulisper
Moræ pretium erit te scire
quæ fœmina sit hic sepulta.
Subtus depositæ jacent exuviæ Katharinæ
Richardi Daston de Wormington
in agro Glocestriensi genere armigeri,
Facultatis gradu juridici purpurati,
Filiæ familia sua dignæ ;
Ægidii Savage de Elmley Castle
in agro Vigorniensi
Armigeri, ex equestri ordine oriundi,
Conjugis æque amantis ac redamatæ :
Quæ viro suo superstes,
Quo melius Christo soli sponso cœlesti nuberet,
Viduam annos quadraginta se continuit :
eadem in rebus domesticis provida,
seu Salomonis mater familias illa,
Eleemosynariis larga quasi Dorcas altera,
Divinis pia velut Anna ipsa.
In amicos, familiares, vicinos, advenas, omnes,
Amœnitate morum suavi prædita.

Mortalitatem exuit, immortalitatem in duit
(Die anni longissimo in æternitatem translatâ)
Mensis Junii 11°,
Anno Christi 1674 ætatis suæ 84.
Effigiem habet Elmley supramemorata
(Una cum conjugis prolisque sculptilibus)
Cœlum animam, sepulchrum corpus,
Exemplum superstites ac posteri :
Δι αυτῆς ἀποθανων ἐτι λαλειλαι.
Dat mundus famam virtuti, dat pietati
Aureolam cœlum, vivit utroque loco."

The monument of Richard Corbet, a Knight
Templar, was probably erected before the four-
teenth century, and is a very plain table monument
without any ornaments whatever ; the sides and
ends of the tomb are covered with tiles, five inches
and a half square, that seem to have been of a red
and yellow colour, like the others with the armorial
bearings. This was drawn in 1778, by Major
Hayman Rooke, who has distinguished himself
much by his Antiquarian Research.

" Margaret, late wife of William Lygon, Esq. and only child
of Thomas Corbyn, Esq. obiit 21st Oct. 1699, ætat. 42."

" William Lygon, jun. of Madresfield, Esq. obiit 4th September, 1716, ætatis, 26."

" Here lies the body of William Lygon, of Madresfield, Esq.
who departed this life 16th day of March, anno dom. 1720,
ætatis suæ 79."

" Hic Jacet Maria uxor Gulielmi Ligon, de Madresfield,
armigeri, filia, Francisci Egiocke de Egiocke militis, et cohæ-
res fratris. Obiit decimo Novembris 1668, ætatis suæ 59.

At the bottom of the stone are these verses :

" Stay, passenger, and from this dusty urne
Both what I was, and what thou must be, learne,

Grace, virtue, beauty had no privilege,
That everlasting statute to abridge,
That all must die: then, gentle friend, with care
In life, for death and happiness prepare.
     Flebilis hoc posuit thalami consors,
     Mortuus est Januarii 29, 1680,
     Ætatis sexagesimo octavo.''

" To the dear memory of Richard Lygon, of Madresfield, in the county of Worcester, who departed this mortal life April 15, 1687, in the 49th year of his age: Anne, his sorrowful wife, eldest daughter to Sir Francis Russell, of the same county, baronet, dedicates this.''

" Here resteth the body of Elizabeth, the wife of John Wallsam, Esq. and daughter to William Lygon, Esq. who departed this transitory life, the 12th day of April, anno dom. 1674.''

N. B. All these inscriptions are in the upper part of the choir.

In the lower part:

" Johannes Dastomus generosus occubuit anno ætat. 70, salut. 1663.''

" John Wodehouse, Esq. third son of Sir Philip Wodehouse, of Kemberley, in Norfolk, Baronet, 26th June, 1718, aged 62 years.''

" Richard, eldest son of Richard Reed, of Lugwardine, in the county of Hereford, Esq. and Mary his wife, eldest daughter of Thomas Savage, Esq. of Great Malvern, died August 13, 1698.''

" John Dickins of Bobington, in the county of Stafford, esq. buried April 25, 1656, aged 78 years, and 6 months.''

" Richard Brindley, died 30 January, 1714, aged 29 years; also Richard son of the above named Richard, and Anne his wife, died Feb. 9, 1719, aged 6 years and 9 months.''

Several other inscriptions are on flat stones, see

Thomas Antiqua, Prior, Maj. Malv. to persons of little consequence; but near the third pillar, on the south side, is an inscription of great antiquity, the account of which is as follows:

" 22 May 1711, as Mrs. Savage's servants were digging in her garden which once belonged to the Priory house—now the Vicar's garden, about 3 feet from the church wall, on the south side the body of the church, and about 12 feet from the south aisle or chapel of St. Ursula, about 2 feet under ground, an old grave stone was found, with this date upon it, 1135, and the following inscription, being the epitaph of Walcher, the second prior of this house :"

PHILOSOPHVS DIGNVS BONVS ASTROLOGVS, LOTHERINGVS,
VIR PIVS AC HVMILIS, MONACHVS, PRIOR HVIVS OVILIS,
HIC JACET IN CISTA, GEOMETRICVS AC ABACISTA,
DOCTOR WALCHERVS; FLET, PLEBS, DOLET VNDOIVE CLERVS;
HVIC LVX PRIMA MORI DEDIT OCTABRIS SENIORI ;
VIVAT VT IN CŒLIS EXORET QVIS QVE FIDELIS. MCXXXV.

This is, in reality, a curious monkish rhyme, and should be written as follows:

" Philosophus bonus dignus
Astrologus lotheringus,
Vir pius et humilis,
Monachus prior hujus ovilis
Hic jacet in cista
Geometricus et Abacista,
          Doctor Walcherus.
Flet plebs, dolet undique clerus,
Huic lux prima mori
Dedit Octobris seniori ;
Vivet ut in cœlis
Exhoret quisque fidelis. 1135."

H

IN THIS TOMB LIES THE BODY · OF
DOCTOR WALCHER,

a Native of the dukedom of Lorrain and prior of this Convent : he was an acute Philosopher an able Astrologer a Geometrician and Mathematician a pious Christian and an humble Monk, his death is universally regretted both by the Clergy and Laity he died the first of Oct. in the year of our Lord 1135 Let every faithful Christian earnestly pray that his Soul may live in Heaven.

This monument was placed in the south side of Great Malvern church, where it remained until the commencement of the repairs, when it was removed to the space it now occupies—the site of Jesus's chapel.

MALVERN MAGNA.

PATRONS.	INCUMBENTS.	REGISTERS.
Prior et Conventus. Majoris Malverne.	Randulphus de I idle, id. 1269............................	Giff. f. 29. a.
	Gareland de Ledebury, P 287......................	ib. f. 21. a.
	Robertus de Bœra, 1313..................	Reg. sede. vac. f. 816.
	Thomas de Blourton, 4 Kal Apr. 1338..........	Hem. f. 15. b.
	Thomas Alyn, pbr. 20 Kal Feb. 1338.	R. sed. vac. f. 148. b. 149.
	(Me Smythes de Poywyke, pbr 10 Julii 1349	Wolst. v. 2. f. 17. a.
	Thomas le Clerk de Hereford, pbr. 21 Aug. 1349.........	Reg. sed. av. f. 128. a.
	Will'us Martyn, pbr 1354..................	Brian. f. 11. b.
	Joh. Smythes, 6 Jul	Barnet f. 2.
	Nicholaus Bn, 6 J 1367..................	Wittlesey, f. 15. a.
	Il pr. 1385.............	wak. f. 41. a.
	Jeronymus Id, 1 Maii, 1424..........	Morg. f. 26. b.
	Ric ap Gryffjth, 471.	Carp. v. 2. f. 23. b.
	1475...............	ib. f. 70. b.
	cap. 21 Aug. 1499............	S. Gygl. f. 8. b.
	Robynr, Will. Jermyne, 15	
Johannes Lumley mil d'us Lumley.	} Will'us Jermayne, cl. 18 Maii, 1575..................	R. 32. Bul. f. 11. a.
Jacobus Rex.	Edmundus Res, cl. A. B. 10 Sept. 1612.	ib. Parry. f. 99. a.
Carolus Rex.	Nicholaus Garret, cl. 25 Febr. 1640.	R. 33. f. 22. a.
Henricus Bromley de Holt, arm.	} Johannes Ballard, cl. A. B. 12 Mart. 1643.	ib. f. 30. a.
	Ricardus Smith, cler. 1656.......... }	Reg. Parochial.
	Jacobus Badger, 1669. .... }	

MALVERN MAGNA.

PATRONS.	INCUMBENTS.	REGISTERS.
Gul. Bromley de civ Wigorn Arm.	Thomas Hassel, cl. 15 Apr. 1692..............................	R. 34. f. 55. a.
Gul. Bromley de Holt.	Thomas Beardmore, cl. A. B. 5 Oct. 1698.	ib. f. 66. a
	Harricus Hill, cl. 17 Feb. 1701.	ib. f. 80. a.
Johnnes Bromley de Holt, arm et de Horseheath.	Johannes Webb, cl. A. A. 24 Jan. 1708.	ib. f. 94 a.
	Johannes Smith, cl. A. B. 12 June, 1730..................	R. 35. f. 15. b.
Thomas lord Foley.	Thomas Phillips* B. A. 8 Jan. 1758.	
Hon. Edward Foley.	Richard Graves † D. D. 19 Sept. 1801.	
Edw.	Henry Card, M. A. 30 June, 1815.	

CAPELLA DE WORDEFELD.

This chapel was not taxed, and was in the patronage of the prior and convent of Great Malverne, to whom it paid a pension of twelve-pence.

CAPELLA DE NEWLAND.

Thomas Hassal, 22 Julii, 1663.......................	Lib. subsc. f. 137.
Thomas Hassal, cler. 18 Maii. 1709.....................	L. subs. f. 137.
Thomas Bell, cl. 10 Feb. 1725.	ib. f. 371.

* Died June 1801, at Malvern, aged 76: he was nearly 50 years Vicar of Malvern.
† Resigned the living in 1815, and died at Mickleton in 1816.

CHAPTER IV.

GREAT MALVERN CHURCH.

Present State.

On entering the village of Great Malvern, the church which is dedicated to St. Mary, rises with picturesque effect. Its lofty square tower, elevated above the interjacent houses, is seen from the centre of the village to great advantage. On a nearer approach, the whole structure presents a very correct idea of the richness and magnificence of the priory, before the dissolution of religious houses. The present edifice so far exceeded the old parish church, which was dedicated to St. Thomas, the apostle, in beauty, and in every other respect, that the inhabitants determined to purchase it for their own use: and Mr. Knotsford, or Knottesford, selling it them for a moderate sum of money, some say 200*l.* it has ever since been deemed the parish church. The outside of this building is very rich in ornament, though light in its architecture, form, and size. It is indeed almost a cathedral in extent, being 171 feet long, and 63 feet broad, the height of the nave is 63 feet, the embattled tower, which springs from its centre, is 124 feet in height; the open work of these battlements give it an air of lightness, which is not, however, unbecoming a christian temple: in this tower are six bells, and a set of chimes. Sir Reginald Bray, who was a favourite of King Henry the VIIth, and a connoisseur in architecture, after shewing his skill in the superintendance of his master's chapel, in Westminster Abbey, and at St. George's, Windsor, built also this church, nearly in its present form and state, or rather he re-edified it; the body is Saxon, but the construction and shape of the arches are altogether gothic. It had abundance of windows curiously painted, but the ravages of time, and the efforts of mischievous boys, in the adjoining house, which for many years was a great school, have very much injured them, and left not one window perfect.. Mr. Dallaway observes "that all the stained glass remaining is but poorly executed." Prince Arthur and the builder, Sir. Reginald, have alone escaped * demolition, except a few armorial bearings, and some other things which appear symbolical of the various branches of Architecture, but by whom or why these have been introduced, it is impossible to explain. That. the church of Great Malvern, as a whole, was one of the finest specimens of Ancient Ecclesiastical Architecture then extant, is allowed by every ancient and modern author: but can the Antiquary com-

* Sir Reginald Bray, placed in the glass windows, the portraits of Henry VII. his Queen, Prince Arthur, and himself, all in surcoats of. armorial blazon.

mand the structure he admires to remain thus far venerable in ruins and no further? The sublime edifice, which to day raises in our minds the most lively feelings of religious awe, must, if that edifice be neglected, nod in dilapidation, and ere many years expire, crumble and fall an unpicturesque lump. Something must be done to arrest the hand of time, and usefulness must give give way to mere embellishment. In the first reparation of this church the encroachment of vegetation became of course constrained, for the ivy had clung to the tracery and threatened ruin in the blandishments of picturesqe beauty, it climbed in masses, and having with freedom, says the author of Reflections relative to Malvern, " crept over a great part of the window, gadding at large about the tracery, and even having insinuated itself, through many parts of the broken painted glass, into the church : there it formed clusters about the side and the mullions, whimsically twisting and wreathing itself about the figures within the niches, sometimes confusing the outlines, yet setting off the rich colours of the window." How shall we finish this description without a sigh? Between the summer of 1812 and 1813 the ivy was cut down by the hard hand of necessity : this occurred some time before the induction of the present Vicar to Great Malvern. The east window has still much of rich gothic magnificence, and though the tower, and so much of the building, consisting of the modern or florid gothic, which prevailed in the times, corresponding with the date of the tiles, about the choir (1453, and 36 of Henry VI. and anno r. H. VI. xxxvi.) part, doubtless, is coeval with the foundation of the monastery. The church of Great Malvern, in the year 1788, at length becoming in too ruinous a state to be used with safety, many plans were suggested to repair the interior so effectually as to enable the inhabitants of Malvern to attend divine service in it, for some time, but without effect: Dr. Booker, in his very pleasing Poem of Malvern, took occasion, in the year 1798, to lament the fallen state of this magnificent pile, in the following appeal to our feelings:

What marvel, that a scene so rich, so grand,
Should admiration e'en in Royal breasts
Awaken? Admiration that inspir'd,
Of old, for yonder venerable pile
Devotion, and Munificence, and Zeal,
To rear those richly tinted windows, now
Alas! with Ivy, and with weedy moss,
Obtrusive, hung: some, by the gusty wind,
Of Striplings—thoughtless in their boyish sports
Fractured, and heedlessly, by hand uncouth,
With ill according workmanship repair'd.

In the year 1802, Mr. Tatham, the architect, was employed to survey and make an estimate of the expences of the necessary repairs; he stated in his report that he was of opinion, that the church was capable of such a repair as might render it fit for divine service; and preserve the building for many years; and as a further inducement to this undertaking, he very judiciously added, "that its antiquity, magnificence, and beauty, combined to render it worthy of being preserved as a specimen of gothic architecture, in which respect it is little inferior to any in the kingdom." It was added, " that as no sufficient fund had existed, for its repair, since the dissolution, when this noble conventual church became parochial, and as the parishioners themselves were now unable to bear the expenses, without assistance, it would be expedient immediately to commence a subscription for the sum of 1000*l.* in order to give it, at once, such substantial repairs as were absolutely necessary for its preservation." The following sums were almost immediately subscribed, and the remainder 25*l.* 17s. made up by a parish rate.

List of the Subscribers, with the amount of their subscriptions, to the OLD FUND, for repairing the church of Great Malvern, in the order in which they subscribed:

	£.	s.	d.
The Hon. Edward Foley, M. P. deceased,.........	100	0	0
The Right Hon. Lord Beauchamp, deceased, ...	52	10	0
Anthony Lechmere, Esq. Rhydde,.................	50	0	0
The Lord Bishop of Worcester, deceased,.........	50	0	0
Richard Morgan Graves, D. D. Vicar, deceased,	30	0	0
Miss Graves, ...	5	5	0
Mrs. Wall, of the Lodge,......................	5	5	0
Dean and Chapter of Worcester,...............	10	10	0
	303	10	0

	£.	s.	d.
Brought over	303	10	0
James Henry Arnold, L. L. D. Chancellor, ...	10	10	0
Thomas Evans, D. D. Archdeacon, ...	5	5	0
Rev. William Calcot, Great Witley, ...	5	5	0
Rev. Reginald Pyndar, Hadsor,......................	5	5	0
Martin Wall, M. D. Oxford,...........................	5	5	0
Mrs. Plumer, ...	21	0	0
Miss Dandridges, Balder Green,.....................	15	15	0
Rev. Martin Stafford Smith, Fladbury, ...	10	10	0
Sir Charles Trubshaw Withers, Knight, deceased,	10	10	0
Richard Bourne Charlet, Esq. Ehmley Castle,...	5	5	0
William Wall, Esq. Worcester, ...	5	5	0
Rev. William Probyn, Pershore,......................	5	5	0
Thomas Hornyold, Esq. Blackmore Park, ...	10	10	0
George Palmer, Esq. London,........................	5	5	0
Treadway Nash, D. D. Bevere, ...	5	5	0
Rev. Allen Cliffe, Mathon,...........................	5	5	0
Thomas Bund, Esq. Wick, ...	5	5	0
Rev. Richard Harrington, Hagley,...................	5	5	0
Mr. Batham, Worcester, ...	2	2	0
Mr. James Oliver, Worcester,........................	5	5	0
Mr. Richard Benbow, Malvern, ...	5	5	0
Mr. Richard Bellers, Malvern,.......................	5	5	0
Mr. William Bullock, Malvern,......................	5	5	0
Mr. William Michael, Malvern, ...	1	1	0
Mr. John Twinberrow, Cirencester,.................	1	1	0
Mr. William Twinberrow, Welland, ...	1	1	0
Mr. Job Twinberrow, Maddresfield, ...	1	1	0
Mr. Samuel Matthews, Malvern,.....................	2	2	0
Mr. John Williams, Ombersley, ...	4	4	0
Mr. William Walker, Hanley,........................	3	3	0
	482	0	0

	£.	s.	d.
Brought over	482	0	0
The Right Hon. Viscount Dudley and Ward,......	50	0	0
Mary, Countess of Harcourt, ...	10	0	0
Rev. James Stillingfleet, Prebendary of Worcester,	3	3	0
Mrs. Williams, Malvern, ...	10	0	0
Mr. John Mason, Birmingham, ...	5	5	0
The Right Hon. Lord Eardley, ...	50	0	0
Mrs. Bridges, Ledbury,.................................	10	0	0
James Laird, Esq. deceased, ...	20	0	0
A Lady from the Wells,.................................	1	0	0
Mrs. Benson, Bath, ...	2	2	0
Miss Benson, Bath, ...	2	2	0
George Nash, Esq. Martley,............................	5	5	0
Thomas Phillips, Esq. Hanbury Hall, ...	30	0	0
Thomas Saunders, Esq. Bristol,......................	20	0	0
Temple West, Esq. London, ...	5	5	0
Right Hon. Earl of Coventry, ...	52	10	0
Lord Bishop of Worcester, ...	50	0	0
Lady Hart, London, ...	5	5	0
Rev. James Bonsquet, Aldridge, ...	5	0	0
Rev. William Smith, ...	1	0	0
A Widow's mite,...	1	1	0
The Right Hon. Lord Foley, Great Witley,......	50	0	0
The Right Hon. Lord Lyttelton, Hagley,..........	31	10	0
Mrs. E. Curling, Blackheath, ...	2	2	0
Charles Dowding, Esq......................................	5	5	0
Mrs. E. Roberts,..	1	1	0
Henry Barry, Esq..	1	1	0
Sir William Pole, Bart....................................	2	2	0
Mrs. Harrington, ...	1	0	0
Rev. H. Hayes, ...	2	2	0
	917	1	0

actually stuck up on its eastern wall, a large pigeon-house, belonging as my conductor informed me, but to which I could not give any credit, to the person presiding over the sacred place wherein I then stood, he being equally happy to see the flights of such innocents, through the aisles and vaults, as to hear the harmonious sounds of the surrounding canine rangers of the sportive fields. I need not, at this time, go into the detail of rubbish, holes, pew lumber, broken altar tables, and the like modern church peculiarities, but shall remark, in referring to the stain edglass, that no more than two pieces then remained perfect, in having escaped the various sorts of rages that have had dominion among us, from the time of Edward IV. to the present school-boy pastime, as above hinted at : these illuminated pieces of glass, gave the small whole lengths of Prince Henry, son to Henry VII. and Sir Reginald Bray, the famous Architect of Henry VII. chapel Westminster, and St. George's chapel, Windsor. Those who from information, by a channel which it is unnecessary to point out, suppose that there are more perfect subjects remaining, will find on a nice examination, that they have been led into an error. Indeed at a first glance, in coming into the church, any one may naturally conclude, when seeing every window full of lineal objects, colours, and shadows, that a general assemblage of whole length portraits, and historical well preserved compositions, pervade every part of the structure, but these suppositions will soon vanish. Hence whatever may be the destiny of the architecture and sculptural beauties of the church for the sake of history and antiquarian instruction, we, Mr. Urban, may warn the subscribers not to consent to the disturbing of the transparent shew, the enthusiastic tinge, " the dim religious light" of Malvern's story, which to the sensitive mind, must ever emit delights inexpressible, when musing on holy rites and former glories. But enough. Depend upon it, Mr. Urban, if the several windows, are gutted, to place a moiety in one window, as has been done at Cirencester, (a proportion of the whole as one 16th part of an inch to a thousand feet) as premised by the subscription receivers, what a disorganized, what a farragoed jumble of heads, arms, and legs, crowns, croziers, shields, swords, and spears, will then meet our sight: what a chaos of lines, and colours, to confuse the inquisitorial antiquary, will then appear, while all around, one continued light of garish day, will break in upon his head, eyes, and soul, in multifarious quarries of modern glazier's work, new cut, squared, diamonded, and leaded! By the bye what is to become of this prodigious mine of illuminated story. May not some stained glass importers from the rifled religious buildings, on the continent, be consulted on this occasion? There have been several sales last spring of these imported articles. J. C.

Surveyor, by inclination, of the various styles
of the ancient architecture of England.

Gentleman's Magazine, Oct. 1802, p. 924.

Mr. Urban, Oct. 17, 1805.

As you have always discovered a laudable zeal for the preservation of our National Antiquities, and have kindly given admission to the communications of your numerous correspondents, I beg permission to add my efforts to theirs. The object to which I am desirous of directing their attention, is the present dangerous and melancholy condition of the church of Great Malvern, in Worcestershire; it is beautifully situated on the slope of the Malvern hills, and belonged to the priory which formerly stood on that spot, and of which only the gate way remains. The building is of stone, large, and exhibits good studies for attaining the knowledge of two periods of our ancient architecture, viz. the Saxon, and that known by the name of the florid Gothic.

In the former style the nave is erected, and the choir and,

tower are of the latter: the altar is adorned with burnt tiles, which are highly glazed and ornamented with mottoes, devices, and armorial bearings, and there are some curious monuments and inscriptions; and all the windows have fragments of beautiful paintings still remaining. It is in fact, for extent, beauty and situation, far superior to most parish churches in England. The profits, however, of the incumbent are small, and there is no fund, at least no sufficient one, for preserving the buildings in good repair, and the consequence is that it is in a state of impending ruin.

The walls and floors are dreadfully damp, and parts of the church sometimes flooded · the ivy is suffered to grow within the building, at least it has pierced through the insterstices, formed by the tracery of the eastern window, and covers a large portion of the eastern end of the fabric. It is, in short, in a state unfit for the parishioners, disgraceful to the parish, and will soon be beyond the power of repair.

The vicar, Mr. Graves, (son of the late rector of Claverton) has made, I understand, more than one endeavour to raise a subscription from the neighbouring gentry and visitors in the summer, for repairing the church; but through a want of proper management, or of a laudable spirit of liberality, the attempt has never fully succeeded. It is my wish, Mr. Urban, to call the attention of the people of the country, and those to whom our antiquities are an object of regard, to the sad state of this church, and I am in hopes that Mr. Graves's wish will be seconded and supported by the rich and liberal. Many indeed of the ancestors of the first Worcestershire families rest in the church of Great Malvern, particularly the present possessor of Maddresfield Court.

Yours, &c.

VIATOR.

It appears, however, that it is indeed difficult to satisfy every one: the lover of picturesque effect clashes with the lover of comfort and antiquity, nor does the poet even escape notice, as may be perceived from the following letter:

Mr. Urban,   April 15, 1813.

The church at Great Malvern, which you, in conjunction with every other person who has seen it, seem to take an interest in, is repaired, and so much improved beyond its late appearance that it might almost be called properly repaired.

But labour and whitewash, however, are in the country by far too cheap to suffer poor country churches to have even a chance of any other remedy for the cure of their distempers, and we are accordingly indulged with a most beautiful quantity of it in the parish church of Malvern.* The ivy, which I presume Dr. Booker lamented, is at the east end of the church, and partly covers the great east window. With the exception of the ivy tree at Mr. Ponsonby's Castle, in the Green Park, it is nearly as large and handsome as can be seen, and however much the poet may lament its intruding upon the sanctity of painted windows, I believe there are but few admirers of nature, or to be a little more confined, of Malvern church yard, that do not require the traveller to give his tribute of praise as he beholds it.

Near the ivy tree is a sun dial, (exalted 6 or 7 feet on a pole) which has four faces, fronting the north, south, east and west, and appears to be one of the few remaining companions of the painted or stained glass: as far as a traveller can guess they are both about four centuries old.

YECATS.

Before the arrival of Dr. Graves, in Malvern, it is said, in addition to the first letter, by Mr.

* If this correspondent had rightly informed himself, he would have found that most of this white wash would, in proper time, be exchanged for a hue, *in proper keeping* with oak wood work.

Carter, relative to the pigeon house, that hounds and a fox were actually kept within the sacred edifice: we are, therefore, not much surprised at reading the following words in a respectable periodical publication:

"Application was made to the Rev. Mr. Phillips, to prevent the cruel depredations committed by a large Ivy bush, on the venerable painted glass, in one of the east windows of Malvern church, but for a time disregarded."

The plan, for the repair of the church, which was delivered to the proper persons by Mr. Tatham, was not acted upon, but the funds raised for that purpose were, in some measure, appropriated to their original intention; for we understand the sum of 2000*l.* was expended in repairing and restoring the ceiling, and in contributing to that quantity of white-washing of which YEOATS so much complains; all this was done about the year 1812.

At this period the venerable edifice became indeed a whitened sepulchre; for although neatness, or, at least, cleanliness, reigned above, ruin and devastation bore sovereign sway below; confusion and dilapidation strove for mastery, and rubbish and dirt mocked all the plasterer's art to restore it to comfort; and in addition to the difficulties of making this place of worship fit for the uses to which it was originally designed, the Rev. Dr. Graves left the vicarage of Great Malvern. So small a sum now remained in the hands of the trustees, that indeed little more could be done than what they had achieved in restoring the roof and white washing the walls. Another effort was however made, towards a further repair of the building, professional aid was again called in, the choice of a proper person fell on Mr. Smirke, the architect, who, after superintending some improvements, not exactly connected with the church, received his dismissal also. It was at this period, June, 1815, that the Rev. Henry Card was inducted to the vicarage of Great Malvern, and it has been fortunate for that village, and its inhabitants, that a gentleman of his knowledge and ability should offer, without the expectancy of any remuneration whatever, to restore his church to its present splendor. He immediately applied to the neighbouring gentry, and having, by his individual exertions, raised upwards of 700*l.* he commenced and has completed his arduous task, with credit to himself, and to the honour of Great Malvern, without the smallest expense to the parish for professional aid; thus furthering the great interests of religion, and the consequent good morals of the residents of that charming village.

The following are the names of the Subscribers to the New Fund, for completing the repairs of the church, in the order in which they subscribed:

	£.	s.	d.
1813. The Hon. Mrs. Percival, Downing-street,...	30	0	0
The Hon. Mrs. Yorke, Forthampton-court,...	30	0	0
	60	0	0

		£.	s.	d.
1813.	Brought over............................	60	0	0
	The Right Hon. Lady Lyttelton,...	21	0	0
	The Right Hon. Lady Bolton,......	100	0	0
	Mrs. Walde,............................	50	0	0
	The Hon. Mrs. Yorke,...............	5	0	0
	Mrs. Williams, Malvern, second subscription,...........................	10	0	0
	Rev. Wm. S. Willes, Astrop-house,	5	5	0
	Mrs. W. Willes,........................	2	2	0
	Lord Dunstanville,......,............	20	0	0
	Dowager Lady Brownlow, ...	5	5	0
	The Hon. Miss Cust,..................	2	2	0
	The Hon. and Rev. Henry Cust,..	10	10	0
	Miss Baker, ...	2	2	0
	Sir Frederick Baker,.................	2	2	0
	The Earl of Hardwicke,.............	31	10	0
	Vice Admiral Sawyer,...............	2	2	0
	The Right Hon. Lady Theodosia Vyner, ...	3	3	0
	Thomas Evans, D. D. Archdeacon of Worcester, second subscription, ...	5	5	0
Aug. 1814.	Temple West, Esq. a crimson velvet pulpit cloth,..................	21	0	0
	Admiral West, ...	5	5	0
	Miss West,.............................	5	5	0
	Miss Sophia West,....................	5	5	0
Dec.	Rev. Digby Smith, Prebendary of Worcester, ...	3	0	0
	Miss Smith, and Mrs. Jones,........	1	1	0
	James Cocks, Esq. M. P.............	10	10	0
April, 1815.	Rev. Edward Neele,..................	1	0	0
		389	14	0

		£.	s.	d.
1815.	Brought over,........................	389	14	0
June	Mrs. Walde, second subscription,	20	0	0
24,	Mrs. Ann Orde,........................	20	0	0
	Holland Gryffith, Esq. Anglesey,	3	0	0
Aug. 7,	Edward Thomas Foley, Esq. Stoke house,...............................	100	0	0
27,	Rev. George Waddington, North-wold, Essex,........................	1	0	0
Sept. 12, 1816.	Mrs. Weston,........................	2	0	0
May 16,	The Right Hon. N. Vansittart,....	50	0	0
	The Earl of Bristol,..................	50	0	0
June 20,	John Taylor, Esq......................	5	0	0
	Lord Dudley and Ward, second subscription,......................	10	0	0
	Temple West, Esq. second sub-scription,.............................	5	0	0
	Henry Clifton, Esq....................	5	5	0
	Rev. Dr. Abbot,......................	5	5	0
	Lady Harcourt, second subscrip-tion,................................	10	0	0
Aug. 3,	Her Royal Highness the Princess Charlotte of Wales, for the completion of the west window	30	0	0
	Lord Elmley,........................	10	0	0
	William Wall, Esq. second sub-scription, ...	17	0	0
	The Hon. Mrs. James Yorke, se-cond subscription,..............	10	0	0
		743	4	0

Subscriptions to be received at the Banking-houses of Messrs. Robarts & Co. M. P. 15, Lombard-street; Biddulph, Cox and Drummond, Charing Cross; Hammersley & Co.

Pall Mall; Birch and Chambers, New Bond-street; at the Crown Hotel; and the Foley Arms, Great Malvern. The smallest donation will be acceptable.

Finding, however, upon winding up the accounts of the repairs at Great Malvern church, that Mr. Card had advanced, from his own pocket, a considerable sum, over and above the money raised, the Honourable Mrs. James Yorke,* with her characteristic liberality, proposed and has set on foot a second subscription to liquidate this debt. The Earl of Bristol also, with the same generous spirit, has concurred in her exertions, to prevent the possibility of pecuniary loss occuring to Mr. Card; and we are informed that it is the intention of the parishioners, in return for the great and actual advantages which his exertions have procured for Great Malvern, not to suffer their Clergyman to be responsible for the smallest sum contracted in restoring their ancient edifice.

Amount of the Subscriptions proposed by the Hon. Mrs. Yorke, at the time this book went to press:

	£.	s.	d.
The Hon. Mrs. Yorke,	10	0	0
The Earl of Bristol,	20	0	0
Viscount Sidmonth,	10	0	0
Lord Arden,	10	0	0
	50	0	0

* This lady is daughter to the Bishop of Worcester, and wife of the Bishop of Ely.

	£.	s.	d.
Brought over, ...	50	0	0
Marquis Camden,..	10	0	0
Earl Bathurst,..	10	0	0
Lord Eardley,..	5	0	0
James Cocks, Esq. M. P................................	5	5	0
Hon. Mr. Bouverie,......................................	5	0	0
	85	5	0

Present account relative to the expenditure for repairs of Malvern church,........................	1254	5	0
Received by Mr. Card, by subscriptions, &c......	1131	17	9
Left due to Mr. Card,..................................	122	7	3

But, while we applaud the zeal and industry of the indefatigable clergyman of Great Malvern, in gaining these subscriptions to assist in the restoration of a place of worship, too much commendation cannot be bestowed on those distinguished individuals, who encouraged him in his exertions, and without whose aid all his good intentions must have been of no avail. It reflects much credit on the good sense, taste and public spirit of the present Lord Beauchamp, for the manner in which he has interested himself, in obtaining a grant from Government of 1000*l.* towards the repair of the church, himself subscribing 20*l.* To Edward Thomas Foley, Esq. of Stoke, to whom most of the village of Malvern belongs, for his very handsome subscription of 121*l.* also to Lady Harcourt, who, not confining her patronage and assistance to the walks and wells, but, having herself subscribed 20*l.* to the church fund, has also materially assisted Mr. Card, in his exertions to obtain many valuable subscriptions from others.

On the 30th of June, 1815, the Rev. Henry Card was inducted to the vicarage of Great Malvern, and on the 12th of February, 1816, the church was closed, for the purpose of continuing the repairs under his superintendance. These repairs being sufficiently proceeded in to enable him to perform divine service, the church was opened on the 20th of June, in the same year, with a sermon from the vicar, whose appeal to the congregation assembled, drew forth the very liberal subscription of 44*l.* in aid of this undertaking, a sum much larger than was ever before obtained for any purpose, in Malvern's ancient edifice. In the July following, the annexed letter appeared in one of the numbers of *The Gentleman's Magazine*:

Mr. URBAN,   Malvern, July 11, 1816.

If I rightly recollect, in some of the numbers of your valuable miscellany, a correspondent deplored, in common with other admirers of what is improperly called the Gothic Architecture*, that one of the most beautiful specimens of it, Great Malvern Abbey Church, should have fallen, as to the interior, into utter neglect and decay. It is gratifying, therefore, to have an opportunity of recording, through

---

* It is recorded, that the first person who applied the term *gothic* to the pointed architecture of our buildings, was Sir Christopher Wren, who called our Cathedrals mountains of stone.

you, what the zeal of an individual, the influence of example, and the rational appropriation of money, have effected within the short space of four months, for the renovation of a structure so ornamental to the county of Worcester. To those who remember Malvern church in its former state, when the bat made her nest within its sacred walls, and the crumbling roof dropped on the uplifted eye of devotion, a short representation of the alterations and improvements which have been made, with a view to restore it to something like its pristine character of dignity and magnificence, must be highly satisfactory. On entering the church, the first object that now meets the eye, in consequence of the removal of two old screens, is the window at the end of the north aisle, which is completely filled up with ancient stained glass: in the approach to the nave, the two circular ends of the church, composed of richly glazed yellow tiles, upon which are the armorial bearings of different great families, cannot fail to arrest the attention. The pavement is of stone, and the two sides of the chancel are now occupied with the old decorated stalls of " the white robed monks," the seats of which are lined with handsome crimson cloth, corresponding with the communion table, the pulpit, and the state pews of Earl Beauchamp, and Mr. Foley, of Stoke, patron of the living, which pews, from their size and costly mode of fitting up, make an imposing appearance. The west now rivals the east window, in richness and beauty of colours. The organ is sufficiently enlarged, and, though it has evidently been the great object to keep an uniformity of design throughout, yet the front of the organ gallery is so conspicuously beautiful, that this, separately, will attract admiration with many ; still there is nothing in it that can violate the general aspect of antiquity which pervades the church, for a due regard to the style of building has been strictly observed in the whole of the ornamental parts. In short, nothing of *modern beautification* is to be discerned.

Such are the principal improvements in this magnificent

structure, and so judiciously have they been made, that they must please the most fastidious taste. The principal benefactors towards these repairs and improvements are the Countess of Harcourt, the Right Honourable Lady Lyttelton, the Earls of Bristol and Hardwicke, Lord Dudley and Ward, the Hon. Mrs. Yorke, Mrs. Waldo, Mr. Foley, Mr. Temple West, and Mr. Vansittart, names well entitled to respect, either for public virtue or private beneficence; but the exertions of the Rev. Henry Card, the present Vicar, under whose personal direction the whole has been conducted, are above all praise. This gentleman, well known to the literary world, from his various productions, seems to have determined that no impediment should have retarded or defeated his pious efforts for the restoration of this monument of the zeal and munificence of our forefathers, and accordingly raised above 500*l.* in a very short time, without causing a single levy to be made on the parish; which, as one of the Worcester Papers justly observes, "is an instance, in these times, of rare and successful exertion, that reflects the highest credit on the character of Mr. Card, as a Clergyman, and ought to ensure the lasting gratitude of his parishioners." AN OLD VISITOR OF MALVERN.

Present internal state of Great Malvern church.

On entering a side door of the north aisle, and over the one which leads to a modern font, and to the entrance to the middle aisle, is affixed a coat of arms, but to whom it relates is at present unknown: it was found, some years ago, by the present clerk and sexton, in digging a grave in the church yard: the arms are, on a shield between a fess, three dolphins; the colours of the bearing, &c. are rendered indistinct by white-wash. To these arms there has been affixed, by way of a crest, though much too large for the shield, a cross, and under the shield, in demy relief, a man's head, taken from some mutilated monument of no ancient date. A kind of scroll margin surrounds this relict, which we have been thus particular in describing, lest the future antiquary might draw inferences from this compound, injurious to the cause of truth.

Proceeding onwards to the left, in the north aisle, we arrived at a mural slab of white marble, on which is the following inscription :

Near this spot
are laid the mortal remains,
of HARRIET HOLLAND :.
She died at Malvern Wells, Aug. 21, 1814.
She was daughter of Henry Holland, Esq.*
A name rendered eminent, by his skill and Genius,
In the profession of Architecture.
From the sufferings of disease, endured without a complaint,
From the painful sympathies of an affectionate heart,
From unremitting labour in the relief of every want, but her own;
She was called to her rest, at the early age of 36.

A little further onward, on a mural slab surmounted by a pediment or obelisk, on which are two urns, and over these, armorial bearings of archer's bows, with arrows in saltire, on a shield sable, crest, an owl, or; is a monument with the following inscription:

Sacred to the memory
of Richard Benbow, of this parish, Gent.
who departed this life, Dec. 19, 1813 :
Aged 73 years.
Also of Nancy, wife of the above Richard Benbow,
who departed this life, Dec. 23, 1813.

* H. Holland, architect of the late Drury Lane Theatre, Carlton-

We now arrive at a recess in this aisle, to which we ascend by three steps; this was formerly Jesus Chapel. Here are two windows composed of fragments of stained glass. In the centre of this recess is a railed-in vault, purchased by the Ladies Hartley and Lyttelton, for a last home; and within the white iron palisades, and on a white slab, decorated with antique vases, is the following inscription:

Underneath this marble,

Lie the remains,

of the Right Honourable Lady Louisa Hartley;

Daughter of Richard Lumley, fourth earl of Scarborough,

And Barbara his wife; a sister,

of Sir George Saville, Baronet,

She was born the twenty first of July, 1773:

She was married to Winchcomb Henry Hartley, Esq.

On the twenty-sixth of Feb. 1798.

She died on the 10th October, 1811,

And left an affectionate Husband,

Two sons, and three daughters,

To lament respectively

Their irreparable loss.

On each side of this tomb are two monuments, the one on the left being that of Walcher, the prior, alluded to in the ancient history of this church; and on the right side the monument of the Saxon knight, in armour, carved in black marble, both of which were removed from the south aisle, on the commencement of the repairs.

House, &c. died in 1808, at the age of nearly 60. He was also architect and surveyor to the East India Company, and in the commission of the peace for the county of Middlesex. He also built the houses facing the Green Park.

On the rails of this monument, was a brass plate, intended to be restored to its place, and on it the following words, under a coat of arms, having as a crest a leopard or tyger's head :

" Here lieth the body of
Maria Giffard Williams,
Late of Mount court, in this
Parish, who departed this life,
March 30, 1785, aged 2 years.

" Now cease afflicted friends, your loss to mourn,
And think me happy, tho' I can't return.''

Passing this chapel, on the side of the opening, on a mural slab, surmounted by the sacramental cup and cloth, we read,

" Sacred to the Memory
of Miss Grace Colt,
Only daughter of Robert Colt, esq.
Of Auldborn, East Lothian,
Died 27 August, 1802:
Aged 21.

His cheerful watch, some guardian angel keeps,
Around the tomb, where youth and virtue lie,
Mourn then no more, her spirit only sleeps,
Such worth, such genuine worth, can never die.

We know not if these lines are original, but their truth and simplicity need no excuse for the poet.

At the further end of this aisle, lighted by another superb window of stained glass, and on the spot which was once also a chapel, but now about to be converted into a vestry room, on the left side, is a mural monument.

To the Memory of
William Hamilton, M. A.
Rector of Evesbach,
In the county of Hereford:
also,
Penelope his wife, one of the daughters
of Francis Woodhouse, of Larport,
In the county aforesaid, gent.
She died May 23,
aged 56.

On the right hand of this monument, inscribed on a more modern mural slab, surmounted by armorial bearings, is the following inscription :

In an adjoining vault,
Lie the remains of Alexander Montgomery Esq.
of Annick lodge, in the county of Ayr,
who died July the 8th, 1802, aged 57 years :

He was second son of y late Alexander Montgomery, Esq.
of the same county,
And brother to the earl of Eglington: he married
Elizabeth Taylor, daughter of John Taylor, Esq.
In the county of Westmoreland,
Whom with nine children, he has left to lament his loss,
And to mourn over the memory of his departed virtues,
To commemorate which, and as a solemn, tho' inadequate
memorial, of her tenderness, and concern,
His surviving widow erects this monument.
Blessed is the memory of the just.

In this chapel, and under their monument, are two projections, which at one time evidently held statues. On the right hand side is an ancient font, or receptacle for holy water. Here is also a book-stand, with the Bible, &c. chained to its desk; a not uncommon way of holding out in many an ancient edifice, an inducement for reformation to the backsliding christian, without the temptation of breaking a commandment.* The back of the altar, where once was a chapel dedicated to our Lady, is ornamented from the ground upwards, with the yellow or orange-coloured tiles, which paved this part of Malvern church. At the end of this chapel, on a mural slab, are these words:

In a vault adjoining this spot,
Lie the remains of Catherine Yarnold,
third daughter of John Dandridge, Esq.
Of Baldens green, in this Parish,
First married to William Bund, Esq.
Of Wick, in the County of Worcester:
Afterwards, to William Yarnold, Esq.
Late of the Town of Monmouth.
She died at Cheltenham, 27 Sept. A. D. 1800,
aged 60.

You now arrive at the south aisle or chapel. This place is at present a scene of confusion. The plumber melts his lead, the carpenter his glue, and here the smoke, from a modern fire place, blackens the few pieces of painted relics of stained

* In the convocation of 1536, it was resolved to publish a new Translation of the Scriptures, in 1538. Henry VIII. jealous, lest his own subjects should become such theologians as to question his tenets, used great precautions in publishing that translation of the scripture which was finished this year. He would only allow a copy of it to be deposited in each parish church, *where it was fixed by a chain:* and he took care to inform the people, by proclamation, " that this indulgence was not the effect of his duty, but of his goodness and liberality to them." HUME.

glass, no longer perfumed by the smell of frankincense, but discoloured by the smoke of a wood fire. In this, the south aisle, you now meet no memorial to strike the eye, except an enriched circular arch, on one side said to have been a place of confession, but which appears more probably, to have once held a tomb.* On each side of the chancel, near the end, is a short rail way of wood work placed bevelled ways, through which, tradition informs us, the people beheld the elevation of the host. Returning down this aisle, until you arrive at the new font,† near the entrance, you proceed up the centre aisle. The back of this entrance is ornamented with the orange tiles, once trodden by monkish feet, but yet in excellent preservation. On one of these tiles, found in a pillar facing the entrance, is an inscription in obsolete character, the only part of which that can be decyphered, is as follows :

> Thenke. mon. yi. liffe.
> mai. not. eu. endure.
> Yat. yow. dost. yi. self.
> of. yat. yow. art. sure.
> But. yat. yow. *givest*
> un. to. yi. lectur. cure.
> And. eu. hit. availe. ye.
> hit. is but. aventure.

* The author of "Reflections relative to the Malvern Hills" calls it a "confessional."

† The old font is still preserved, it is merely a large circular stone receptacle for water, without either letters or tracery, to afford conjecture to the antiquary, or pleasure to the eye of taste.

In the floor of Little Malvern church, "says the author of Reflections relative to the Malvern hills," I have observed tiles exactly corresponding with this; on one or two the inscription is still perfect. Nash, in his account of Stanford, in this, county, addns. p. 70, has inserted a fac simile of a tile of the same size, with characters, which appear the same in shape and dimensions.

The inscriptions correspond, except as to one obscure word, with this; and the rest at Great and Little Malvern, all of which agree with each other, as far as I can trace them. The tile, he says, is supposed to have belonged to the old church of Stanford. He does not any where notice these tiles at Malvern, nor does Thomas. Under the fac simile are the words, 'upon a tile on the outside of Stanford church,' but Nash elsewhere says, 'the tile is in the possession of Sir Edward Winnington.' It cannot now be found, but there is good reason to suppose it agreed in size with the engraving. The present church of Stanford was built about 40 years ago. It is not improbable, that the tile was brought, by some person, to the old church, from Malvern. If not, it is rather curious that a tile, with the same inscription, should occur in a place so distant. The word, with respect to which these lines differ from the representation of that at Stanford, is *givist*, (givest.) If that be, as I suppose, the true reading, Nash's fac simile, which might here, in a perplexing part, be copied conjecturally, has the words '*be just*,' which certainly differ from the Malvern inscriptions.*

Mr. Card informs us, some persons are of opinion that the square bricks or tiles, which form the tesselated pavement of Malvern church, and

---

* On the tile at Malvern, spoken of by Vigorniensis, that, which is in the place of Nash's ' *be just*,' is *one* word only, no stop intervening, as between every two words in other parts. (Nor does a stop intervene in Nash.) The first letter a good deal resembles his. The second is e. Then occur characters, the outline of which (though they are larger,) is tolerably represented by ⎵ The next letter is one long, straight stroke, which is probably f. Then follows t.

If the word was intended for *gevist*, (givest,) which there seems little reason to doubt, it is to an experienced antiquary that the removal of the obscurity is chiefly owing.

I find *geve* and *gef*, for give, in the Glossary to Percy's Rel. Vols. 1 and 2. *Cure*, for care, heed, regard, is in the ballad of Harpalus, ibid. Vol. 2. We still say ' *cure* of souls.' *But that thou gevist unto thy lectur cure.* But see that thou givest heed, attention, to the good advice afforded thee. Probably it would not be difficult to find, in old writers, instances of *that* used nearly as the French *Que. Qu' il vienne.* Let him come. In Greek *That* is sometimes used for *See that.* Viger. de Idiotismis, Cap. 7. Sect. 10. Reg. 6: where this use of the French *Qua* is noticed. And V. ibid. note, part 3.

It has been suggested to me that the sentiment, *That thou dost thyself of that thou art sure*, was probably designed to point out to the reader the expediency of being pious and virtuous in his own life, rather than of trusting to the masses said by the priest. And it has been, at the same time, supposed that the lines were written not earlier than the period, when the opinions, which led to the Reformation, began to be made public. This supposition, however, does not seem absolutely necessary to warrant the explanation. Even without hostility to the masses of the priest, it is possible that the reader might be admonished to place *far* which are painted over, in a coarse style, with mottoes, devices, and armorial bearings; among the latter those of England, Westminster Abbey, Mortimer, Earl of March; Bohun and Beauchamp, Earls of Warwick; and some of which tiles have the letters I. H. S. and others the date 1453 and 36 Henry VI. have the appellation of Alhambra tiles, being manufactured at Alhambra, in Portugal, and are, upon that account, considered as valuable, from their antiquity and rarity: he by no means subscribes to this opinion. On

greater reliance upon his own exertions. Should the above interpretation appear doubtful, the only one which I could offer agrees much less aptly with the words themselves: viz. That which thou dost thyself, of thy own rash will, respecting that, or the issue of it, thou feelest securely. But see that thou, &c.

The meaning of the whole, perhaps, is this:

Think, man, thy life cannot endure for ever. That which thou dost thyself, rather than trust to the acts of others, of the effect of that thou art sure. But see that thou give attention to the advice afforded thee. And yet it is but a chance that it ever shall avail thee.

Lecture in more modern English sometimes signifies *Reading*. V. Johnson. And that may be the meaning here. *To thy reading, or to what thou readest.*

The date of the tiles about the choir is 1453. 36 H. VI. &c. V. p. 37. Is it probable that these others are more modern?

We see of how long standing is the use of $\overset{e}{y}$ for *the*, *y*, or *yat*, for *that*, which, in writing, is not yet wholly laid aside. Y S for *this*, and Y T for *that*, occur on the monument of Shakespeare, at Stratford. The reason, I learn, why *th* is represented by *y*, is that the Saxon *th*, which a good deal resembles that letter, was commonly used in manuscript many centuries after the use of the Saxon language had ceased.

In the floor of M. church, are some other old inscriptions. Nothing is said of them by Nash or Thomas.

entering the centre aisle, under the organ, the eye is struck with the extreme neatness of the whole interior of the church; a quality, however rejected by the antiquary and the lover of the picturesque, is certainly necessary to the comfort of a house of God. The pews are painted in imitation of wainscoat, and the front of the organ gallery with the hue of old oak, relieved by a clay-like tint. At the south side of the middle aisle is the pulpit, painted in imitation of old oak, at the back of which are two long pews, the upper of which is destined for Thomas Foley, Esq. cousin to Lord Foley, and the one underneath, for Lord Beauchamp. These pews are lined with a maroon coloured cloth, and are furnished with chairs. Over these pews is a painting which once served as an altar piece, but which is now removed in order more fully to expose the large window at the end of the middle aisle. This altar piece, composed of the Virgin Mary, Moses, and Angels descending and singing Hallelujahs, was painted by Ponty, a Worcester Artist, of whom there is an account in the history of Worcester. This painting is not so despicable, as a work of art, as might be expected from the style of the artist's advertisement, as drawn up in the book alluded to. His production is not mended in effect, from the manner in which it is now exhibited, for the heads of Moses and the Virgin are so cut across the throat as to present rather a risible appearance. The remaining part of the painting over the communion table still retains its place : on this are painted the Lord's Prayer, Belief, and Commandments, between and under columns, and an entablature of the Ionic order, in very poor taste, probably by the aforesaid Ponty. The ancient stalls are removed to this place, and they are painted to imitate dark oak, the carved grotesque figures being of a clay-like hue, en suite with the front of the organ gallery. On the left of the altar is the tomb of the Knottes-fords, alluded to in the ancient state of Great Malvern church : this monument has been lately repaired and restored with scarlet and gold, by a descendant of the family, still living in this parish. The steps, &c. leading to the altar, are paved with the orange or red coloured tiles, which we have before-mentioned. On the north side of the wall of this centre aisle are three marble memorials : the first, as you enter the church, is dedicated to the memory of Sarah Francis Abbot, wife of Dr. Abbot, Latin master to Mr. Roberts, who, about thirty years since, kept an Academy on the spot, now occupied by the Crown Hotel : the other two inscriptions belong to the Snelson family. The front of the organ gallery is to be decorated with the armorial bearings of her Royal Highness the Princess Charlotte of Wales, and those of his Serene Highness Prince Leopold of Saxe Cobourg,*

* An application having been made to the Princess Charlotte to increase the fund already raised for completing the west window of Malvern

which are now painting by Mr. Humphry Chamberlain, of Worcester, son of the celebrated china manufacturer, and nephew to the present Mayor of that city, who has, in the most handsome manner, offered the exertion of his abilities gratis, for this ornament to Malvern church. These arms are to be emblazoned in colours on the present vacant shields, and are to occupy those immediately in the centre under the organ, and should there be any of these shields unoccupied, by the quarterings of this illustrious pair, these are to be ornamented with the armorial bearings of the principal contributors to the revival of Malvern church. The ceiling of this edifice is embellished, between the ribs and groins of the roof, with coloured leaves or mullets, said to be executed in imitation of the ancient raised work; that part over the communion table, being painted by Mr. Solloway, of Malvern, and the part over the organ by Mr. Lucy, of St. John's, Worcester.

THE ORGAN.

During the many attempts made to restore the church of Great Malvern to a state to which it was originally intended, a few individuals, lovers of music, began to interest themselves in procuring that aid for an instrument to assist their devotion

church, and, for permission to put up her arms and those of the Prince of Saxe Cobourg on the centre pannel of the organ gallery, her Royal Highness has transmitted a liberal donation and granted the liberty required. Worcester Herald, Aug. 1816.

in which they at length succeeded; and it is only justice in us to declare that, but for the exertions of the present organist, Mr. Southall, who engaged to play on the instrument, and also to instruct the children to sing, gratis, this part of the divine service might have wanted much of its present effect : assisted by liberal subscriptions he undertook, though uncertain of remuneration, to purchase the present organ, and volunteered his services as musician, for which he has received no pecuniary salary or reward whatever.

The annexed is a list of the subscribers who immediately came forward, in aid of so useful a purpose, with the following liberal assistance :

	£.	s.	d.
Edward Thomas Foley, Esq...................................	21	0	0
Viscount Dudley and Ward,..................................	21	0	0
Lord Foley,..	21	0	0
Mrs. Waldo,..	20	0	0
The Lord Bishop of Worcester,.............................	10	10	0
The late Lord Beauchamp,.................................	10	10	0
Dean and Chapter of Westminster,.........................	10	10	0
Lord Elmley, now Lord Beauchamp,.........................	10	10	0
T. C. Hornyhold, Esq.....................................	10	0	0
Lady Lyttelton,...	5	0	0
A. Lechmere, Esq...	5	0	0
Admiral West,..	5	0	0
Temple West, Esq...	5	5	0
Rev. Mr. Stillingfleet,....................................	3	3	0
Mrs. Wakeman, ...	3	3	0
	161	11	0

	£.	s.	d.
Brought over, ...	161	11	0
Lady Southampton, ...	2	2	0
Hon. Mrs. J. Yorke, ...	2	2	0
Mrs. Stillingfleet, ...	2	2	0
W. Dandridge, Esq.	2	2	0
J. Pyke, Esq.	2	2	0
Mrs. Baker, ...	1	0	0
Mrs. Plumer, ...	2	0	0
Mr. Chavasse, ...	1	0	0
Mr. Walker, ...	1	0	0
Mr. Steers, ...	2	2	0
Mrs. Ford, ...	1	0	0
	171	3	0

For a trumpet stop, a flute stop, and a long octave :

Viscount Dudley and Ward, ...	10	0	0
The Rev. Henry Card, from the fund for the interior decoration of the church, ...	30	0	0
Amount to complete organ, ...	210	3	0

It may be necessary to remark, that the Rev. Mr. Morgan was also one of those who assisted Mr. Southall in his exertions.

This instrument is built by Green, and was used originally in a concert room. It is constructed on an extensive scale, and is much admired for its power and sweetness of tone, particularly of the stops, diapasons. A new trumpet stop, by Elliot, has been added to it, which is considered equal to any in the kingdom. The swell has a charming and sublime effect in the service.

In speaking of the interior of this church, it may not be improper to say something of some of her most humble servants. "That good old chronicler of the church," says Mr. Rudd, "now sleeps under the turf she has so often trodden." She died May 12, 1812. Her husband still holds the situation of sexton and clerk, which he has filled for more than forty years; and, at the advanced age of seventy, forms a useful appendage to this venerable pile.

THE ABBEY-HOUSE

Was erected on the ruins of the priory. This house exhibits a good specimen of the style of domestic architecture of the reign of Elizabeth and James. It is now used as a Boarding-house, and has a venerable long room lined with *varnished* oak. At this hotel are hot and cold baths.

THE ABBEY GATE.

A building, whose style of architecture is that of the reign of Henry VI. and VII. It is, outwardly, in good or tolerable preservation, and adorned with niches, in which, formerly, were the statues of various saints. The windows, though now devoid of glass, are ornamented with tracery. It formerly led to the monastic part of the building, of which there are now but small remains.

SUNDAY SCHOOL.

In the church-yard is a highly useful structure of brick and flint stones. This was erected by the munificence and at the sole expense of the dowager Lady Lyttelton.

It were much to be wished that the taste of the person, employed to build this structure, had borne an equal ratio with the charitable disposition of the donor. But the Sunday School of Great Malvern, instituted by her Ladyship, will nevertheless remain a beautiful monument of her liberality and goodness of heart. Its internal arrangement is highly favourable for the ends proposed, and a very little trouble would give it an outward appearance more in *accord* with the gothic air of the nearly adjoining church. The ground, on which the school is built, is glebe land, and it was granted to her Ladyship, for this erection, by the Vicar of Great Malvern. This Sunday School, at present, consists of about one hundred children, and is supported by voluntary contribution; but the funds of this very charitable institution being much reduced, from the unavoidable expenses attending it, a general solicitation is made to all visitors to contribute their mite into the hands of the land-lords of the various hotels.

In addition to the sums gathered from the visitors at Malvern, there have been two charity sermons preached for its benefit, by the Vicar of Great Malvern, and the contributions gained on these occasions have enabled the managers of the Sunday School to increase the number of the children from sixty to its present respectable state.

THE VICARAGE,

The residence of the Rev. Henry Card, is visible soon after you enter the village of Great Malvern; it wears the appearance of a cottage ornée, its front is covered with jessamine, and it is almost invisible to the eye, from the laurels and other evergreens planted near it. It is situate near the church, the Post-office being to the right, and is almost facing the Crown Hotel, whose stables, near the Abbey House, are a disgrace to this charming village.

THE POST OFFICE

Is situate about the middle of the village. Here a bag, containing all letters addressed to the residents of Great Malvern or houses contiguous, is left by the Hereford mail coach, which leaves Hereford at half past six in the morning, and passes through this place from London three times in the week, viz. Tuesdays, Thursdays, and Saturdays, between three and four o'clock in the afternoon, and returns on the following mornings, through Malvern, about nine o'clock, on its way to London, taking with it the letter bag from this office.

On those days which the mail does not bring letters, viz. on Wednesdays, Fridays, and Sundays, a person on horseback is sent to fetch them from the Worcester Post-office, as soon as they arrive at that place. A separate bag is likewise sent from The

Wells Boarding-house, by Mr. Steers, the proprietor, for such letters as are directed to his house.

HOTELS AT GREAT MALVERN.

The Crown, opened about the year 1796, as an Inn, was originally a School. It is the oldest house, for general accommodation, in the village ; before the opening of these premises, the company visiting Malvern were accommodated at the Abbey-house with board and lodging, or at the neighbouring farm houses: until lately there were attached to these premises a coffee and subscription newspaper room. It was formerly kept by Mr. Roberts, but is now in the occupation of Mr. Harrison. From the gardens of this house you may ascend the hill to St. Ann's Well, to which it is the nearest road.

BELLE VUE

Is a new Hotel lately opened by Mr. Beard, who was landlord of the Crown to which this house is situate next door. It possesses all the advantages of a house of modern construction, fitted up with corresponding taste. Here is no table d'hote.

THE FOLEY ARMS.

The name of this very handsome and modern Hotel is appropriate, the ground on which it is built, with a considerable portion of the village, and a very large tract of land, being the property of the Foley family. This house was built by the

present proprietor, in the year 1810, and considerable additions made to it in the years 1812 and
1817. At the back of this Hotel are bow windows,
commanding an extensive view over a beautiful
variegated country. The landlord of this well-
furnished Hotel is Mr. Downes. At both the Crown
and the Foley Arms post horses and open carriages
are to be had, for the accommodation of travellers
pursuing their journey, or for occasional tours.
Here is no table d'hote.

About the spots, occupied by these Hotels, the
owners of Jerusalem ponies ply for hire : here are
also to be let, Donkey carts, where the patrons of
the whip may drive these animals curricle or tandem.

CIRCULATING LIBRARY.

There was an infant institution of this kind
opened by Mr. Deykes, near the Foley Arms.

Mr. Southall, the organist of Great Malvern, has
removed the reading room to his house, No. 1,
Paradise-row, where novels and other publications
are to be had, and he hopes, so much from the
increased popularity of Malvern and its numerous
visitors, to be able to make such arrangements,
with respect to his Library, as to render it worthy
the patronage of the scientific reader as well as
those who read only for amusement. Here are to
be hired musical instruments, music may be procured and advertisements be seen relative to the

place, its charities, accommodations, &c. and a book is kept with a list of the visitants of Malvern for the last three years.

The following persons reside constantly in Great Malvern:

Mrs. Bridges,

Wm. Wall, Esq. Banker, Worcester,

Mr. Chavasse, Surgeon,

Mrs. Baker, Laurel Cottage,

Rev. Henry Card, Vicarage,

Mrs. Saunders, Ladies School,

S. Surman, Esq. The Lodge,

Mis. Laird, Holly Lodge,

Rev. Dr. Stillingfleet, Prebendary of Worcester: the Shrubbery,

Mrs. Plomer,

Admiral West,

Besides upwards of 22 lodging houses, Tradesmen's, and houses of entertainment.

The Link* is a common on which, latterly, many houses have been erected, and lies between New-land and Great Malvern, close to the latter place.

Here, about the year 1781, was found, many feet under ground, a celt, weighing ten ounces, about five inches and a half long, of a mixed metal between brass and copper, with a small ring or loop, as engraved in Nash's Worcestershire. It has a beautiful patina upon it: antiquaries are not agreed whether the celts are Romish or Gaulish instruments, or for what purpose designed, whether

* Link, perhaps the same as the Scottish word. The *Links* of Edinburgh, &c. To the Links of the winding river Forth. "The *Links* of Forth shall bear the Knell." (vide Lady of the Lake, Canto 2, Stanza 30.) The word belongs perhaps to a different idea.

In the *Links* of Ousenam water
They found him sleeping sound.

Note on the Lay of the Last Minstrel, Canto 4, Stanza 34.

as chissels to cut stone or weapons of war. Dr. Stukely, a great admirer of the Druids, supposes them druidical, and that they were the golden or rather brazen hooks, with which they cut the misletoe ; but as they are often found in great quantities, in or near Roman camps or stations, they probably belonged to the Romans or their Gaulish auxiliaries. The learned and ingenious Dr. Lort, in his observations on celts, in the fifth volume of the Archœlogia, p. 106, mentions some that were found in Herculaneum, and gives engravings of many different sorts. The one represented in Nash's Worcestershire comes nearest to fig. 3, in plate 8, of Dr. Lort's specimens.

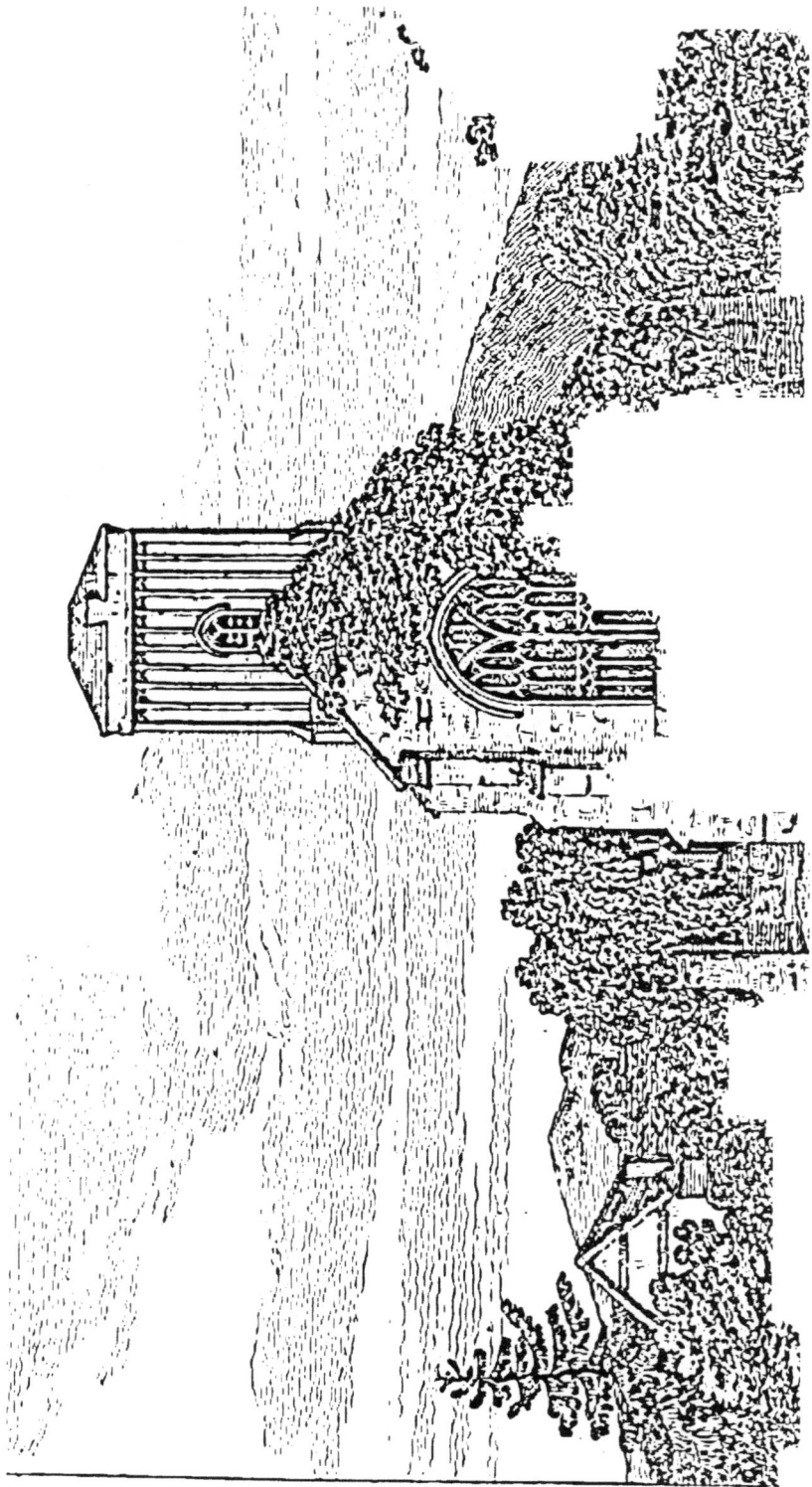

CHAPTER V.

LITTLE MALVERN.

Situation, Extent, and Antiquity.

The parish of Little Malvern is situate in the lower division of Oswaldeslowe hundred, and the deanery of Powick, in the county of Worcester; it lies on a recumbent slope, near the entrance of a great recess in the Herefordshire beacon,[*] and is bounded on the east by Hanley Castle, on the west by Colwall, in the county of Hereford, on the south by Castle Morton, and on the north by Great Malvern, to which it forms a separate parish, and from which the distance is three miles and a half, and not far from the turning-off of the new road to Ledbury. Little Malvern was once a considerable village, and appears to have been at one time fully inhabited, for in Bishop Sandys' return to the privy council in the reign of Elizabeth, it is said to contain 37 families. About the year 1781, when Dr. Nash wrote his Worcester, it contained only six families, according to the return made by Bishop North. This decrease may

---

[*] Hanley Castle has also a narrow slip of land returning to the top of the hill, which divides Great and Little Malvern, " vide Nash."

o

be owing to the dissolution of the priory, and the disafforesting of the chace, the former supplying the poor with provisions, the latter with firing, and food for their cows, pigs, fowls, &c. &c. Little Malvern, says Dr. Nash, pays to the land tax at 4s. in the pound, 63*l.* and to the poor 12*l.* At present, this parish contains nine houses, including the mansion belonging to Mrs. Wakeman, farmhouses, cottages, &c. the land tax is redeemed, the number of families is eleven, and the number of persons fifty-two.

At Little Malvern was originally a religious house, but not so large or magnificent a one in its buildings as that at Great Malvern. It was founded from the same cause, and originated in the same date and manner as the neighbouring priory.

A congregation of monks of the priory of Worcester, having entered into the wilderness of Malvern, and determined to lead an austere life as hermits, Jocelin and Edred of the order of St. Benedict are said to have founded and dedicated this house and church to St. Gyles, an abbot of royal blood, some where about the year 1171, in the reign of Henry II. see Stevens's Monas. vol. 1. p. 353, taken from Habingdon M. S. when it became a benedictine cell to Worcester.* The principal

---

* So Annales Wigorn in Angla, vol. 1, p. 476, "but yet the charter referred to in Heming, p. 532, mentions the uniting of the two Monasteries of Little Malvern and St. Giles, by Bishop Simon temp. R. Hen. 1, of which quære. And also of the Monastery of St. Giles, distinct from

benefactors were William de Blois, Bishop of Worcester, from the year 1202 to 1236, and Kings Henry the II. and III. Gilbert de Clare, Earl of Gloucester, and Lord of Malvern Chace, was also a great contributor to Little Malvern, and John Alcock, Bishop of Worcester, from 1476 to 1486, chancellor of England, and president of the council, 1 King Edward IV. rebuilt the church here and dedicated it to St. Mary, St. Giles, and St. John the Evangelist.

In the ancient ledger of the priory of Worcester it is recorded that Simon, Bishop of Worcester, granteth, confirmeth, and decreeth that Little Malvern and the church of St. Giles, there situated, built in the bishop's see, and enriched with a monastic order, be eternally in frankalmoigne, and as one inseparable body with the church of Worcester, and be made the same in cohabitation and profession as Worcester church, in such manner as that no person shall be admitted to the monastic habit, in Little Malvern, without the consent of the bishop, prior, and convent of Worcester, but be received with their joint will and

Malvern, which I have yet met with no other account of, and believe will appear upon examination to be a mistake in the abstracter. For the Monastery of Little Malvern was, as I take it, the same with that of St. Giles, and this union might probably be nothing more than some act made by the Bishop for its dependance on, and subordination to the priory of Worcester. However it ought to be observed, that Bishop Simon died 20 years before the time commonly assigned for the foundation of this priory; therefore quære if it is not more ancient.'—TANNER.

benedictions, and thus it shall be lawful for the said prior of Worcester, by way of correction, to remove the monks of Little Malvern to Worcester, and place monks of Worcester in their stead, and that the prior of Malvern shall be chosen by the chapter of Worcester.

Mr. Habington thinks this Simon might be that bishop who died the 20th of March, 1149,—50, if so, we must date the foundation of this house somewhat earlier, but it might be Simon de Monteacuto or Mountagu, who was bishop in the year 1337. The church of Worcester retained their superiority, for, in the year 1378, John of Worcester, prior of Little Malvern, resigned his priory into the hands of Henry, Bishop of Worcester, upon which the said bishop, by and with the consent of the prior and convent of Worcester, created Richard Wenlake, a monk of Worcester, prior of Little Malvern, the patron of which appertained to the bishoprick.

By the ten seats which remain in the choir, it is probable this house consisted of ten monks, although 31st of August, 1534, only John Bristow, prior of Malvern, and six others, subscribed to the King's supremacy; and we read, in Rhymer's Fœdera, vol. xiv, p. 506, that they subscribed unanimously *uno ore.* Among their possessions were lands and tythe, at Naunton, in Gloucestershire, and the manor of Horewell, in Worcestershire.

Having lost divers possessions in Ireland, in

consideration thereof, they obtained leave to appropriate the church of Watcote, in Warwickshire, though it doth not appear that they made use of this privilege, for they presented to the rectory from 1392 to the dissolution of their house. They had portions in the chapel of Berlingham and Nafford, 3, Edward IV. They had a yearly allowance of forty shillings from Elmley Castle, and were patrons of the church of Cuberleye, three miles south from Cheltenham, A. D. 1230. The abbot and convent of Lyra, in France, conveyed to the priory of Little Malvern, in fee farm for ever, whatever they had in the church and parish of Hanley, paying yearly sixteen marks; they had beside the scite of the house and manor of Little Malvern. At the dissolution the revenues of this house, according to Dugdale, were estimated at 98*l*. 10s. 9d. per annum; but according to Speed they amounted to 102*l*. 10s. 9d. per annum.

In the reign of Phillip and Mary the dissolved monastery, with the lands and the perpetual advowson of the church of Little Malvern, were granted to John Russel*, who left it to his heir, Henry Russel, from whom it fell to his son, Mr. John Russel: they are a branch of the Russels of Strensham, see their pedigree at

---

* The author of the article " Malvern" in the Beauties of England and Wales, is therefore wrong, when he says it was granted, at the dissolution, to Richard Andrews and Nicholas Temple.

length in Dr. Nash's Worcester, the heiress of which estate was married to Thomas Williams, Esq. of Treyllinnie, in the county of Flint, a descendant of whom, Mary Williams, who remained unmarried in the year 1780, and who resided in the house now occupied by Mrs. Wakeman, was by her father's mother, Elizabeth Mornington, the last of the blood of Owen Glendwr. See Stephens's Supplement, vol. 1, p. 353, also a little account of the priory from a M. S. in the hands of Francis Canning, of Foxcote, in Warwickshire, Esq.

THE CHURCH

Of Little Malvern, says Dr. Nash, is mostly in ruins, but it still forms a very picturesque and interesting object, particularly where the ruins of the cross aisle on each side, with their gothic windows and fine tracery, still remain. The outside of the body of the church, as well as the ruinous parts, is covered with mantling ivy, whose deep green, in some places, is well contrasted with the glow of some remnant of painted glass, whose armorial blazonry speaks of times long past. The floor of Little Malvern church exhibits the remains of a tesselated pavement; and on a beam is a piece of carving of most exquisite workmanship, but there are but few monumental inscriptions. Only part of the nave remains, the two side aisles being in ruins. The windows were curiously painted with storied ornaments rivalling those of Great Malvern, but now

they are all broken, leaving only paintings of the
Prince of Wales, part of the Queen, the Prin-
cess Elizabeth and her three sisters, Elizabeth,
Cecilia and Anne*.

In the east window of the choir are six large
compartments. In the middle one is represented,
Edward IV. in a robe of ermine, with an imperial
crown on his head. In the next compartment is
his queen with the like diadem. In the pane behind
the king is painted his eldest son, the prince,
afterwards Edward the 5th, though never crowned,
his surcoat Azure and his robe Gules turned down
and lined with ermine, on his head a prince's
coronet. In the last pane of that side is his brother
Richard, Duke of York, his surcoat also, Gules
and his robe Azure, turned down with ermine, one
row to the feet, on his head a duke's coronet. In
the pane behind the queen, her eldest daughter,
the lady Elizabeth, the only branch whence sprung
all the Kings of England and Scotland, behind her
sister who left no issue. In the last pane is John
Alcock, Bishop of Worcester, kneeling and praying.
In the highest part of this window, which is divided into four panes, is represented, in the
principal one, the arms of France and England
quarterly, and over an imperial crown, supported
by two angels, Argent winged Or. and below, with
two lions Or. In the next pane the queen's arms,

* These portraits were copied from this painted glass, and engraved in
Green's History of the Queens of England.

consisting of six pieces: 1 a lion rampant, 2 quarterly Gules and Vert, On the Gules a star Argent, on the Vert a fleur de lis Or. 3 Barry a lion rampant, 4 and 5 broken, 6 Argent a fesse and quarter Gules, supported with angels as before and over all a royal diadem. Next pane behind the King's Arms were the princes, being quarterly, France and England, supported with angels and lions, like the kings: on the shield a label of three Argent, and over all, on a cap of maintenance, Argent turned up ermine a prince's crown. On the next pane behind the queen's arms, Argent on a fesse between three cock's heads, erased sable, combs and gills Gules, a bishop's mitre Or. the coat supported with angels like the others, and over all a bishop's mitre. In the south pane of this window below, is cheque Or. and Azure; in the lower part of this window is written:

"Orate pro anima Johannis Alcocke Episcopi Wigorniensis, qui de novo hanc ecclesiam sanctorum Dei genetricis Sancti Egidii, & Sancti Johannis Evangeliste ædificavit quondam cancellarii Angliæ & presidentis concilii Edwardi regis quarti primo regni."*

In a seat on the south side of the choir is 1 Argent, an eagle displayed with two heads, Vert. legged and beaked Gules; 2 Argent on a fesse between

---

* Bishop Alcock not only built the church, but reformed the monks, who were grown very profligate, and gave them many wise rules.

three cock's heads erased sable, combs and gills,
3 Gules, a bishop's mitre Or. 3 the five wounds
of Christ, 4 Azure a cross argent.

In the north cross aisle, the first pane of the
north window, Or. three Chevrons gules. In the
next pane Gules, two bars Argent, between six
Cinquefoils Or. 3, 2, 1. In the third pane Or.
a maunche mail taile Gules. In the uppermost
part of the west window of the same cross aisle,
Gules three lions passant Argent. In the east
window of the south aisle of the church are
Alcock's arms, as before, and in the south part is
written :

"Orate pro animabus Roberti Skinner & Isabelle uxoris
ejus & filiorum suorum & filiarum."

On the north side was an ancient raised monument, with the figure of a man all armed except
his face; under his head an helmet with his crest,
being a lion's head; at his feet, a lion; on his
right hand, his wife, richly dressed; at her head,
two angels; at her feet, a little dog with collar and
bells.

In the south aisle, on a raised tomb, was the
figure of a knight, armed, saving his face, his
right hand on his sword, which he is drawing; on
his left arm, his shield, his legs crossed, shewing
him to be a knight of the holy crusade against the
Saracens; on his right hand lay his lady, with her
arms crossed over her breast, which Habington
supposes alludes to her having accompanied her

husband in his military religious pilgrimage. There was another monument of a knight, armed, cross legged, and drawing his sword, as the former, but having no wife. It is not known to whom these ancient cross-legged monuments belong; but their bodies were buried before the year 1311, and the knight, with the crest on his helmet, (who perhaps was Gyfford, of Bromfield,) died since the year 1388; for few or none in England, before that time, quartered their arms or wore crests. These monuments are now gone:

Dominus Gilbertus de Berkeley legavit corpus suum sepeliendum in ecclesia Parve Malvern, viz. in cancello ejusdem loci coram imagine Sti. Egidii & confessoris & cor suum sepeliri in cancella Sti. Egidii de Cuberlege circa an 1294.

Mrs. Wakeman, the present incumbent of Little Malvern, being a Roman Catholic, and of course having no power to present a living in a Protestant church, has devolved that right on Lord Somers, whose family indeed for near 200 years have presented; and we have heard it is the boast of the incumbent, that there has never been a difference on that point or any other, between the two families, during all that period.

Little Malvern is served by a curate who is sometimes licenced, but as no institution or induction is required, I can give (says Dr. Nash) no regular list of Incumbents.

Ricardus prior, 1268..........	.....Lib. Alb. Ep. Wig. f, 60 and 67
Will'us	weye, 16 Kal. Maii. 1268.............	
Will'us	Wherwan, 1279...............	
Johan.	Wigorn, 10 Kal. Jan. 1287.........	Reg. Giff. 290. b.
Johan.	Dumbleton, 2 non. Nov. 1300.	ib. 447. a.
Roger	Pyribroke..........	
Hugo	ribroke, 4 id. Apr. 1326....	Reg. 5. Cobham, s. 112. a.
	Staunton, 25 Jun. 1360....	R. 11. Brian, vol. 1. f. 30.
Johan.	Wigorn, 30 Nov. 1369,.....	R. Brian, v. 2. f. 8. b. R. 13. f. 20. a.
Rich.	Wenlat, 1378,.....	Ledg. Priorat, Wig.
Rich.	4 Oct. 1392.........	R. 15. Wakefield, f. 101. a.
Will.	435............	
Johan.	1445............	R. 22. Carp. v. 1. f. 57. b.
Johan.	cut, 1462.....	ib. f. 172.
Johan.	Wytesham, 1476.......	Alcock, f. 74. b.
Henric	orton, 1486....	ibid.
Johan.	tow, 1534............	Rhymer Fœd. vol. 14. p. 506.

The present state of Little Malvern church.

On entering this edifice you are indeed struck with the little approximation it bears to its former grandeur: the exterior of the building, it is true, is highly picturesque, but the interior does not in the least partake of that quality. One narrow aisle, with a few broken forms, present themselves at the entrance near the railed partition which separates the chancel from the aisle; and on the south corner is the remains of a once gothic pulpit, threatening with a fall the daring preacher who ventures to ascend its disjointed steps. In the chancel on each side are remains of some stalls, and over the communion table a window, where a few particles of stained glass, dimly lend a ray: a grotesque carving of antique nonentity is placed in a corner near the stalls on the north side, where is, in stained glass, the remains of a figure kneeling, to which popular tradition has given the name of King David: the colour of his robe is red and of a most brilliant clearness. Two modern achievements occupy that part of the wall usually destined for the Belief, the Lord's Prayer and the ten Commandments. On the south side of the aisle, near the pulpit, is a nearly-effaced black letter inscription: the floor still exhibits some few remains of the tesselated pavement similar to that of Great Malvern, and the west end, which was open and dilapidated, is now closed up, and while we contemplate this interesting ruin with feelings of regret, at its fallen grandeur, let us chear our hearts with the recollection that the sacred duties, which were once performed under its venerable roof, are again regularly and devoutly attended to, and that "the poor have the gospel preached to them." The Rev. Mr. Jeffries, who is also curate to the Rev. Mr. Turberville, the rector of Hanley, performs duty here every Sunday, to a numerous congregation; for, until the praise-worthy exertions of this gentleman commenced, divine service was only performed once a fortnight, during the summer, and once a month, during the winter season, to, at most, a congregation of three or four persons.

CHAPTER VI.

THE SPRINGS OF MALVERN.

Description, Medical Importance and Chemical Analysis.

There is no river, nor scarcely a brook of any consequence, that takes its rise in the Malvern hills, but throughout the whole extent there are several small springs, some of which are to be found mineralized. Dr. Hopkins,* a prebendary of Worcester, makes mention of these springs in his addenda to Camden's Britannia. The pure Malvern springs, according to Dr. Townshend, in his work on the Deluge, p. 308, originate in the red ground, for they break out in the south-east side of the hill, in what he conceives to be beds of sand.

THE CHALYBEATE SPRING

Is situate, near the village of Great Malvern, on the eastern side of the mountain, about a quarter of a mile from the church, and at the end of a pleasing lane, from which a portion of the church is here and there seen. A small area is sunk in

* I can only find the name of *Wm. Hopkins, B. D.* 1675, in Green's Worcester.

the green sward, and before some thick hedge-row of hazel you perceive the chalybeate spring. In one of the sides which are bricked up, in parts hidden by the grass, damp, and moss, the spring trickles into a basin of brickwork, over a stone; the mouth of which, where leaves of trees are placed to serve as spouts for the water, is stained with ferruginous incrustations. The simplicity of the spot has been lessened, but the usefulness of the spring is increased, for close to it is erected a covered seat, as a shelter from the heat or coming shower, and we believe it is in contemplation to add to this convenience by a small room for glasses, &c. The Chalybeate Spring, according to Dr. J. Wall, approaches to the Holy Well, nearly in point of purity, for two quarts of this are found to contain only one grain of earth, one grain of iron, and nearly the same quantity of muriatic salt, which grows moist in the air, and therefore appears to be Bittern. On this account it seems to challenge one of the first places among the waters of this class, for though it be not so highly impregnated with iron as some others, yet it is sufficiently so to answer all our expectations from it as a Chalybeate; and being much less loaded with earth than any other, it seems probable that the ferruginous particles, will, for that reason, be more readily and intimately mixed with the blood and juices, while the water, by its extreme purity, pervading the finest vessels, washes away the acrimonious salts and obstructing viscidities. From the most accurate analyses, it appears that, at the spring head, *Paukon Spa Water*, contains four times more of the Chalybeate principle than this spring, but at the same time, is loaded with four times more earth: *Tunbridge Water* contains three times more iron, but has six times more earth: *Cheltenham* and *Scarborough* waters have only the same quantity of iron, but are very much loaded with earth. Cheltenham water, in particular, contains 88 times more than this spring; and to instance no more, Bath water has nine times less of the Chalybeate principle, and contains 28 times more in soluble parts than the Malvern water does. Thus far, says Dr. Wall, I have considered the purity of these waters in respect of earth; but they are also possessed of a *mineral spirit*, and some other principles, not so easily discoverable by experiments, to which, notwithstanding, their virtues may probably be in a great measure owing. This water, at the spring head, instantly strikes a fair purple with galls, and if carefully taken up and close corked, will retain that same property several hours, but the colour gradually grows more and more pale, and at last approaches to the orange. To have this water therefore in full perfection, it must be drank at the source. Dr. Wall mentions the following cases, to shew the superior efficacy of the Mavern waters at the spring head:

Case 6.

A young lady who used the water with great success, for a scaly roughness, which covered her whole forehead, ears and the crown of her head, tells me, that when she applied the water at Malvern, though it was brought fresh from the well, in close corked bottles, it never gave her the least uneasiness, but when she bathed under the spout it made the parts smart very much: these, with several other instances of the like kind, sufficiently prove that the waters, at the Holy Well, contain some very active parts, on which, probably, their efficacy very greatly depends, and that these particles are volatile, but do not fly off entirely, in a very little time, though it is manifested that their energy is much the greatest at the spring head, and is gradually impaired by keeping afterwards.

Case 7.

Miss Baron, of Hanley, has been long subject to the Cardialgia, or heart-burn, a painful sensation arising from a superabundant acid in the stomach, which therefore is usually relieved by absorbents, but increased by any thing, either acid or acescent. She has several times attempted to drink Malvern water, but it constantly gives her great pain and uneasiness at the stomach, an effect not produced by common spring water. Several other patients were obliged to desist from the same reason.

o

ST. ANN'S WELL

Is situate also in Great Malvern, about a quarter of a mile from the church; it rises from the hill immediately at the back of the Crown Hotel, the pleasantest road being through the garden of that house, to which the approach leads from the level of the first floor. The ascent to this spring is here so steep, that paths are made to lead to it, in a zig-zag direction, but as they are very neatly kept, and have seats at proper distances, from which there are enchanting prospects, the invalid may receive pleasure while resting, and gain strength to pursue his journey. The principal walks and seats towards St. Ann's Well were formed by the Hon. Mr. Damer, Lady Southampton, and Mrs. Wall, the latter the lady of the Worcester banker, and these accommodations reflect much credit on the taste and philanthropy of the projectors. This well is protected by a house or cottage which affords every convenience for hot and cold bathing ; and here patients, whose maladies render it necessary, may receive from a spout upon the parts affected, the healing element. A commodious apartment is here provided for company resorting to the well to drink the waters, who are furnished with glasses by the person who resides at the cottage.

THE HOLY WELL.

The source of this spring is secured by a decent building, containing a bath, and several apart-

ments, small, but suited to the various purposes
that using the waters require. This spring rises
on the east* side of the hill, about the middle,
and almost equally distant from both the extremi-
ties, and nearly as much above the vale as below
the summit.

This well is distant two miles to the southward
from the village of Great Malvern, and is the
source of that much-esteemed clear aliment, called
Malvern water: from whence it derived the appellation of holy is not certainly known, but tradition
informs us, it was in great repute with the ancients,
who ascribed the virtues of the water to a super-
natural effect, communicated by some celestial
benefactor, and therefore this well was dignified

---

* Dr. Mackenzie, formerly a physician in Worcester, in a Treatise on
Health, has introduced an *old remark*, that Springs which have this
aspect are generally distinguished by their purity and medicinal qualities;
see also Hoffman; and Mr. Boyle gives this as his second rule to observe
whether the spring-head or other receptacle do chiefly regard the *east*,
the north, or the south. Memoirs for the History of Mineral Waters,
Sec. 2. So MILTON,

> Wherever fountain or fresh water flowed,
> Against the eastern ray.—SAMPSON.

In the next place the waters that are exposed to the rising of the sun
must needs be clear, of a good smell, soft and pleasant, for the sun,
by rising and shining upon them, prevents any bad effects from the
damps of the morning, which the air diffuses for the most part every
where. Again, but such are chiefly to be commended whose springs
break out towards the rising of the *sun*, especially in the summer
season, for they must needs be clear, of a good smell, and light: in a
word, these waters, whose springs lie to the east, are the very best of all.
Clifton Hippoc. p. 7 and 10.

with that sacred epithet, and this assertion is not
repugnant to the superstitious notions which prevailed in former ages. But there is a spring, called
Ditchford's well, which rises in an ash coppice,
about five hundred yards from Little Malvern
church, on the Ledbury road. This spring, we
are informed, is the original one, and that it was
noticed long before the holy well, when an ancient
dame conveyed the water, in bottles, to Worcester.
To Dr. John Wall, late of Worcester, we are
indebted principally for our knowledge of the
Malvern waters, and the further experiments of
his son, Dr. M. Wall, of Oxford, were presumed
to throw fresh light on their contents. Dr. Johnson, an eminent Physician, who also resided at
Worcester, made several experiments on this water,
and although his results were somewhat different
from those of Dr. Wall, yet he fully confirmed
their efficacy, added to the salubrity of the air of
Malvern, in scrophulous and other cases.

But it was left to Dr. Phillip, of Worcester, to
produce at this period of time, when chemical
knowledge has made such rapid strides towards
truth, a more perfect analysis; and he seems to
prove that the Holy Well and St. Ann's Well are
impregnated with certain active ingredients to
which their good effects are greatly attributable.

The following extracts are from his book on
the Malvern waters, (published in 1815.) These
waters have been long celebrated for their purity,

and to this alone their effects have generally been ascribed. From the following analysis of these waters, however, it would appear that this opinion is erroneous, and that their good effects, as in the case of other mineral waters, arise chiefly from the foreign ingredients they contain.-— This will hardly be doubted if it can be shewn that they contain substances which have long been celebrated medicines in the same diseases in which the effects of the Malvern waters are so strikingly beneficial. That they contain but a small quantity of such substances is no argument against this opinion. We well know that the effects of medicines are not in proportion to the dose merely. How many chalybeate springs, which contain but a small quantity of iron, are more efficacious in restoring vigour, than the most powerful artificial chalybeate; yet we know that the effects of such waters depend on the iron they contain, because when deprived of it, they lose at the same time their invigorating quality. Whether the same quantity of iron dissolved in the same quantity of pure water, would produce the same good effects, independently of the other ingredients of such waters, we cannot tell; most probably it would not. But when we reflect on the intimate union which takes place between bodies, when one exists in very great, and the other in very small quantity, of which a thousand instances might be enumerated, we have reason to suppose that the effects of many mineral waters depend on this intimate union, by which, perhaps, a greater quantity of the medicine is received into the system, or is received in a state more capable of producing its peculiar effects, than when it is taken into the stomach and bowels, in a mere concentrated form. To the seventy-six cases, republished by Dr. Martin Wall, in his Father's book, in 1780, Dr. Phillip could, were it necessary, add some equally striking effects of the Malvern waters, which have fallen under his own observation. The complaints, in which these waters have been chiefly celebrated, are the various forms of Scrophula, Cutaneous Diseases of different kinds, and Gravel. Drs. John and Martin Wall are the principal writers on the Malvern waters. The holy well and St. Anne's well are supposed to be of the same nature. It seems to be the opinion of both these gentlemen, that the effect of these waters are chiefly to be ascribed to their purity.* " The efficacy of this water," the former observes, "seems chiefly to arise from its great purity, whereby it passes through the smallest vessels, and not being loaded with any salts or earth it is capable of dissolving more than those

---

* The purest water, in the city of Worcester, contains more than 50 times..............................

The hot well at Bristol 20 times ....

The spring at Henwick Hill, near Worcester, which has been always thought extremely pure, contains 12 times

as much earth as the Holy Well water at Malvern does.

See Dr. J. Wall's Analysis.

waters which are already saturated with them." Its effects externally, both in lotion and bathing, may, in a great measure, depend upon the same, since it is past all doubt, that fluids may enter the body this way, by the absorbing vessels; and Dr. M. Wall remarks, in his appendix to his Father's, Dr. John Wall's, observations, that "its principal virtue then must depend upon its extreme purity, assisted by the fixed air which it contains."* Dr. J. Wall, however, was led by several observations to doubt the justice of the popular opinion. "It has been the opinion of some person," he observes, "that the water of the holy well is only pure element, devoid of mineral spirit, and almost all other principles." Indeed, were this the case, which for many reasons I am convinced it is not, that purity alone would make the spring of great value. No spring can more justly deserve the term of pure water than this does, but that there is also a fine subtile penetrating spirit concealed in these waters,

* Dr. M. Wall, we shall find, has shewn that his father was deceived, with respect to the quantity of the foreign contents of this water. It is certain, however, that compared even with the springs in common use, it must be considered a very pure water. From the apparent purity of the water, Dr. Wall adds, one would expect that it should keep well, yet on the contrary, after some time, it is apt to acquire an offensive taste, and sometimes it contracts great foulness, and this when it has been taken up and preserved with the greatest care. *Query.*—Does this proceed from the putrefaction of its oily or bituminous parts, or does it not rather shew that there may be some latent substances in the water which our experiments have not yet discerned?

is evident, from the following observations: Dr.
Mackenzie informed me that he knows a gentleman, in Warwickshire, who has a cancerous ulcer
in his face, which he uses to bathe, every day,
with Malvern waters, before he applies his other
dressings to it: the water, when used alone, frequently makes the ulcer smart, to a degree which
he is not able to bear, until he adds a certain,
proportion of common water to it; he can then
bear it very well. Dr. J. Wall also relates that
this was, in some measure, confirmed to him by
Dr. Turton, who, at first, felt the same smarting
pain, on swallowing the water, during the time he
had a putrid fever, accompanied with ulcerations on
the throat and tongue; this subsided on his washing
his mouth frequently. Before relating his experiments, Dr. Phillip points out those experiments of
Drs. J. and M. Wall, which seem to contradict
his, and the circumstances which reconcile these
contradictions. Dr. M. Wall has noticed what
appears to be a principal cause of Dr. J. Wall's
having obtained so small a residuum from the Malvern water, by evaporation, viz. that he performed the evaporation in open vessels—the fact
is, that some parts of the solid contents of this
water, if the distillation is not performed very
slowly, comes over with the water, even when it is
performed, as Dr. M. Wall, advises, in a retort
and receiver luted together. Dr. J. Wall was led
to believe that the Malvern waters contained sul-

phuric acid, in a disengaged state. "The water of the holy well, when drank immediately as it comes out of the hill, leaves a peculiar tartness in the throat; this is by some, likened to the taste of brass or alum, and is most perceptible to those who have not been used to the water, but this taste is soon lost, and the water grows softer after it has been kept some time, though the bottles be ever so carefully stopped. With this water, either acids or alkalies mix without the least alteration in transparency, and without any precipitate or conflict, and yet it seems to contain a concealed acid, because iron laid in the water is corroded, and with a solution of silver, though at first it mixes without any milkiness, yet, by standing some time, the water grows gradually whitish, and then muddy and of a dirty reddish purple, and at last a powder of a deep purple colour is precipitated which is the effect of the vitriolic acid." Dr. M. Wall attributes this precipitate to carbonet of lime: it seems not, however, to proceed either from this or the sulphuric acid. Dr. M. Wall justly observes, that if it arose from the presence of sulphuric acid, infusion of litmus and syrup of violets would give evidence of acidity which they do not: with respect to the carbonet of lime, Dr. M. Wall seems to have been misled by his correspondent, who says that no turbidness takes place on the addition of a solution of nitrat of silver, after the water has been distilled in close vessels, although acetat of lead occasions a precipitate. Dr. J. Wall has always found the turbidness to take place on the addition of nitrat of silver, when a precipitate could be obtained by acetat of lead. Were Dr. M. Wall's explanation just, the turbidness should be prevented by the previous addition of nitrous acid to the water, which is not the case, unless the water has been distilled. Besides, there is no precipitate on the addition of oxalic acid, whether the water has been distilled or not. Dr. J. Wall states, as another proof of the existence of a disengaged acid in these waters, that effervescence ensued on mixing the water, of the holy well, with a saturated solution of carbonat of pot ash. The way in which the experiment was made sufficiently points out, that the appearance of effervescence arose merely from the extrication of air, with which all waters are impregnated. A far less quantity of acid than is necessary to occasion any degree of effervescence would affect the above-mentioned tests of acidity. Carbonate of ammonia has also been supposed to exist in the Malvern waters, and one of Dr. M. Wall's correspondents thought he had ascertained its presence, as indeed there was reason to believe, when he found that, after distillation, this water gives a precipitate with acetat of lead. Dr. M. Wall refers to another experiment, of the same correspondent, in which he found, that the nitrat of silver occasioned no precipitation nor turbidness in the distilled Malvern water, which, Dr. M. Wall justly observes, it should have done, had this water contained an alkali ; but, in this experiment, there seems to have been some inaccuracy, for, as Dr. Philip has observed, the Malvern waters, though distilled in close vessels, may still give a precipitate with nitrat of silver, a circumstance which tends to invalidate Dr. M. Wall's explanation of the precipitate, from the distilled water, by acetat of lead, viz. that it arises from the water retaining its carbonic gas after distillation, which we cannot surely suppose. But this explanation is wholly set aside by a circumstance which was overlooked, both by Dr. M. Wall and the gentleman he alludes to, viz. that the addition of an acid prevents the precipitate, and this seems to confirm the account of the precipitate given by the latter : we shall find, however, that it is not owing to the presence of carbonate of ammonia, but to another cause, which Dr. Philip alludes to, in the course of his observatons, as detailed by him, in his analysis of the Malvern waters. In the twenty-fourth experiment, related by Dr. M. Wall, potash gave a precipitate with three-quarters of a pint of Malvern water, boiled down to half an ounce; and, in experiment twenty-six, a solution of ammonia gave a precipitate with this water, boiled down in the same manner, and this precipitate being removed by filtration, it became turbid in about a minute after the addition of a few drops of a saturated solution of carbonate of potash. From these experiments, Dr. M. Wall infers that the Malvern waters contain selenite. This inference seems, on more than one account, to be inadmissible; had the water contained selenite, it must have been precipitated long before the evaporation was carried to this length. Besides, the presence of some other earthy salt may have occasioned this precipitate, or that with the ammonia may have been produced by carbonate of magnesia, which is not wholly precipitated by boiling till the water is evaporated nearly to dryness. The precipitate which Dr. M. Wall obtained by potash, after the addition of the ammonia, demands more particular attention. There can be no doubt, from the following circumstances, that this precipitate proceeded from the impurity of the solution of ammonia which had been employed. Unless this solution is prepared with care, it may contain a small quantity of the lime used for obtaining ammonia from the muriat of ammonia. When Dr. Philip repeated Dr. M. Wall's experiment with Malvern water, it evaporated to less than a twentieth part of its bulk, and a solution of ammonia, which he had by him, and he found the result as Dr. M. Wall has stated it.

The following are the contents of a gallon of the Holy Well water, according to the analysis of Dr. Wilson Philip:

Carbonate of Soda...............6.33 grs.	
Carbonate of Lime................1.6	
Carbonate of Magnesia 0.9199	
Carbonate of Iron 0.625	
Sulphat of Soda..................2.896	
Muriat of Soda 1.553	
Residuum..........................1.687	

14.6109

The following are the contents of the water of St. Ann's Well:

Carbonate of Soda...............3.55 grs.	
Carbonate of Lime................0.352	
Carbonate of Magnesia 0.26	
Carbonate of Iron 0.328	
Sulphat of Soda..................1.48	
Muriat of Soda 0.955	
Residuum..........................0.47	

7.395

On the medicinal effects of the Malvern waters.

As the following observations concern the public at large, equally with the chymist, Dr. Philip lays aside the language peculiar to the latter, which may here be done, as the few substances he has occasion to mention are such as are commonly known. The general reader will understand many of the terms used in the analysis, and have a clearer knowledge of what the Dr. is about to say, when the terms carbonic gas ar cabonat are explained to him, which may be done in a few words. By carbonic gas, the chymist means fixed air. This air is an acid which, like every other, has a tendency to unite with certain substances when it is brought into contact with them; when it is united to any other substance, chymists call the compound, a carbonat, as the carbonat of soda, of iron, &c.* It appears, from the foregoing analysis, that the Malvern waters differ from the other celebrated waters of Britain, and agree with several of those of the continent, in containing carbonat of soda. To the spa water they bear so striking a resemblance, that the solid contents of these waters differ in little else, than the greater proportion in which they exist in the spa water, as the reader will perceive from the following table of the solid contents of a gallon of the Malvern and Spa waters. The proportion of the contents of the spa water is

* When it enters into combination, it loses the form of air, which, however, it immediately assumes, if it is displaced by a stronger acid, or any other cause; hence the effervescence which ensues, when we mix a solution of carbonat of soda with lemon juice, in making the common saline draught, or drop lemon juice on chalk, which is the carbonat of lime, from the property of being, as it were, fixed in bodies with which it combines. It was in a less perfect state of chymistry, when this property was supposed to be peculiar to it, called fixed or fixable air; chymists do not allow it the name of air or gas, their term for air, except when it exists in an aereform state. The cause of this requisite distinction in chymistry, it is not necessary here to enter on. After the explanation Dr. Philip has given, he allows himself to call it here, fixed air, whether it exists in the aereform of fixed state.

taken from the analysis of Bergman, reduced to the English measure, by Dr. Saunders, in his *Treatise on Mineral Waters* :

	Holy Well.	St. Ann's.	Spa.
Soda, combined with fixed air,	5.33	3.55	11.76 grs.
Lime, combined with fixed air, i. e. chalk,	1.6	0.352	11.76
Magnesia, combined with fixed air. i. e uncalcined Magnesia,	0.9199	0.26	35.68
Calx of Iron, combined with fixed air, i. e. rust of Iron,	0.625	0.328	5.86*
Glauber Salt,	2.896	1.48	
Common Salt,	1.553	0 955	1.376

The solid contents of the Malvern and Spa waters, it appears, from the foregoing table, if we except the difference in quantity, differ only in their being no Glauber salt in the Spa water. The Spa water differs also from the Malvern waters, in containing a considerable quantity of uncombined fixed air, none of which is contained in the Malvern waters. How far the effects of the Spa waters depend on the presence of the uncombined fixed air, we cannot say: we should not be inclined to attribute much of them to this air, because water, as much or more charged with it, is not found to produce the same effects; but a similar observation applies to every other ingredient of these waters.

The effects of mineral waters do not seem to

---

* Dr. Saunders gives the quantity of calx of iron. Dr. Philip here gives the quantity of calx, saturated with fixed air.

arise from any one of their contents, so much as from the peculiar combination and manner in which they exist in the waters. We cannot infer that all waters having any one ingredient, although their most active ingredient, the same will produce similar effects; but we certainly have reason to expect similar effects from waters, the greater part of whose most active ingredients are the same, and exist in them in the same state. Whether the Malvern waters will be found serviceable in the various cases in which the Spa water is so celebrated, it is impossible to say, as a trial of them, in many of these cases, has not been made, but that they are calculated to produce similar effects in relaxation of the system, and the various diseases which arise from it, is probable from their effect in scrofulous debility, which are, perhaps, more beneficial than those of any other mineral water of this country. The smaller quantity of the foreign contents, which, however, is in some measure, compensated by the Malvern waters being used in greater quantity than the Spa water, will probably render them less effectual than the latter, in many cases; but it is not unlikely that, from the same circumstance, they may be better adapted to others, and they derive from it no small advantage in being perfectly safe. A trial of them, though often attended with some inconvenience, never produces any seriously bad effects. In estimating the probable virtues of a mineral water, we must not

attend so much to the mass of its solid contents as
to the activity of these contents. Many waters, in
common use, contain a much larger proportion of
solid contents than some of the most powerful mineral waters.

Of the ingredients found in mineral waters, iron
and soda are among the most active ; and the reader will observe, from the foregoing table, that
the difference of the quantities of these, in the
Malvern and Spa waters, is not so great as of some
other of their contents. The solid contents of the
Buxton water, though rather more than those of
the holy well, may almost, perhaps, from the inac-
tivity of their nature, and their similarity to the
contents of many waters in common use, be overlooked in explaining its effects. Writers have
consequently, with great probability, attributed
these effects to an air of a peculiar kind, which it
contains. The effects of the Tunbridge water, on
the contrary, are attributed chiefly to its solid
contents, although the whole of these, according
to Dr. Babington's Analysis, amount only to 5 grs.
in a wine gallon; about a third part of the solid
contents of the holy well water. But one grain is
calx of iron. The sensible effects of the Malvern
waters are different in different cases, and they are
generally most felt on first using the waters. It is
not uncommon for them to produce a degree of
nausea, and they afterwards prove aperient; sometimes considerably so. In many cases they produce

a

the opposite effect on the bowels, so that some aperient medicine is necessary. When drank largely, particularly by those who are not accustomed to them, they frequently produce some vertigo, drowsiness, or even pain of the head. In some, they produce a degree of feverish heat. Many instances have been known, in which it was necessary to lay aside the use of them, on this account. The most constant of all their sensible effects, is that of a diuretic, and they seldom fail, after they have been used for some time, to increase both the spirits and the appetite. To what part of their contents each of these effects are to be ascribed, it is difficult to say positively; many of them seem to arise from the iron they contain. That the increased heat proceeds from this cause cannot, I think, be doubted; and it is remarkable, that many of the other effects, which have been enumerated, are the same which attend the use of other chalybeates.

Many of the effects of the Tunbridge water, for example, although more powerful in proportion, as it is a stronger chalybeate, are similar to those just mentioned. It also produces nausea, drowsiness, and vertigo, which, as in the case of the Malvern waters, are most felt on first using it. Dr. J. Wall's explanation of these effects, though ingenious, can hardly, thinks Dr. Philip, be admitted. He supposes that they arise from the great purity of this water, in consequence of which it enters the vessels very rapidly, and thus produces a temporary plethora. But it appears, from all that has been said, that the Malvern waters, particularly the water of the holy well, are by no means so free from foreign contents, as has been supposed. Besides, were this explanation just, distilled water ought to produce a greater degree of the same symptoms, which is not found to be the case.

The diuretic effect, probably one of the most beneficial effects of these waters, we cannot hesitate to ascribe to the carbonat of soda, which has long been used in medicine, for the purpose of producing this effect, although, in the artificial forms in which it is given, it is seldom so effectual a diuretic as the Malvern waters are. In these it is doubtless assisted by the large quantity of water in which it is taken, probably by some other part of their contents. To this effect, and to the iron which the Malvern waters contain, we may partly ascribe the good appetite and spirits which attend their use. These must, in some measure, be ascribed to the pleasant situation, and the pure air of the Malvern hills. The quantity of the carbonats of lime and magnesia, and of the salts found in these waters, seems too small to permit us to attribute any of their sensible effects to them. They may, perhaps, modify the effects of the other ingredients in a way we do not understand. In scrophula and cutaneous diseases, in their various kinds, soda and iron have long been celebrated medicines; and on soda, in some form or other, we chiefly rely for relief in gravel.

The Malvern waters seem to be better adapted to the two former cases than to gravel, because they depend more immediately on the fault of the habit in general, in which we find that minute quantities of medicines, given frequently and for a considerable length of time, are often more efficacious than larger doses. Such, however, is the relief, often obtained by these waters, in gravel, probably, in part, from their acting merely as a diluent, and, in part, from the soda they contain, that Dr. Wall thought they possessed the power of dissolving urinary concretions. "It is, perhaps, too much to expect," he observes, "that a formed stone can be dissolved by this water: but that sabulous matter may, I am fully convinced, from the effects I have observed in those who have used it." That it may tend to wash out sand, lodged in the kidneys, and to prevent its formation, seems highly probable, and there is reason to believe that it has some degree of the effect of waters more strongly impregnated with soda, which seems often to allay the irritation occasioned by urinary concretions, even where they have no effect in dissolving them. That a weak chalybeate, impregnated with carbonat of soda, which passes off so freely by the kidneys, should allay a variety of other disorders of the urinary passages, which Dr. J. Wall says he has found it to do, cannot appear surprising.

Wherever there are eruptions, &c. these waters should be used externally as well as internally.

Indeed, like many other mineral waters, the Malvern waters were, at first, only used as an external application. Their good effects, employed in this way, are chiefly to be ascribed to the carbonat of soda they contain; a simple solution of which, applied externally, has long been used as a remedy in the same diseases.

The existence of a carbonat of fixed alkali, in this water, accounts for many observations which have been made respecting it. It is remarked, that clothes may be washed in it with less soap than in any other, and that vessels, which are incrustated by hard water having been boiled in them, are cleaned by boiling in them the holy well water. "Upon the whole," Dr. J. Wall observes, "too much care cannot be taken, by those who send for this water from the well, that their bottles be perfectly clean, since it is known that this water will dissolve those foulnesses which common water will not touch. Waters, full of earthy particles, are found to foul and incrust the vessels, in which they are boiled, as is evident in tea kettles, &c. which vessels may again be perfectly cleaned by boiling some of these pure waters in them." But the effect of the purest water, in removing this crust, will not be found equal to that of the holy well water, and indeed is very trifling, the crust formed being sulphat of lime, which is very insoluble in water, but is readily decomposed by all the alkaline carbonats. The late Edward Popham, Esq. of the Lodge, Tewkesbury, rebuilt a bath, under the spout at the holy well, in return for the marvellous cure of the gout which he experienced.

It may, however, be necessary to add, (for we had rather be accused of redundancy than leave out ought which may be interesting to the invalid reader,) that Dr. Wall found, especially in those who used the waters for complaints of long standing, that they were apt, at first, to bring out a slight fever and inflame the parts. This adventitious heat is commonly soon relieved by drinking freely of the waters, which washes out of the habit any morbid particles, which may have been received into the circulation, but the fever usually goes off in four days, at farthest: sometimes where the water is applied to indurated glands or in cysted tumours the heat rises higher, so as to bring on suppuration, an event by no means to be dreaded. The common people about Malvern are from long observation, so well apprized of these effects, that they think the assistance of a Surgeon upon no occasion necessary, and the usual phrase is, " that the water will break any humour and afterwards heal it;" this, however, of course is carrying the virtues of the Malvern waters too far, and getting rid of the Surgeon at the expence of their judgment. Dr. Wall repeats, that there is not the least danger of repelling any morbid humour from the skin, either by the internal or external use of the water, both of which have been frequently experienced to promote eruptions, and propel them very forcibly. He never remembers, in all his practise, to have seen one instance, where it injured the constitution by repelling any peccant matter which nature had before endeavoured to eliminate. So that all calumnies of that sort, he is convinced, are false, and that whoever propagates such injurious reports, is unjustly prejudiced against the virtues of these springs, either from ignorance or a worse motive. Indeed, in glandular swellings, or in internal tumours, where morbid matter has long stagnated out of the common course of circulation, if the tumours are resolved, and this matter thereby thrown into the blood, unless care be taken to correct its acrimony and carry it out of the habit, it must disorder the patient, or obstruct other glands where the vessels are small and scarce permeable, but, as this is the case with every other deobstruent or discutient, no blame can attach to the use and effect of the Malvern water. In cutaneous diseases the internal use of the water is apt, for some days, to increase the eruptions; but, in a longer continuance, it washes them off and clears the skin. In scorbutic habits it also produces similar effects, when applied externally; but, by continuing its use, all these angry pimples are commonly soon healed and disappear. Many instances prove the efficacy of these waters alone, without any help from the shop. "Indeed," Dr. Wall affirms, "I have not found it requisite to give many medicines along with them; some circumstances and some constitutions may, occasionally, require assistance from pharmacy, but, in general, I think a course of mineral waters ought, as little as possible, to be broken in upon by the shop compositions, which, oftentimes, may rather obstruct than promote a cure."

It may be necessary to imprint upon the mind of the ignorant or impatient, that the water performs no miracles. In all cases patience and perseverance are absolutely necessary, for a great length of time: and a steady pursuit of proper remedies is required to affect a total change of the fluids, and restore a due tone to the solids, without which a perfect cure is not to be expected. Those, therefore, who unreasonably flatter themselves with the hope of regaining and establishing their health, by using these waters a short time, will most frequently be disappointed; and they who leave them off, as soon as they begin to feel some amendment, must not be surprised at a relapse.

WALM'S WELL,

Or Wa'am's well, is situate in that part of Newen's Wood, in the parish of Ledbury, called Tippin's Rough, on the Ledbury turnpike road; and not more than three miles from the holy well, there is a road (nearly impassable for a gentleman's carriage) to this well, which is little more than half a mile from the turnpike road, down a steep valley below the giant's cave. This well, which is much resorted to for the cure of scorbutic eruptions, has a small building contiguous to it, where there is just room for one person to go in. "I was informed," says Mr. Horner, in his Geological Essays, by Mr. Wallet,* Surgeon, of Great Malvern, "that a spring, on the western side of the Herefordshire beacon, known by the name of Walm's Well, had been long used by the country people, as an outward application in cutaneous diseases. The water flows in a pretty copious stream, and, at the place where it issues from the hill, is collected by an embankment of wood and mud, so as to form a large bath. "Through the kind assistance of Dr. Marcet," he continues, "I have made the following examination of the water, with a view of ascertaining merely the nature of its contents, without any regard to proportions, as the quantity I brought away was much too small for the purpose. This water, as it issues from the hill, is perfectly transparent, and remains so after exposure to the air. It produced no change or tincture on red cabbage. Its specific gravity is 1000.0. Six cubit inches of the water were boiled for some minutes, and the gaseous contents were received over mercury, on the admission of caustic

---

* Mr. Wallet has left Malvern.

potash no absorption took place, the transparency of the water remained undisturbed. The following tests produced no change :—litmus paper, violet paper, tumeric paper, lime water, muritete or nitrat of barytes, tincture of galls, and prussiate of potash, even after the addition of a little muriatic acid.

"Caustic, potash, oxalate of ammonia, and nitrat of silver, all occasioned a turbidity. On the addition of barytic water, there is also a cloudiness, even after the water of the spring had been boiled. Although, neither muriate nor nitrat of barytes produced any effect, super carbonat of ammonia, with phosphate of soda, occasioned at first no change; but, after standing for some time, the rod left white streaks wherever it was drawn along the sides of the glass vessel.

"Eight ounces of the water, slowly evaporated to dryness, yielded 0.75 grs. of solid ingredients. On adding cold distilled water to this, only a small part was redissolved to the solution : the following tests were applied :

a. Violet paper, slightly changed to a green.

b. Oxalate of ammonia, no change.

c. Muriate of barytes, a cloudiness.

d. Nitrat of silver, a dense precipitate.

e. Super carbonat of ammonia, with phosphate of ammonia, a slight cloud, and the rod produced white streaks on the sides of the vessel.

f. Nitrat of lime, a considerable precipitate.

g. There was no change produced by tincture of galls, or by prussiate of potash, even after the addition of muriatic acid.

h. To the residuum, insoluble in water, there were added, a few drops of dilute muriatic acid, which dissolved the whole with a brisk effervescence.

i. Oxalate of ammonia, a copious precipitate.

k. The solution, from which the lime was thrown down, by the last experiment, was filtered, and the same test applied as in exp. a. which produced a similar effect, but in a very slight degree.

" The waters of Walm's well, therefore, contain about 12 grains, of solid ingredients in a gallon, which appear to consist of

1. Carbonat of lime, as the principal ingredient, by exp. h. i.

2. Carbonat of magnesia, in minute quantity, by exp. a. k. and by the effect of the barytic water in the preliminary experiments. From the change produced on the violet paper, in exp. a. and from the action of the barytic water, which last test occasions a precipitate with carbonat of soda, I suspected that there might be a small quantity of that alkali existing in the water of the spring; but, by comparative trials, I found, that on applying these tests to a solution of carbonat of magnesia in water, exactly the same effects were produced.

3. Muriate of soda or magnesia, by exp. d. e. probably the latter, for, in one experiment, the entire solid ingredients were by accident dried at a heat that must have decomposed the muriate of magnesia, the earth being found in the insoluble residuum, in greater quantity than when the evaporation had been carried on with a gentle heat,

and there was only a trace of it discovered in the part soluble in water.

4. Sulphate of soda, or magnesia, by exp. c. e. f. probably the former, as the proportion of sulphuric acid indicated, is much more considerable than that of magnesia, and that earth seems to be combined with muriatic acid."

MOORARL'S WELL

Is situate on the Herefordshire or western side of the hill, in the parish of Colwall, directly opposite to the holy well. There is also a bath and a cottage near it: formerly there was a bath, lined with bricks, in this tenement, but it is, at present, filled up: we understand, however, it is in contemplation to restore this bath to its original state, for the use of the public.

THE EYE WELL.

This spring flows about 100 yards higher up the hill than the holy well: its water has been more particularly used for disorders in the eyes; "but as it does not appear," says Dr. Wall, "to differ in quality from the water at the holy well, I do not deem it necessary to take further notice of it." Mention is made of this spring in Bannister's Breviary of the eyes, printed A. D. 1622, in these lines:

" A little more I'll of their curing tell,
How they help sore eyes with a new-found well:
Great speech of Malvern hills was late reported,
Unto which springs people in troops resorted."

In the addenda to Camden's Britannica, by Dr. Hopkins, are the following words :

" Near the division betwixt Worcestershire and Herefordshire, is a spring that has been long famed for the virtue of healing eyes and other parts of the head, called, therefore, eye well; and beside, there is another spring called holy well, heretofore much resorted to for curing all scorbutic humours, &c. by bathing and drinking of the waters."

And in the " Geography Reformed," these wells are taken notice of in these words :

" There are two medicinal springs, in Malvern hills, called holy wells, and of which, one is good for the eyes, and diseased livers, the other for cancers."

There are also two or three other springs which rise from the west side of the hills, the one in the parish of Colwall, and the other in the parish of Eastnor, which have a petrifactive quality. This is evident, says Mr. Barrett, from the moss and vegetables immersed in their streams, which, for a considerable distance from the springs, are incrusted with a lapidious matter.

These concretions are of various sizes, some of them several inches in diameter, and are the effects of a calcareous matter, contracted by the water in its current through beds of limestone.

There is also a spring, the property of Mrs. Waldron, a few yards from her house, Pomona Place. Besides these springs, known by the name of Pewtris's and St. John's well, are numerous others of too little importance to require mentioning. It may here be necessary to add to our account of DITCHFORD'S WELL, at p. 116, that this well has also been called Mary's and Nancy's well, all of which names have been presumed to be belonging to the woman who carried the water of this spring, in bottles, on horseback, to Worcester. Ditchford's spring no longer rises, as we had stated, in an ash coppice, this fissure being closed up, but flows on the other side of the hedge, about 150 yards from the finger post, at the foot of the hill, in Little Malvern, and on the road leading to that church, running into Mr. Price's garden, supplying his house, from thence falling into a drain, and emptying itself into a pool, at the top of the north field or orchard adjoining.

In most complaints, for which the Malvern waters are prescribed, they must be used both by drinking and lotion. In scrofulous and scorbutic cases, bathing the whole body and drinking freely from the fountain are absolutely necessary, and in ulcerous cases the admission of water, to the part affected, as it falls from the spout, and the application of wet linen, are found to be most beneficial. Early rising and a proper degree of exercise, either by riding or walking on the hills, previous to using the waters, and also at intervals afterwards, should by no means be omitted, as such exercise will promote a requisite circulation of the blood, and prove a powerful auxiliary in the cure of these diseases for which the waters are recommended.

Dr. Woodyatt, an eminent Physician, residing in Worcester, considers the Malvern waters as an invaluable natural beverage, its trifling foreign contents giving it little medicinal power. As a diluent, he has, during a long practise, in and round Malvern, observed its cooling and refreshing effects, in various diseases, especially in the scrofulous hectic. And he thinks, that many chronic ailments sooner give way to proper medical treatment, upon those hills, than in less happy situations. In most chronic diseases, an improvement of the functions of the stomach is of the greatest importance, and this generally occurs during a course of the waters, assisted by exercise, pure air, and a total restriction from all fermented liquors : a careful attention to these rules he thinks highly salutary, particularly to the sedentary, the artizan, and others, whom a visit to Malvern may take from pernicious habits or an impure air. Dr. Woodyatt also considers the salubrity of the air of Malvern greatly increased, even in his memory, by a circumstance which has not generally been adverted to, he means the draining of that large tract of common called Malvern Chace.*   He remembers this extensive

* Lord Somers suggested and took some pains to promote an inclosure of the waste lands, in Mathon, Colwall, and the adjoining parishes, which his Lordship proposed doing as a public benefit, but from the variety of claims, the perplexity of boundaries, and probable litigation likely to ensue, he was induced to abandon his plan.

surface covered with large sheets of water, the constant evaporation of which, rendered the air, blown from it, upon Malvern, damp and unwholesome, particularly to those affected with pulmonary complaints. Invalids are now able to extend their visits later in the season than formerly; and one of the diseases which originates in the neighbourhood of marshy effluvia, the ague, which, at the time he alludes to, was epidemic in those districts, has now wholly disappeared. It was the custom of many families, at Malvern, before the inclosure of the chace took place, to serve out, regularly every Sunday morning, to the neighbouring poor, snake root and bark, as a preventative from the baneful effects of the marshy effluvia of the fens.' In addition to this highly respectable reference, in favour of the Malvern waters, we are authorised to state that Sir Everard Home relates the case of a young gentleman, who had nine wounds in his foot, from scrophula, and that the use of the Malvern waters certainly saved his life. The patient had resorted to Brighton and other watering places, but without effect, when, after a residence at Malvern and taking the waters, he became convalescent.

Sir Francis Millman and Dr. Baillie have also highly recommended these waters of Malvern, and it has become the practice of late, for many eminent Physicians to send patients, with consumptive cases, to this spot, instead of Devonshire or other places.

It has been said, on the authority of a Dr. Beal, whom we are informed wrote a Treatise on the Malvern Waters, " that a bishop, some years ago, endowed the hospital of Ledbury with certain revenues, that were to be applied to the use of distressed travellers who might be passing to these springs of Malvern for the relief of their disorders." This, however, is contradicted, by the following communication, politely sent us by the Rev. James Watts, Vicar of Ledbury :

" St. Catherine's hospital, at Ledbury, was founded by Hugh Foliatt, bishop of Hereford, A. D. 1232, for the use of poor and sick persons, resident therein. I am informed that there is no mention made, in the charter rules or history of this hospital, of travellers to Malvern springs or to any other place."

CHAPTER VII.

THE HEREFORDSHIRE BEACON.

Situation, Antiquity and Military Importance.

In the parish of Little Malvern, about two miles northward from the ruins of Bransil Castle, on the summit of one of the highest ridges of the Malvern hills, and on the very verge of Worcestershire, are the immense works of the Herefordshire beacon.* This eminence is the highest and in the

---

* Beacon: the word is derived from the Anglo Saxon *becnian*, to shew, by sign or beckon; it was usually placed upon a high ground, and sometimes on a tumulus. From Lord Coke, we learn (4 Insti. c. xxv. p. 184,) that before the reign of Edward III, beacons were but stacks of wood, set up on high places, which were fired when the coming of an enemy was descried : different methods have been taken in different countries and times in making these beacons or signals; they were always used for the better securing a kingdom against foreign invasion, to convey the notice of any impending danger to distant places, with the greatest expedition. But no kind of signals have more generally prevailed than that of fires in the night. That this was practised by the Jews, we learn from the sacred writers. Hence the prophet, Isaiah, in allusion to that custom, threatens them that they " should be left as a beacon upon the top of a mountain, and as an ensign on a hill." (Chap. 30, v. 17.) See also other passages in Jeremiah, &c.

Among the Greeks, these beacons were called Φρυκτοὶ; and their use is particularly described in the Agamemnon of Æschylus. The ike custom of nocturnal fires was also used by the Romans, as appears from a

centre of the range of hills, but its elevation, above the other two, is not very apparent: on the eastern side of the range, it rather falls back from the general outline, and is stated, in the table taken by the board of ordinance, to be 1444 feet in height, vide pages 23 and 24 of this work. The Herefordshire beacon is one of the strongest and most important hill fortresses, in this island, the vast labour employed in its construction, its amazing belts of ramparts and trenches, its great extent, its well-chosen situation, its singular irregularity of form and evident dissimilitude to the modes of fortification, observed by the Danes, axons and Romans, all combine to establish its origin to the Britons. The same reasons, also, evince that it was not constructed for temporary purposes, but rather for permanent security, as a place wherein an entire district might seek refuge with all their possessions, either of flocks or herds, in case of invasion or any other emergency. "Some authors," says Dr. Nash, " have imagined this intrenchment to be Roman, because of the prœtorium or centre part, and the name of the parish in which the greater part of it is situate, Colwall, that is, *collis vallum.*

passage in Cicero's speech, on the misconduct of Verres: see also Pliny. They were also used in the east, vide Aristotle de Mundo.

There are modern beacons also used in the marine and other service. The corporation of the Trinity-house are empowered to set up any beacons or sea marks, where they may deem them necessary.

Some Roman remains, in Herefordshire, are called *Walles*, and Severus's wall, in the north, is called *Gual Sever*, or Vallum Severi.* "But the shape of this camp does not," continues Dr. Nash, "shew it to be Roman, though he knows not to what age to attribute it, as it is not mentioned by any author, either in print or in manuscript. It was certainly prior to the partition trench, before mentioned, which divides the counties of Worcester and Hereford; for the outward trench of the camp serves for part of this ditch.

The whole circumference of the beacon is 2970 yards, the length is 1100, and the whole camp contains 44 statute acres. The general shape of this hill, or at least of the portion occupied by the works, approaches, at each end, to an ellipsis, and the disposition of the banks and ditches correspond with that figure. The area of the centre and highest part is an irregular parallel ogram, measuring about 60 yards in its largest diameter, and nearly 40 in the shortest : this is surrounded by a high and steep rampart of stones and earth, now covered with turf, and that again defended by a very deep ditch. Considerably below this, on the acclivity of the hill, ranging towards the S. W. or rather S. W. by South, is a very extensive outwork or bastion, of an oval form, containing a sufficient area for the stowage and even pasture of horses

* Some of these remains are also to be seen at Wall, near Lichfield.

and cattle; this is connected, by means of a narrow slip of land running beneath the S. E. side of the upper ditch, with a similar kind of bastion or outwork, ranging eastward, and is manifestly intended for similar purposes.

Both these works are surrounded by a high rampart and deep ditch, and the enclosed areas have evidently been levelled by art, as far as the natural shape of the eminence would admit.

Still lower, on the acclivity, are successive ranges of ramparts and ditches, very steep, deep, and high, encircling the sides of the mountain.

"On that part of the Malvern hills, called the Herefordshire beacon," says Mr. Barrett, "are the remains of an old camp; but by whom it was formed, or at what period of time, cannot be ascertained, as there is no history extant that mentions the circumstance: but it may be conjectured that it was formed at a very distant period; if not before history was known in Britain, yet, before any progress was made in that science; otherwise it is probable, that history would have afforded us some information concerning its origin. Some have imagined that it was a Roman or Saxon, and others a British camp; the latter opinion seems to carry the appearance of most probability; for it is natural to suppose, that when the Britons were driven, by the Romans, beyond the Severn, they posted themselves in some situation where they might be able to make a stand, and repel the further progress of their enemies. Now the Malvern hills being advantageously situated for that purpose, they probably availed themselves of the eligible position.

The existing remains of this camp consist of two intrenchments, or what is usually termed a double ditch, formed in a circular direction round the declivity of the eminence. The uppermost, which is very near to the summit, is about 700 feet in extent. The other is formed lower, on the descent of the hill, and is much more extensive, being upwards of half a mile in circumference. These trenches are from 6 to 12 feet deep, and, in some places, more than 30 broad, and supposed capable of containing an army of 20,000 men. The avenues or passes are still to be seen, and some part in good preservation. On a protuberance of the hill, about a mile and a half further to the southward, are the remains of another camp, consisting of only a single ditch. The form and appearance of this, seem to bespeak that it was not made by the same people as the above-mentioned; and, perhaps, was formed at a more remote period.

On the declivity of this Herefordshire beacon, at a small distance from its summit, and on the south side of the camp, is a cave, cut in the rock, rather of an oval form, but of rude workmanship and small dimensions. The entrance is about four feet wide, and six feet high. The concavity, or hollowed part, is 10 feet in length, 6 feet broad,

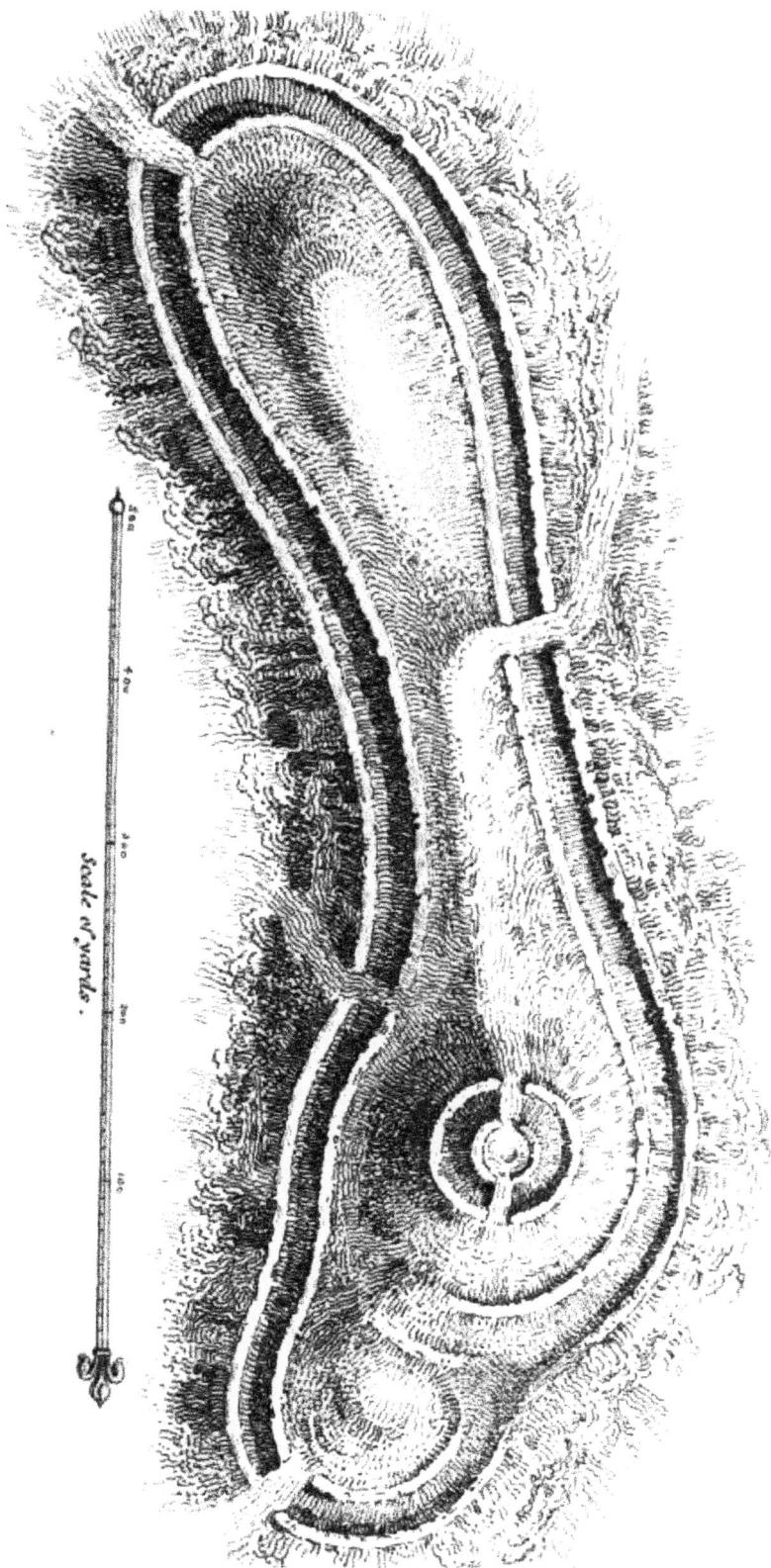

Scale of yards.

and 7 high. It is unknown for what purpose, or by whom this cell was made; but it is not unlikely to have been the retreat of some recluse individual.

Returning along the ridge, towards the Worcestershire beacon, we arrive at a rude building, erected on the very summit, close to the Earl of Gloucester's ditch: it is constructed of sods, and having a comfortable range of seats, serves either for a resting place or a retreat from the coming shower; a short distance further leads to a steep precipice which looks down upon the Witch.*

"A notion has long prevailed," says Mr. Barrett, "among the inhabitants of the adjoining country, that much treasure has been lost or deposited in the Malvern hills; but from whence such an opinion originated we are at a loss to conjecture. However, a quantity of silver coin was found, about 40 years back, on the west side of the hills, in the parish of Mathon."

It is said that it amounted to a considerable value; but there are no further particulars of it. But the most valuable, as well as singular discovery, was the coronet or crown of gold, and its appendages, mentiond by Camden, and other writers and historians. There is a manuscript account of the particulars of this discovery, kept in

---

* Leave me those hills, where harbrough (harbour) nis to see,
Nor holy bush, nor briar, nor winding *witch*.

Johnson, from Spencer.

" Witch, a winding sinuous bank, from wic Sax."

the library of Jesus Coll. Oxon. of which the following is a copy:

"Within the distance of a musket shot from the trenches of the camp, in the parish of Colwall, in Herefordshire, was found, in the year 1650, by Thomas Tailer, near Burstners-cross, as he was digging a ditch round his cottage, a coronet or bracelet of gold, set with precious stones, of a size to be drawn over the arm and sleeve. It was sold to Mr. Hill, a Goldsmith, in Gloucester, for 37*l*. Hill sold it to a Jeweller, in Lombard-street, London, for 250*l*. and the Jeweller sold the stones, which were deeply inlaid, for 1500*l*. as Mr. Clough, of Lombard-street, reported."

It was supposed that the gold alone of this coronet, might have been worth 1000*l*. which, added to the value of the diamonds above-mentioned, amounted to the amazing sum of 25,00*l*. for which the peasant who found it, received but 37*l*.

This curious relict should certainly have been preserved as an invaluable piece of antiquity; but being only in the possession of mechanics, and of such great value, profit prevailed against curiosity; therefore it was soon demolished, even before the discovery was made public, or any of the learned got the inspection of it. The opinion of some is, that this was the diadem of a British prince, who might have been slain in some contest near the spot where it was found; for, according to Roland, the Princes of Wales wore on their bonnets or helmets, a coronet of gold, being a broad head band, indented upwards, and set with precious stones. Richards, in his Welch dictionary, calls it a torch or tyrch, a wreath or collar, a torquis, which was worn by the nobility and great commanders among the ancient Britons.

It appears, from the registers of Colwall, that there were several of the name of Thomas Tailer, living there about the year 1650. On examining the deaths, there was found, the entry of two of that name, one who died in 1654, and another who died in 1661. In the margin of the register, opposite to the name of the latter, is prefixed an asterisk, which, in all probability, was inserted, both to distinguish this was the person rendered memorable by the above discovery; and also as a reference to some particulars made relating to it.

On the declivity of the Malvern hill, in the parish of Eastnor, are the ruins of Bransil castle. A vestige of the wall is the only part remaining of this ancient structure, which was fortified with a double ditch, faced with stone. The appearance of this venerable ruin, immured in wood, together with the obscurity of its situation, and stillness of the surrounding water, fills the mind of the beholder with a contemplative melancholy. Who was the founder of Bransil castle, or at what time it was erected, is not known, but the general opinion is, that it was built by the Britons, soon after the Romans left this island. It is said, some ancient records shew that this castle came to the crown by forfeiture, from the earl of Dorset; and that Henry VI. granted it to the great Talbot, earl of Shrewsbury: it afterwards became the property of the Reeds, of Lugwardine, in the county of Hereford; from a descendant of which family it was purchased about the year 1778, by Lord Somers, the present proprietor.

The view of the country, from the Herefordshire beacon, assumes a very distinct character to that of the contiguous districts of Worcester and Gloucester; it appears to be composed of an immense continuation of oblong, conical and irregular hills, principally covered with fine timber, the deep shadows of whose luxuriant foliage, project over the most beautiful vales, abounding with orchards, corn fields and hop grounds. The distance, in the west, is finely marked by the range of the black mountains and the hills of Radnorshire; and the Herefordshire beacon is of itself most eminently conspicuous for many miles round; forming an object of sublime and uncommon grandeur.

CHAPTER VIII.

MINERALOGY OF THE MALVERN HILLS.

WHEN Mr. Horner first began to examine the rocks of which the hills are composed, he was particularly struck with the great variety that presented itself, for almost every specimen, which he detached within a very limited space, offered a new character ; a closer examination, however, shewed that there is a greater uniformity than he at first suspected, and that the diversity of appearance depends on the different proportions in which the same materials are united together. Felspar, hornblende, quartz, and mica, forming different compound rocks, and varying, as much in the size, as in the proportions of their ingredients, constitute the greater part of the range. There are very few rocks, in which the size of the component parts is so minute, as to give the internal structure a homogeneous appearance.

If every compound granular aggregated rock, composed of felspar, quartz and mica, is to be considered as granite, a very great part of the Malvern hills is composed of it ; but, among the various compounds of that nature, found in this place, there are very few which present the same appearance as the granite of alphine countries. They have not the decided chrystalline structure which these granites usually exhibit, nor are the several parts so intermixed; the felspar is generally red, and predominates considerably in the mass; sometimes the quartz and sometimes the mica is wanting, but more frequently the latter. Mr. Horner then proceeds, by distinguishing the rocks of Malvern by the name of granite, however disproportionate the quantities of felspar, quartz, or mica may be to each other;* and also for the sake of brevity, he occasionally distinguishes these rocks in which hornblende† is found by the name of sienitic rocks. The general structure then, of the great masses, the central part of the range and nearly the whole of the eastern side, consist of the different compounds of felspar, hornblende, quartz, and mica, already alluded to: these are irregularly heaped together in large masses, and in no part were they discovered disposed in any way that

* Granite rocks are those in which the different particles, composing it, vary in quantity, so that sometimes the one and more frequently two of them predominate; felspar is generally the predominating, as mica is the least considerable ingredient of the rock: in some varieties the quartz is wanting; in others the mica, and these have received particular names; such distinctions, however, are useless.   Jameson's Gregory, p. 102.

† The hornblende is forced through the strata of the Malvern hills.
Bakewell's Geological Lecture.

could be considered as a continued stratification. In some instances, the materials of the rock are so arranged as to give it a fissile appearance, and in these cases, the slaity structure is either vertical or very highly inclined: but the masses themselves Mr. Horner never found to be of any great extent, and they are frequently inclined to various points of the compass, within a very short space: except in regard to the granite, he did not discover any uniformity in the occurrence of any one compound in particular situations, but all seemed confusedly heaped together. The granite is sometimes found in the highest part of the hills, but chiefly prevails in the lower parts, particularly towards the northern extremity, either in large masses, or, what is very common, forming veins, which traverse the other rocks: these veins or shoots are for the most part narrow, and, as far as he had an opportunity of ascertaining, they generally became more so, the higher they ascend. The stratified rocks, which occupy the country to the westward, rise, in some places, to a considerable height, on the side of the range; the highest point, where he found them, was on the Herefordshire beacon, at about one third of the elevation of that hill.

Mr. Horner has deposited, in the collection of the Geological Society, a series of specimens, illustrative of the mineralogy of this district, and these were accompanied by the valuable paper from which we have made our extracts, and which may be seen in the transactions of the society alluded to. In the year 1711, one William Williams, of Bristol, sunk a mine, about a mile from the town of Great Malvern, on the top of the hill, as you go to the holy well, on the eastern side, between the Worcestershire beacon and the Wytch: he took a lease from the bishop of Hereford, and at first worked by a level of 80 yards; he then sunk a perpendicular shaft, near 220 feet deep; he built several furnaces and a smelting house, at a small distance from the spot, but never extracted any considerable quantity of metal, though he asserted, that both tin and copper were to be found. He persevered in his trials till the year 1721, at the expence of about 600*l*. and then gave up the project: a Dr. Dudley was his great assistant. Trials, for the same purpose, had been made here some years before Williams commenced his operations. It has been asserted, that the miscarriage of the scheme, by Williams, proceeded from the deficiency of the skill in the workmen employed in the operation; a common excuse, by the bye, set up by projectors, as well in modern as in ancient times, when treasures were to be found either in the strata of a mountain or at the bottom of an alembic; but it is still insisted on, by some, that it is still practicable to be brought, at least, to some extent of profitable production. That tin or copper ore is to be gained in the Malvern hills, has been contradicted by recent experiments, which have proved this substance, so mistaken for copper ore, to be a kind of mica, not furnished by any proofs whatever.* But though this is the precise nature of the ore, taken at a considerable distance from the surface of the hill, yet the interior parts may contain ore, not only fusible, but even valuable, at least such has been the opinion of many, conversant in mineralogical researches. Mr. Barrett thinks it may be proper to observe that the trials, made about the year 1715, were never carried to any great extent, being in some measure cramped by the narrow circumstances of the projector, who possessed a sum by no means adequate to such an undertaking : among the mica, so mistaken for copper ore, was found, that curious production, asbestos, an inconsumeable matter, which is well known and which was once so much esteemed by the ancients. "It is very probable," continues Mr. Horner, "that the metallic lustre, of the micaceous rock, was the cause of this speculation, and to this day the country people call the scales of mica, which are washed down by the streams, in this part of the hill, gold dust." They are, however, so far aware of the difference that they save themselves the trouble of collecting

* In many rocks of a granite character, in which hornblende is a constituent part, a micaceous substance, having the lustre of bronze, and by no means the smoothness and elasticity of true mica, is often observable. Such is the cat gold as it is sometimes called of a part of Malvern hill.
Geo. Essay, Kidd. p. 65.

it. There is now no appearance of the level, and the shaft is almost completely filled up; a large heap of stones, however, are to be seen upon the sides of the hill, immediately below the mouth of the shaft, which is probably the rubbish of the mine, although it is so long since it was worked; for there are no rocks above, from which they could have fallen down. "The lime-stone,"* continues Mr. Horner, "does not form a continued ridge, but, for several miles along the range, rises up in many places, forming low hills, the longitudinal bearing of which, is in general parallel to the Malvern hills: the dip of the strata is in general towards the west, but, in this, is subject to much more variation than the bearing. It is, in general, of a bluish grey colour, but is sometimes of a pale brown, especially in the strata, near the surface. It contains a great many organic remains, particularly terebratulites, and, occasionally, vertebræ of the encrinite, so common in some of the lime-stones of Derbyshire: these organic bodies are most distinct in the upper strata. From the point, where the road turns to the westward, the ground, for a considerable way to the south, is covered with trees: there are very extensive plan-

---

* The metalliferous lime-stone, incumbent on Malvern hill, on the Herefordshire side, towards Ledbury, is sometimes so charged with argillaceous matter as scarcely to effervesce on the addition of acid.

Kidd. E. 99.

tations of the ash and the alder, along the side of the Malvern hills; the former being used in making the hoops for the cyder casks, and the latter for hop-poles.

In Chamberlain's quarry, to the north of Pearly quarry, Mr. Horner obtained a specimen of the vertebræ of an enchrinite, which, he was informed by Mr. Parkinson, is one of a very rare species; the only other specimen of it was in the British museum.

In the road which leads from the Wych to Colwall green, and immediately at the foot of the range, the argillaceous rock occurs in strata, bearing N. and S. but dipping east, at an angle of 60°; it is mixed with calcareous particles as usual, balls of lime-stone, and abounds very much in petrifactions: he obtained specimens of the following varieties, for a description of which he is obliged to Mr. Parkinson:

a. A small madreporite, the stars of which are bounded by circles: in the cells of these there is a small quantity of red sulphat of barytes.

b. Different species of the porpital madreporite.

c. A termined madreporite, with a longitudinal section of a ramose madreporite.

d. A ramose madreporite, with terebratulites.

e. A coralloid, neither the form or structure of which can be defined.

Mr. Horner is informed that the chain coral is also to be met with in this place, but he did not find any specimens of it.

"In the western declivity," says Mr. Barrett, "is a bed of lime-stone, which is the course of a vein that commences near Pensax, in the county of Worcester, and terminates at Ledbury, in Herefordshire : it produces excellent lime, at least in the vicinity of the Malvern hills, where large quantities are made annually, particularly in the parishes of Colwall and Mathon, the stone, which is of a blue cast, is interspersed with veins of a whitish colour, which, together, take an excellent polish : it is sometimes used for chimney pieces, and when properly finished looks little inferior to the Derbyshire marble. That beautiful elevated ground, called Old Castle Bank, which branches out of the hill, and extends in a transverse direction, about a mile to the westward, is chiefly composed of water stone, a brittle substance not sufficiently durable for the exterior purposes of building. When it is applied to the repair of the public roads, or long exposed to the weather, it dissolves to a greyish soil, favourable, it is said, to vegetation.

Mr. Horner mentions an extensive lime-stone quarry, to the south of Old Castle Bank, in a wood belonging to Lord Somers, and immediately at the foot of the Herefordshire beacon; also an extensive lime-stone quarry, on the right hand side of the road to Ledbury, and near that town : the bearing of the strata is, in one part, N. and S. with a dip to the east of $18°$. In these quarries of lime-stone, he found large veins of calcareous spar, which, in

some places, had red sulphat of barytes dissemi-
nated through it; he also observed that mineral,
in the interior of those shells, which are found in
the lime-stone. In the quarry, on the opposite side
of the road, he found a specimen of a madreporite,
resembling, in form, the lithostration of Lhwyd,
but much smaller in size. This is the same fossil
that is represented in plate v. figure 3 and 6 of the
2d vol. of Parkinson's Organic Remains.

At the foot of the hills, the ground is quite un-
broken, and, at the termination of that part of the
plain which is opposite to the Worcestershire beacon, the right bank of the Severn is nearly 70 feet
high, and is of a red argillaceous sand-stone, with
occasional beds or long patches of a white quartoze
sand-stone. It is the same red stone which prevails
over the great part of Worcestershire.

According to Mr. Barret, the component matter
of the Malvern hills is so rugged and brittle as to
render it unfit for carving, but that it is of an exceeding durable nature, and possesses the chymical
property of resisting acids : both the grey and the
red take a good polish, and the latter then somewhat resembles cornelian.

There is also some excellent gravel lately met
with on a terrace-like shelf, about half way up to
the eastern side of the range. Several quarries
are worked in different places and at different
heights, beside which the mineralogist has the
opportunity of observation from the chasm, called

the Wych, in the northern road, across the hills, and also in the Ledbury road, near Little Malvern, in the making of which, the rock has, in many places, been cut down to the depth of 20 or 30 feet.

"In our own island, the Malvern hills, on the side towards Worcester," says Mr. Kidd, "terminate almost abruptly in a level plain of rock marl, out of which they seem to rise, while on the opposite side they give support to a variety of beds of a very different nature, and forming a rugged surface."

Townshend, in his work on the Deluge, tell us that the Lyas beds surround Malvern hills, and the metalliferous or mountain lime-stones are lying against their ascent; and that these precipitous cliffs, and disrupted mountains, carry with them equivocal marks of dislocation.

"Lime-stone resting on the west part of the Malvern hills," says Dr. Gilby, "I have seen: it generally occurs in a strata of considerable magnitude: the strata, however, of the Malvern lime stone seemed to me never to exceed the thickness of a foot or a foot and a half. Mr. Horner considered them as decidedly transitions, and as it appears that they rest on the sienite of the Malvern hills, which is indisputably lime-stone; "and since," as Dr. Prichard informs us, "they dip under the old red sand-stone of Herefordshire:" there can, I think, be no doubt of their being entitled to this denomination. Upon primitive rocks, rest those of the transition formation, consisting of grey wacke, lime-stone, and grey wacke slate, which, however, sometimes as at Malvern, and in Cumberland, &c. are found unsociated by the older rocks. " Mr. Farey," in his account of Derby-shire, " when enumerating the beds," as he calls them, the products of the red ground, mentions after gypsum, and sand-stone strata, sienite, and roof or clay slate : " and probably," says he, " the sienite of Malvern belongs to this formation." " It is quite unnecessary for me," continues Dr. Gilby, " to make any comment upon so strange an error, as that of placing the sienite and slate of Derbyshire and Malvern hills (which certainly belong to the transition series, but which some have called primitive) in the same formation with the gypsum, of the red ground, between which and the sienite, in point of regular succession, there intervenes the red sand-stone, mountain lime-stone, and coal deposit, &c. But Mr. Farey in fact seems to despise every thing like a sys-tematic arrangement, and calls forsooth the confu-sion which he seems to introduce, Geology." Vide Geological Observations, by W. H. Gilby, M. D. Philosop. Mag. Sept. 1815, p. 182; also Mags. for Sept. and Nov.

. Mr. Barrett remarks, " that in the lime-stone, found in the parishes of Colwall and Mathon, are an almost infinite variety of marine productions, particularly the remains of shell fish, such as cockles and muscles, of various sizes, some of them partly, and others of them only petrified or changed to a perfect lime-stone : he has also seen the fragments of different kinds of fish, in a state of petrifaction, but retaining their natural figure. These strata also abound with the relicts of several kinds of zoophites, a most singular marine production, which are always found in a petrified state, and are commonly known by the name of screw stones. These are the remains of substances that possessed animal and vegetable life, and which are therefore considered, by naturalists, as the grand concatenation of the animal and vegetable kingdoms. Mr. Barrett recently discovered, in this lime-stone, the fragment of a horn which probably belonged to a cornigerous marine animal. It was in a petrified state, but not totally divested of its original testaceous matter. Here is also found the *cornu ammonis,* specimens of which are often seen of different sizes, but always divested of their native shell. He likewise found here the nautilus, the head of an exceeding large enchrinus, several species of gryphites, corals fungi marini, &c.

Many of these marine relicts are in great preservation: the shell fish retain their striæ, and the other kinds their respective vertebræ—with their figures so extremely perfect, as leave no room to doubt of their species, and incontestibly prove that they belong to the aquatic element.

" It undoubtedly exceeds," says Mr. Barrett, in

conclusion, " the limits of human abilities to de-
monstrate the origin of the Malvern hills,* or to
ascertain the period of their existence. Nevertheless it is obvious that they are either primary
productions of nature, or were produced at some
very remote æra, and might probably have been
rocks involved by the ocean. This latter idea,
at the first perception, may appear rather romantic, till it be recollected that the globe has suffered
various revolutions, and that its surface, in many
parts, has undergone a similar alteration. Those
marine productions contained in the lime-stone, as
before recited, form the principal basis of this
conjecture. The method of their arrangment in
the *strata* evidently shews, that they were thus
deposited by water : hence those parts must be
pervaded by that element. That vast aggre-
gate mass, or rock, which composes the hills,
is perfectly exempt from any marine production;
an indication, not only of their primary existence, but, that they had acquired their solidity
previous to the lime-stone. It was before observed, that the remains of zoophites, by some
termed sensitive plants, were extremely numerous;
which substances, when in a living state, always
inhabit the cavernous recesses of rocks in the sea,
such places only being adapted to the nature of
their existence—hence the discovery of these

---

* The Malvern hills were at one time higher than at present.

Vide Bakewell's Lectures.

relicts plead strongly in favour of the conjecture. The beds of lime-stone, which contain those marine bodies, when the water subsided, which might have been either at the grand deluge or some subsequent period, were probably banks of soil, which, from being saturated with water, were subject to petrifaction. Various other productions of the natural kingdom abound in the environs of the Malvern hills, from which inferences might be deduced to favour the idea that these mountains, in common with other similar productions of nature, were compacted together by some sudden convulsion, at least it is the only basis of conviction, that human reason can rest on, to account for their formation and appearance."

The more elevated parts of the Malverns hills, which are not enclosed or cultivated, chiefly belong to proprietors of land in the adjoining parishes. The surface, in some places, is productive of gorse and fern; in others it is a sweet turf, affording an excellent sheep pasture : large numbers feed thereon, and the mutton, which is small, is much esteemed for its mild flavour.

"With the exception of the small bed of redsandstone," says Mr. Horner, in continuation, "on the eastern side of the Worcestershire beacon, all the unstratified rocks seem to belong to the primitive class of the Wernerian system; and in general accord very much with the account given by Mr. Jameson, in his Geognosy, of the third or newest granite formation. The structure of the granite is very irregular, it is generally of a red colour, and it is found in veins that probably shoot from a great body of rock: it is frequently traversed by veins of quartz, and is not stratified. The rocks, in which hornblende exists, correspond with some of the varieties of primitive trap, and of sienite, as described in the same work.

"The stratified rocks on the western side, are probably of very early formation, as the organic remains that are found in them are such as only occur in the oldest of the secondary rocks.

" The characters of the lime-stone quite agree with those of the transition lime-stone of Werner, and though the argillaceous rock does not exactly correspond with any of the transition rocks enumerated by Mr. Jameson, yet as the organic remains are found in it as in the lime-stone, and as it occurs, in some places, on both sides of the lime-stone strata, in conformable stratification, it is very probable, that both belong to the same class. The argillaceous rock may perhaps be a grauwacke slate, as that name has so very wide a range, but it is in general much less indurated than any rock I have yet seen, to which that denomination has been applied.

" Whether I am correct or not in the application I have made of the Wernerian names to the individual rocks of the Malvern district, will be shewn: if we consider their geological arrangement we

z

shall find they exhibit appearances very inconsistent with the Wernerian system of Geognosy. The most remarkable feature of this district is the very great contrast between the two sides of the range. On the eastern side, a level plain extending for many miles; on the western, a constant succession of hills. Now if the unstratified rocks, in the centre, are to be considered as the oldest, and if the stratified rocks have been deposited upon them, how does it happen that they are only found on one side, that not a vestige of the strata, that occur on the western side, is to be met with on the eastern; and *vice versa*, that the red sand-stone of the eastern side is not to be found on the western, at least for three or four miles all along the range, beyond which my observations did not extend. Besides, if the stratified rocks were deposited on the unstratified central rock, we should expect to find their bearings always parallel to the direction of the range, and their dip, uniformly towards the west; corresponding with the slope of the hill: supposing what is maintained in the Wernerian system—the possibility of a stratified rock being deposited on any other than a horizontal or nearly horizontal position. We should also expect, in so short an extent as that of the Malvern range, that the same kind of stratified rock would always be found next to the unstratified, but I have shewn that neither of these things occur. It is true that the direction of the strata is in general parallel to that of the range, but there are some remarkable exceptions to it, as in the lime-stone of Stonyway quarry, where the direction of the strata is from E. to W. exactly at right angles to that of the range : again, the strata, nearest the range, is in general quite vertical, and even, in some places, dip towards it, that is eastward, at an angle of 60°. and so far from the same stratified rock always occurring near the unstratified, it is, in some places, sand-stone; in others, the argillaceous rock; and in others, lime-stone. The unstratified central rocks are so much concealed that any inferences, with respect to them, are liable to more uncertainty than those we are able to draw from the frequent exposure of the stratified rock on the western side; but wherever they can be seen, to any extent, they exhibit a great degree of irregularity, the different kinds of rock being found in large masses, confusedly heaped together. The granite chiefly occurs in the lower part of the hill; and the veins of it, which penetrate the other rocks, become more slender as they ascend, in all those places, where they can be distinctly traced.

"Such remarkable variations, in the direction and dip of the stratified rocks, can only be accounted for on the supposition of some violent force, that has elevated them from the horizontal position in which they must have originally been deposited, and thrown them into the different situations in which they are now found, and the Huttonian

Theory offers, in Mr. Horner's opinion, a more
satisfactory explanation of this phenomena than
any other with which we are yet acquainted. The
situation of the granite, and the veins of it that
penetrate the other rocks, in almost every part of
the range, perfectly accord with the supposition of
its being of later origin, and of its having been
thrown up from beneath them : it is also probable,
that the elevation of the granite has produced the
great disturbance in the strata, which Mr. H. has
described. The direction of the force seems to
have been from west to east, and its action appears
to have ceased, where the unstratified rocks broke
through and appeared above the surfaces ; and as
these have been thrown up in a line between N.
and S. the bearing of the elevated strata ought in
general to be parallel to that line, and this has
been shewn to be the case. The force would be
greatest at the point where the unstratified rocks
burst forth, and accordingly we find the strata there
in general vertical, and in those places, where they
dip towards the range, they seem to have been
raised, not only into a vertical position, but even
thrown back, and in some degree inverted; the
elevation of the strata in different places, forming
the low hills which occur on the western side of
the range, and in which the strata exhibits such remarkable changes, in their position, as at Stonyway quarry, Eventon quarry, and the quarries near
Ledbury."

Mr. Horner concludes his valuable essay, to which we regret our limits do but imperfect justice, with the following excellent observation: " if the geologist strictly guards himself against the influence of theory, in his Observations of Nature, and faithfully records what he has seen, there is no danger of his checking the progress of science, however much he may indulge in the speculative view of the subject."

CHAPTER IX.

The Sunday School, Lodging and Boarding Houses, Walks, &c.

THE excellent establishment of the Sunday School, at Little Malvern, owes its existence chiefly, not to the splendor of royal or even noble patronage, but to the exertion of an humble individual, whose enviable feelings, resulting from a good conscience, has hitherto been his only reward.

In the year 1812, Mrs. Barry, a widow lady of good property, commenced a subscription for the purpose of erecting a building and establishing a Sunday School for the instruction and reformation of the children of the poor, residing in the neighbourhood of Malvern Wells. But discouraged by the smallness of the sum she received, deterred by the voice of her friends, who suggested she had undertaken more than her spirits would enable her to accomplish, and worn out by the many obstacles thrown in her way, she was at length, though reluctantly, obliged to desist from her purpose. Thus had a plan, so beneficial to the interests of society, been entirely abandoned, when Mr. George Phillips, who, at that time, lived servant with Mrs.

Barry, and who had been employed by her in her benevolent intention, being fully aware of the profligacy and ignorance in which the surrounding peasantry were plunged, and fondly hoping something might be done for the reformation of their morals, resolved to adopt the idea suggested by his worthy mistress, and, as far as his humble means would allow, commenced his scheme of education, but without, at first, informing Mrs. Barry, until his plan should, in some measure, be crowned with success. From the funds carefully amassed in his situation of servant alone, and without the smallest idea that any greater extension of his plan would be necessary, than these funds would satisfy, he hired a room and engaged a person, at three shillings a week, for the purposes of teaching a few children to read gratuitously, and also volunteered his own services, as far as his leisure would permit, to instruct those who were willing to attain a knowledge of reading the bible ; " being firmly persuaded" says he, in a letter to us, " that the reading this holy book, attended by the divine blessing, is calculated to produce the most beneficial effects to every class of the community." " As to my own religious opinions," he continues, " they are agreeable to the Articles and Liturgy of the Church of England; but, at the same time, I am willing and thankful to avail myself of the assistance of any class of christians, provided they do not teach contrary to this my confession. With these sentiments and wishes, I commenced my school at North Cottage, Dec. 5, 1813, with twenty-two children : this number kept increasing so fast that the two rooms, at North Cottage, became too small to contain all my pupils.

" About this time my worthy and pious mistress, who had now become acquainted with this prosecution of her favourite idea, permitted me to make use of a long room, over her coach house and stables : she also encouraged me to build a school-room on a piece of ground of my own, and made over to me the sum of 50*l.* she had collected, 30*l.* of which was her own free gift.—Here my school-room is now erected, and a book for subscriptions opened at the principal Hotels in Malvern, to register any sum which the benevolent may please to contribute towards defraying the sums advanced from my own private resources.

"In the year 1815, the number of children instructed were two hundred and eighty-three, being one hundred and twenty-five boys and one hundred and fifty-eight girls ; the number that attend, at present, do not amount to many more than 60, probably, owing to a Sunday School since established by the Rev. Mr. Tuberville, at Hanley, and also from my having, at the suggestion of a lady, adopted Dr. Bell's plan, which, however preferable in itself, the parents of the children are prejudiced against, preferring what they call the old way. The children come from the different parishes, from Hanley, the Wells and Castle Morton, Little Malvern, where the school is held, and Colwall: they attend Little Malvern church, which is about a mile from the school. Prayers are also read in the School-room, and the Monitors, and some of the best behaved children, meet every Thursday evening, at six in the Summer, and the whole of the afternoon in Winter, when they are taught writing and arithmetic, the Sunday instruction being dedicated to reading, spelling and catechising only."

Mrs. Barry, the benevolent projector of the Sunday School, did not long survive to witness the exertions of her faithful servant. She died Sept. 30, 1814; her daughter is, however, the inheritor of her mother's virtues, and, though at present residing in Ireland, continues a warm friend to the Sunday School of Little Malvern.

The persons to whom Mrs. Barry more particularly owed the aid of their exertions and subscriptions, were Lord and Lady Riversdale, Lady Kent, Admiral West, The Hon. and Rev. Ludlow Tonson, The Rev. Mr. Greig, Mr. and Mrs. Wigram, and the late David Pike Watts, Esq.

The following is an extract from the subscription book, illustrative of the expenses of the Sunday School, at Little Malvern:

" Mr. George Phillips, servant to the late Mrs. Barry, erected a very eligible building for a Sunday School, at an expense of 389*l.* 12s. 6d. including all expenses: he has received subscriptions amounting to 215*l.* 14s. 0d. also books from the Countess of Harcourt and Lady Olivia Sparrow; thus the cost of the building, &c. exceeded the subscription 173*l.* 18s. 6d.

"Mr. Phillips has been actuated by the most benevolent motives, gratuitously devoting his time to the religious education of children, of this and the adjacent parishes, and regularly attending them to the Parish Church of Little Malvern : he renounces all salary, his sole support being derived from his attendance to the interest of Miss Barry, letting Piano Fortes, and repairing musical instruments, &c. The friends of this disinterested man indulge the fond hope that every christian, solicitous for the diffusion of the light of the Gospel and the temporal and eternal welfare of the rising generation, will liberally contribute to defray the cost of the building, " recollecting," as St. Austin well said, "Men must live ill, if their belief in God be not right, and they that turn many to righteousness shall shine as the stars for ever and ever." The smallest donation will be gratefully received by Mr. Steers, Mr. Essington and Mr. George Phillips."

The following notice was written, in June, 1816, by the Rev. S. Alworthy, Rector of Roscall, Staffordshire, in the hope of stimulating the rich and benevolent to contribute to the aid of this excellent institution :

"It ought not to be unrecorded, to the honour of this second man of Ross, that he has not only reared this Sunday School at his sole expense, without either the hope or expectation of return, but he has also purchased the ground on which it stands, a quarter of an acre, for which he paid 80*l.* Had not rumour led a gentleman to make a strict enquiry into this almost unparalleled act of christian benevolence, the statement of it would never, in all probability, have met the public eye, or sympathy and benevolence ever have been solicited; for *this man* sought not the praise or liberality that cometh from man, but the praise and reward that cometh from God only. Mr. George Phillips's place of residence is not two hundred yards from the Well-house, and he may be seen and conversed with by any one desirous of further information on the subject."

The following is a list of the Subscribers to the Sunday School, in the order in which they subscribed. Those names marked with an asterisk denote persons who have also contributed their personal assistance, in tuition, &c.

	£.	s.	d.
* Mrs. Barry and Friends,..........................	50	0	0
* Miss Barry,...	7	0	0
Dr. Woodyatt,......................................	1	0	0
Miss Berwick,.......................................	1	0	0
* Lady Olivia Sparrow, ...	5	0	0
Mr. Essington, ...	5	0	0
Mr. Curteis,...	1	0	0
Miss Curteis,..	1	0	0
Miss Caroline Curteis, ...	1	0	0
* Mrs. Arbuthnot,..................................	1	0	0
Mr. and *Mrs. Wigram,...........................	5	0	0
* Countess Harcourt,..............................	3	0	0
* Hon. Mrs. Cornwall,.............................	5	0	0
* Lady Wigram,.....................................	10	0	0
Earl Harcourt,.......................................	2	0	0
Mr. J. Phillips,......................................	1	0	0
* Mrs. Hare,...	1	1	0
* The Miss Hares, ...	1	1	0
Mr. Dan. Crauford, ...	1	1	0
Mr. Holland, ...	1	1	0
Lady Hayes,...	1	0	0
* Mrs. Empson,.....................................	5	0	0
Mr. Bright,...	3	0	0
Earl Harcourt, second subscription,...	2	0	0
* Countess Harcourt, second subscription, ...	2	0	0
* Hon. Miss Trefusis,..............................	1	1	0
Mr. Webster,..	1	0	0
* Mr. P. W. Crowther,†	2	0	0
	120	5	0

	£.	s.	d.
Brought over, ...	120	5	0
* Miss Clements, ...	1	0	0
Mr. Wigram, second subscription, ...	5	0	0
Col. Barry, ...	1	0	0
Mrs. Pritchard, ...	1	0	0
* Mrs. Forrest, ...	1	0	0
Major Davidson, ...	1	0	0
* Rev. Dan. Price, ...	1	0	0
Miss Bayley, ...	1	0	0
Mrs. Delancey, ...	1	0	0
Miss Delancey, ...	1	0	0
Mr. Henry Willock, ...	1	1	0
The Bishop of Meath, ...	1	0	0
Mr. Biddulph, ...	1	0	0
E. I.	1	1	0
Mrs. Gabagan, ...	1	1	0
A Friend, ...	1	1	0
Lady Carnagie, ...	1	1	0
Mr. Atwick, ...	1	1	0
The Miss Milligans, ...	1	10	0
The Rev. Mr. Bowdler, ...	1	0	0
* Miss Empson, ...	1	1	0
Mrs. Kinderley, ...	1	1	0
Rev. Mr. Bowdler, second subscription, ...	1	0	0
Mr. A. Guinness, ...	1	0	0
A Passenger, by G. Phillips, ...	10	0	0
Mr. Bright, second subscription, ...	2	0	0
Lady Hayes, second subscription, ...	1	0	0
	162	3	0

† This gentleman has also conferred a benefit on the public, by the publication of the following work : " The Christian's Manuel, compiled from the Enchiridion Militis Christiani of Erasmus, with notes, life and correspondence, &c. published for the benefit of the city of London Auxiliary National School, 8vo. May, 1816."

	£.	s.	d.
Brought over,......................................	162	3	0
Mr. Tighe, ...	1	0	0
Mrs. Tighe,..	1	0	0
Major Newenham, ...	1	0	0
Mrs. Frewen Turner, ...	1	0	0
Mr. and Mrs. Wigram, third subscription,....	5	0	0
P. W. Crowther, Esq. second subscription....	1	1	0
* Rev. S. and Mrs. Holworthy,...................	1	1	0
H..	2	0	0
Countess Harcourt, third subscription,.........	3	3	0
Mr. Grainger,......................................	1	1	0
Mr. Baillie,..	1	1	0
Hon. Miss Trefusis,† second subscription, ...	1	1	0
Earl Harcourt, third subscription, ...	2	0	0
Lady Wigram,‡ second subscription,...........	2	0	0
Mrs. W. Dundas, ...	1	0	0
The Hon. W. Dundas, ...	1	0	0
A Friend, ...	1	0	0
Mr. Charles Morris, ...	1	0	0
Mr. Thos. Calvert,.................................	2	0	0
Mrs. Thos. Calvert, ...	1	0	0
The Miss Calverts,.................................	1	10	0
* Miss Parry,......................................	1	0	0
Mrs. Woodhouse, ...	1	1	0
Mr. Parry,...	1	0	0
Mr. Bright, second subscription,.................	2	0	0
Subscriptions under a pound,......................	13	10	0
Rev. Mr. Atwick, second subscription,.........	1	1	0
P. W. Crowther, Esq. third subscription, ...	1	1	0
Mr. Matthews, ...	1	0	0
	215	14	0

† This lady is niece to Lady Harcourt.

‡ This lady gave also 1l. to be distributed as rewards to the children.

In the year 1814, the Hon. Mrs. Cornwall, in addition to her assiduity for the prosperity and usefulness of the School, gave a dinner, every Sunday, to a certain number of the children, while she remained at Malvern. And, in the year 1814, on signing the preliminaries of peace, Mr. Essington, of the Hotel, gave a dinner to a hundred of the children; Mr. Steers has also treated them with a dinner, and Miss Steers has assisted in their education.

Mr. Phillips is anxious to acknowledge the assistance he received from Mrs. Biddulph, during the second year of the school; also that which he received, during last winter, from Mrs. and Miss Stephenson; for the exertions of Mr. Bright, in inducing children to frequent the school; and to Mrs. Woodhouse, for her offer of procuring him instruction in the manner of the National Sunday School, he begs to offer his grateful thanks.

We regret to state that, from Mr. Phillip's not having the same means of support as he had, at the time the Sunday School was first established, resulting from the patronage of Mrs. Barry, he is obliged to give up his gratuitous services, it therefore remains with the inhabitants of Malvern, to judge how far an individual, who has done thus much for the benefit of society, ought to be encouraged by them in the furtherance of a plan which owes every thing to him for its completion and success.

LODGING HOUSES AT LITTLE MALVERN.

At a small distance from the Holy Well, and on an eminence, overlooking the road to Upton, Cheltenham and Tewkesbury, is a lodging and boarding house, kept by Mr. Steers, called the Wells House.* From the back part of this house, which is built on a declivity, you ascend the hill from a window on the one-pair floor, and may here commence your journey upward through walks, laid out, with regard to picturesque effect, where seats are placed at convenient distances. The prospect, from the front of this house, is extensive, and the situation congenial with health; but the view across the road presents little interest, being composed of various parcels of inclosures, fringed with young hedge rows, and these have not been unaptly compared to the plot of an estate upon paper. This Hotel is the resort of much company,

* This house, with many others of various descriptions, extending half a mile from the Holy Well, on the east side of the hill, are chiefly in Hanley Parish. These residences consist of Belle Monte, occupied by R. Wigram, Esq. M. P. Mrs. Barry's cottage, two farm houses, two hotels, including Steers' and Essington's, five lodging and boarding houses, with twenty-six cottages. The population of this part of Hanley Parish being about two hundred persons, seventy of which are conceived to be poor children, most of whom under the age of twelve years.

drawn here by the contiguity of a charming landscape: here is a table d'hote, with the usual accommodations of houses of this description, bil-
liard table, piano fortes, chess boards, &c. &c.
In the dining room is a large painting, representing a view of Covent Garden market, at five
o'clock in the morning, and is probably the production of John Collet, a pupil of Hogarth, who
died at Chelsea, in the year 1780. The two
smaller paintings, suspended at each side of the
room, are said to be painted by a gentleman's
servant, a self-taught artist, and, under the un-
propitious circumstances of his situation, are
worthy observation: they are presumed to be
copies from Opie. In this room hang the various
advertisements relative to the place, among which,
in the cause of charity, are the following lines:-

"The humble address of Ann Farmer, who, at the age of
seventy, sweeps the walks near the Well-house, relying, for
support, on the visitors of Malvern.

    "This humble petition I beg leave to shew,
    For sweeping the walks, above and below,
    From the top of the hill, down to the Well-house,
    There is not a stone so large as a mouse."

May the scribblers of bad lines be as easily for-
given as Ann Farmer's Poet.

This lodging house is seldom visited in the winter, the air here being very sharp during that
season, but, in the summer months, this spot is
most delightful, rendered, indeed, particularly so,
in the morning, by the rising sun, whose meri-

dian rays are tempered by a refreshing breeze, peculiar to the Malvern hills. Besides these premises, Mr. Steers is the owner of a residence, close to the holy well, called the Rock-house, which is calculated for persons who wish to live in a private manner.

A regular penny post-office is established at the Well-house, from the 6th of May to the 6th of November, which goes out every day, except on Mondays: the remainder of the year, letters are circulated from this house on Tuesdays, Thursdays and Saturdays only; and a person is sent to Worcester, for letters, on those days which the mail does not arrive at Little Malvern. Divine service is performed at Mr. Steers's Hotel, every Sunday morning, from May to October, at one o'clock, by Mr. Turberville, the rector of Hanley, or his curate, or any visitor of the clerical profession, who may be staying at this hotel.

ESSINGTON HOTEL

Is a boarding house, kept by a person of that name: here are, attached to the house, hot and cold baths, a wood, garden and a hermitage. The following lines were written at this hotel, by Mr. Bissett, of Leamington, author of several literary productions:

At Malvern Wells, where health bears the belle,
All visitors notice the famous hotel,
By Essington kept, where you meet with good cheer,
Good wines and good liquors, good ale and good beer:

Of damp beds and rough treatment, no person's in danger,
Whilst civil attention is paid to each stranger ;
Then honour the house if you please, if you call,
The Essingtons cheerly will wait on you all :
To serve you with zeal, and obey each behest,
They'll endeavour to please you by doing their best.

The annexed rules and orders, to be observed at these boarding houses, may serve to give the stranger, at Malvern, some idea of the accommodations to be found at this romantic spot.

1.—Each person to be provided with a lodging room, properly furnished, from eight shillings to fourteen shillings per week ; and so in proportion for as many rooms as any lady or gentleman may have occasion for.—Each person to pay one shilling and sixpence a week for candles.—Five shillings will also be charged for the servants of the house, for each bed room.

II.—Each lodger to pay two pounds two shillings per week, (or six shilling per day, for a shorter period,) for their board, which includes every article except tea and sugar ; and twenty-four shillings and sixpence per week, or three shillings and sixpence per day, for each servant's breakfast, dinner and supper ; and if a single bed room is required for a servant, then to pay five shillings per week for such room.

III.—Each person to be supplied with wine, spirits, &c. by the master of the house, and to find themselves with tea and sugar ; or the master of the house will supply them with tea and sugar, charging the same.

IV.—The company to assemble and dine together, at the public table, in the great room, at three o'clock each day ;—the first bell will be rung at half-past two, and the dinner bell at three o'clock.—No lodger to dine privately in the house, unless sickness render it necessary.

V.—Every lady and gentleman is requested to settle with the master of the house, for board, lodging, &c. at the end of every week, commencing from the time of each person's arrival.

VI.—All persons not lodging in the house to pay four shillings and sixpence each for dinner, and two shillings and sixpence for supper.

VII.—No petition from travelling beggars suffered to be presented, nor any petition whatever obtruded on the company, or hung up in the long room, without permission of the master of the house.

No deduction for children in the above rules.—Fires to be paid for.

Any persons engaging lodgings must pay for them from the day they are engaged.

Dogs will be charged for, but will not be permitted in the parlour or long room.

Besides these houses are many others, ready furnished, dispersed about the neighbourhood, nor is any accommodation wanted in the vicinity of Little Malvern.

PICTURESQUE RIDES, WALKS, &c.

At the distance of two miles from Great Malvern is a public road, over the hill, through the Witch or chasm, cut by art, at the summit, in order to shorten the ascent, and render the passage, over it, safe and easy. This road is rather steep and uneven, and therefore seldom used for carriages. It is, however, convenient as a shorter way for travellers, on horse-back, from Ledbury to Malvern and Worcester. The ride from the Well-house to the Herefordshire beacon is generally the first excursion, proposed by the guide, and, to the mere traveller through Malvern, a better cannot be taken, nor any other from which he may behold a finer specimen of the grand panorama of nature, visible from this hill. A very short walk, from this road, will lead us on the Herefordshire side of the hills, past this chasm, and from thence to the Worcestershire beacon, from whence, still keeping to the northward, we descend into a deep winding vale, without either cottage or shrub to relieve the eye, and, for a few minutes, we may suppose ourselves in the wildest deserts of Africa, until we catch a winding walk, which we may cross towards the ascent of the north hill, and then return by it into the village of Great Malvern; or the traveller may commence another tour from the remains of the Abbey gate. In one of the Malvern tours, "we find that there was a road made about eight years since, by means of which, carriages may be taken round the north part of the hill. This undertaking was promoted by the late Sir Hildebrande Jacob, Bart. whom, it is said, contributed largely towards defraying the expenses of the execution." Of this circumstance, we have, however, been able to gain but little—the result was of scarce any importance, nor is it supposed Sir Hildebrande Jacob's efforts were very strenuously exerted to gain his purpose.

There is, at present, in execution, a recent plan for an intended new road, along the east side, and round the north end of the Malvern range. It is proposed that this road shall commence and gradually ascend from the seven-mile stone, on the link, in a proportion of one inch and a quarter per yard, for 1600 yards, when it will join the present high road, in the parish of Cradley, near adjoining the parish of Mathon. The road, already finished, through the latter parish, skirting the western limit of the hills, is, at present, in excellent repair, for a considerable distance; and when the above-mentioned 1600 yards are added to it, the estimate of which was near 400*l*, it is intended that the overplus of the subscription money, raised for that purpose, shall be expended towards extending the projected road along the western side of the hills, to connect it with the present high road, above Little Malvern; so that a good carriage road will then encircle these beautiful hills, and enable even the most valetudinary to enjoy, at ease, their delightful scenery.

The following are the names of Subscribers who have come forward in aid of this desirable improvement :

	£.	s.	d.
Lord Harcourt,	10	0	0
Mr. Foley,	100	0	0
Mr. Branch,	15	15	0
	125	15	0

	£.	s.	d.
Brought over,..	125	15	0
W. Wall,...	20	0	0
T. Hornyhold,......................................	15	15	0
Lord Beauchamp,..................................	50	0	0
Hon. W. B. Lygon,...............................	25	0	0
A. Cliffe, ...	21	0	0
Lord Foley,..	25	0	0
The Dean and Chapter of Westminster,........	20	0	0
W. Leighton,......................................	5	5	0
W. Woodyatt,......................................	5	5	0
Miss Benbow,......................................	2	2	0
Thomas Jones,......................................	3	3	0
Mrs. Ann Jones,....................................	1	1	0
L. Bright,..	10	0	0
Mrs. Barry,..	1	0	0
Miss Barry,..	1	0	0
Rev. Daniel Price,...............................	5	0	0
	336	6	0

Thus it appears, that a sum of money is yet wanted to complete the first 1600 yards; and it is hoped that so desirable a plan, as that of completing the road round the hills, will not be suffered to languish for want of further encouragement.

Two drawings, shewing the line of this new road, may be seen at the Old Bank, Worcester.

To describe, more particularly, the romantic rides and walks, about Malvern, will be, it is true, to recapitulate much of what we have already said; for, indeed, every part of the high roads,

and numerous paths around it, may be considered
as leading to new beauties ; but, in describing to
our readers those points of view most deserving
notice, we must not forget to award due praise to
the benevolent exertions of a lady, to whom Malvern is under no small obligations, if we consider
her either as aiding its charities or contributing to
the enjoyment of its picturesque effect.   It is
here, in the walks at Malvern, that the name of
Harcourt will be aspirated by the invalid, and the
lover of pure nature : the facilities she has procured for the former to visit heights where the gale
more salubriously blows, will not be forgotten, and
the latter will hail her name, as he looks up
through nature to nature's God.

If we might be allowed to alter the words of
Pope, we would say,

"Whose causeway parts the vale and shady rows,
Whose seats the weary traveller repose,
Who spreads the scene with joy to glad our eyes,
'Tis Harcourt, Harcourt every grove replies."

When Lady Harcourt first visited Malvern, there
was but one small path to the top of the hills, and
this led to the least interesting part of them :
this, we believe, was made by Mr. Berkeley, of
Spetchley.

It has ever been her ladyship's delight, and un-
wearied solicitude, to form several walks in the
most picturesque parts of the Malvern hills, particularly round the beautiful camp hill, for a distance

of about five miles, the road being formed without gravel, but with decomposed granate, of which that part of the hill is composed.

"In planning these roads and walks," says her ladyship, in a letter she honoured us with in answer to one requesting information relative to the walks, &c. "I owe the place much, for the health it has procured me." But, in order to convince us that selfish gratification was not alone her ladyship's stimulant, we learn, that so anxious is Lady Harcourt, that the seats and the rough stone building, which she has erected, should remain, after her death, for the benefit of the visitors of Malvern, that her ladyship has left, in the hands of Mr. Bright and Mr. Hornyold, the sum of 100*l.* the interest of which, after her decease, she has desired may be employed in the repair of the different seats, in the hope that this may stimulate some other persons further to prosecute what her ladyship has commenced, the preservation of those seats, and to add to the beauty of those walks, which it has been her delight to embellish. Nor would her ladyship have stopped here, in the improvement of Malvern, for we are authorized to say that she would have proceeded in her exertions and extended the walks still further, and have carried them from the wells to Great Malvern, had she not been constantly checked by the different proprietors of the hill, who, with the exception of Mr. Hornyold, impeded her progress, in

which her ladyship had no other view than to make
the magnificent scenery of Malvern easier of access
to those who resorted to it for the benefit of the
waters.

It is not only our duty to mention these acts of
philanthophy of her ladyship, but it may be useful to record this bequest of 100l. which the
worthy donor has left for the future preservation
of the walks, after her death, as these legacies,
from a change of hands in which such sums are
invested, are often applied to purposes for which
they were never intended.

For the gratification of the sojourner, at Malvern, and more fully to point out its many beauties, we shall conclude our account of the walks
and rides, in its vicinity, by the following extracts
from a tour performed by two gentlemen, under
the signatures of Academicus and Vigorniensis, as
detailed in "Reflections relative to the Malvern
hills."

" Vigorniensis determined that they should go
up the hill, the Worcestershire Beacon, as it is
called, the highest of the whole range, by the
simpler and ruder ascent, and return by way of St.
Ann's Well.

" They began to ascend by the common pathway,
over pieces of rock. They soon came to a part of
the ascent, opposite to which a cottage was pointed
out by Vigorniensis, on the other side of a little
runnel, that trickles down through the turf, and

faintly bubbles beside you, during a great part of your walk up the hill. Somewhat higher up, the sloping, craggy sides of two hills begin to open, as parts of the diverging sides of an angle, and leave a slanting valley between them, their edges being rugged with fern, furze, bushes and bits of rock. Vigorniensis singled out two views, one from a lower, and one from a higher, point; taking care in the former, to exclude, as far as could be, the tops of houses below, to retain, in the right fore-ground, a spreading witch-tree,* that hangs over the scene; and, in both views, to keep Worcester a good deal to the left of the landscape, (in the lower, indeed, almost close to the hill,) and, in the upper, by no means to make it central between the sides. In this upper view, these two sides rise high above the distant horizon, and between them is admitted, in front of the spectator, a wide, rich, soft and varied scene, Worcester, with the Cathedral, and the spire of St. Andrew's, being the chief object. The landscape is sometimes clear; sometimes blended and mellowed by a sort of transparent mistiness; sometimes pleasingly confused, in parts, by a bluish dimness.†

---

* These trees are so called by the peasants: properly witch-hazels.

† The former of these views, being so near the foot, is liable to alteration in its foregrounds. The tree mentioned has been reduced in size.

A small farm-house, at the bottom of a cornfield with winding furrows, should not be left out of the *lower*

" They had passed a path, which, at a point nearly opposite to the cottage, turned aside to the right of them, as they ascended, leading to another part of the hills.

" They turned into an ascending pathway, shovelled along the slopes; and strolled on, observing the hills in different aspects; which here heave forward in huge, gigantic swells, there retire into sloping vallies; and, for the most part, are clothed with short green turf, though much roughened with rocky fragments of course granite-stone, with furze and fern, and sometimes with ivy, bushes, and stunted trees.*

" When they had proceeded a good way, there appeared, in a retiring part of the hill, a large rugged projection of rock, splintered down, in parts, almost perpendicularly; of a hoary grey and white, but stained with various colours by moss and lichens and weeds; and, on a portion of the top, thickly covered with clustering ivy bearing marks of great age. And the rock was partly bordered by high, thick fern. In one or two of the cavities, resembling fragments in the ruin of some artificial fabric, sheep were reposing. Oppo-

landscape. This landscape should be viewed, from a point just above a little natural basin in the turf, serving for a well to the cottage. About the point, whence the upper should be viewed, some stones, large enough to sit on, were lying in 1812, when these visitors were at Malvern.

* The granite is generally mixed with ' some heterogeneous matter.'

BARRETT, p. 10.

site to this rock is another of less size; and small ones jut out, at various distances, in the slope above. From points near the bottom of both rocks, are fine views of the distant country. They sat down just beyond the furthest of the two. From the top of this hangs a hawthorn : and another (smaller) is seen shooting out above the ivy, on the former.

"Here, said Vigorniensis, (though slightly blemished on the right,) is one of the choicest Malvern views. I know not that the church and abbey-gate are elsewhere seen together to such advantage. In the south extremity, less conspicuous than Worcester, but discernible, is Gloucester.* And what a scene lies between the cities ! Academicus joined in its commendation. How exquisitely, said Vigorniensis, have nature and man together disposed of the trees and underwood in the meadows: though the alders near the church may be more striking !

"They returned, and re-entered the path which leads up to the highest hill. While they were preceding up a smooth slope, we have, said Vigorniensis, the choice of, at least, three ways. Were we to diverge, on our left, by this accommodating path, and to retrograde a little, the ascent would be longer, but more gradual and easy: and we should have a wider view of the Worcestershire

---

* The Cathedral, at least, may often be seen plainly.

prospect. But we shall descend by that path, and, in ascending, will take the rudest and boldest, though the most laborious, of the three. You perceive, a little before us, two ways meeting in an angle. The right leads to the top of a lower hill, by a gentle slope, buried among other slopes, and admitting scarce any thing of the distant scene.

"At length they reached the ridge; and part of the Herefordshire prospect was before them. They forbore to pause there; but climbed on to the summit.

"In front, and to the south of us, said Vigorniensis, are Welch mountains. The Sugar-loaf, in Monmouthshire, points itself out by its form. The black mountain, in Brecknockshire, one of those which appear largest, is nearly in front of us. It is distinguishable by the abruptness of its north extremity. The order of the counties (besides Hereford and Worcester,) is, on the Herefordshire side, Monmouth, Brecknock, Radnor, Salop; on the Worcestershire side, part of Salop, Stafford, Warwick, Oxford, Gloucester.

"The Worcestershire prospect, though grand from its extent, is, in its richness, luxuriancy and beauty, more smooth and tranquillising than the other. The Worcestershire has more of Claude; the Herefordshire of Salvator Rosa, with his characteristics, perhaps, a little lowered.

"Have patience, continued Vigorniensis, to follow me in this tour. I notice nearer spots, before I begin upon the circumference of our circle. Worcester, the leading object, so interesting from various causes, we dwelt upon below. Some way to the left of it,* is Hartlebury, once the abode of Stillingfleet and of Hough, and lately of Hurd. Not far distant from this is Bewdley, with Winterdyne; and the rest of its beautiful neighbourhood. At these places I guess; but Hagley, at the end of Clent hill, stately, classical Hagley, ennobled by the taste, talents and virtues of Lyttelton,† I can behold. I can discern the hill, on which stands the Obelisk, if not, by somewhat straining the sight, the Obelisk itself. A few miles distant, ('a step, methinks, would cross' from one to the other,) is the Leasowes,‡ all simplicity, all nature; a place still delightful, in spite of neglect, and changes and injuries : which once, I conceive, more than rivalled Hagley, (when both were in their perfection,) but which Hagley now excels. Shenstone, (too much blamed by you Academical critics, though too much praised by common readers; part of whose poetry has no small merit of its kind;) he, doubtless, has often 'wasted his inoffensive day,' upon these hills, as 'beside his flowery lawn,' at the Leasowes.

---

* Not far from a tall spire, (Ombersley,) which, when the day is clear, may be seen on lower parts, if not from the highest point.

† 'Still true to virtue, and as warm as true.'

Thus Pope speaks of him,

IMITATION OF HORACE, B. 1. Ep. 1.

‡ In a great measure, if not wholly, behind Clent Hill.

"I must interrupt you, said Academicus, (though I feel interested in your reverie,) by asking what is that town and church with a tapering spire, near a conspicuous turn in the Severn, with a bridge, and what appears a high red bank of that river.

"It is Upton, said Vigorniensis. You have brought me near to a most interesting spot, Tewkesbury, and its church, a square tower, to the right of Upton, near another similar bank. Within and about that structure, so ancient, so memorable for the occurrences in its precincts, lie the bones of those who fell in the battle. Near the church is the Vineyard, where Margaret's army passed the night, and a little further from it is Bloody Meadow, where was the chief slaughter. To the left of Bredon, (on which is a camp,) we touch on the fertile vale of Evesham; a place noted, like Tewkesbury, for its battle, nor without interest to the ecclesiastical antiquary.

"I now turn to the extreme point of the horizon Northward. The Clee hills first strike my view. Near them are the ruins of Ludlow Castle. Comus, you may remember, was performed there as a mask. To the right of these appears the Wrekin. I am reminded of 'all friends round it.' I carry my eye more Southward. Thereabouts is the 'Toyshop of Europe,'* with its crowds of me-

* So Burke has called Birmingham.
It must be behind Clent Hill, or Bromsgrove Lickey.

chanics, the products of whose skill and labour, whether baubles, or of solid use, travel to all quarters of the globe. But, as we advance along the line, a very different object strikes my recollection. Kenilworth, that proud mass of weather-stained, ivied ruins, that memorial of Leicester's chivalrous magnificence, frowns over the meadows, once his domain, in that direction. By it is Warwick, not in decay, but entire, as when the castle of a feudal Lord. Leamington, with its waters, (different from those of Malvern,) should not be overlooked. Somewhat nearer to us is, (how shall I speak of it with due warmth!) the birth-place, the early abode, the last retreat, the burial-place of—Shakespeare. We know that the house in which he was born, the site of his latter residence, and his grave and his effigy, and the epitaph, with which we are so familiar, may be seen there.

" I pass on to ground above a point in that portion of the distance, which, from the village, has a beautiful, baylike appearance. Here Edgehill catches my eye,* and I think of its battle, and of its prospect. Thereabouts begin the Cotswold hills, famous for games and sports, a relic of which remains. We should see more of Broadway, which itself commands no vulgar view, but Bredon intervenes.

"Further on, I perceive the smoke of Chel-

* It cannot, I believe, be seen from the village.

tenham; and the surrounding hills are easily re-
cognised. Here again, in a spot not a little beautiful, waters spring forth for our relief, prepared
by the chymistry of nature.

"Much more to the South, I discern Gloucester
and its sublime Cathedral. Berkley cannot be far
off, on the banks of the Severn, which once ' re-
echoed with affright'——

          Shrieks of an agonizing king.'

"Last of all, just over our own camp, and the
obelisk in memory of Somers, glimmers the Severn
Sea, and brings to our thoughts the world of
waters with which it communicates."

We cannot resist copying the following description :

"I sometimes go back, in imagination, to the
state of things at Malvern many centuries ago. I
see beneath these hills, instead of this diversified,
cheerful scene of cultivation, a vast, straggling
forest, interspersed with heathy pastures, with
much fewer dwellings visible, chiefly huts and
cottages, and here and there a great man's
castle, bosomed in trees,—the wide, forest scene
having a rich and noble, but far more lonely aspect. Archers, at a distance, appear and disappear among the trees, traversing the chace in
quest of deer. Solitude, nevertheless, strongly
characterizes the scene. I have before me the
grey Gothic Abbey, and its conventual buildings.
Its bell sounds among the rocks. Cowled monks

walk among the thick alder-clumps below. Some are setting out on a spiritual visit to the peasants, or to the household of some baron. Others return with water from the Holy Well, two miles distant. Some are here upon the hills. One sits reading, among rocks and tangled bushes : and two or three are above, near the summit, looking down on the expanse below.

"*Acad.*—You have traced a pretty just Malvern scene, during part of the middle ages.

"*Vigorn.*—In the twelfth or thirteenth century. That was in the morning or at mid-day. About the spot, where we are now sitting, I figure to myself a pair of the reverend brethren, strolling calmly after their vespers, in some sober, summer eve, after having, perhaps, on the top of the hill, 'with wistful eyes pursued the setting sun,' sublime emblem of the just, which 'shall anon repair its beams,' and 'flame in the forehead of the morning sky,'———strolling calmly, I say, on this spot ; discoursing in serene, lofty, moralizing mood, on some subject friendly to pious hope ; and then, with a sacred serenity and elevation of soul, sinking down, in twilight, through the bushes, to their place of repose, in the peaceful, holy receptacle below.

Acad.—In the best periods of this monastery, such cases probably existed. But beware lest your imagination, under the influence of the ' loci ad-monitus,' and this rudeness and majesty of nature, should impose on you, and lead you to too indulgent a retrospect of the monastic character. Often it was a strange mixture of belief, blended with superstition and of hypocrisy; of craft and of imbecility; of learning and of darkness; of needless self-denial, and of luxury and intemperance; of heavenly-mindedness which was strained and affected, and of ambition and avarice; of quaintness and gloom, united with debauchery.

" We have not leisure to take one of the most beautiful rides here, that by Barnard's Green to the farther part of Sherard's Green, but let us turn off, at the top of the Link, by a road parallel with the range. On the right of the road, small hills rise out of the wide, open country, slope upon slope, heaped thick together, consisting of cultivated lands, and parts of extensive running woods, rich, though rather low, of a somewhat bristly surface, forming knolls of various shapes, sometimes approaching to the conical, or sugarloaf, above and about the cornfields. One of them is particularly distinguished by a little peak, (or cone,) which it forms under the knolls. You ride on, with bold and picturesque scenery of this kind, (by varying,) to your right, and you have still, occasionally, some very fine distance, on the side, and in rear of you. By windings in the road, steepish and rutty, you come to a close, confined part of it, and pass almost imperceptibly, from the eastern to the western side. Most rich and beautiful portions of the wide scene on that side, softened and mellowed, (rather brown and dusky,) with distances fading one into another, in the horizon, begin to glimmer through the trees in the hedge-row, opening more and more upon the view, as the boughs become thinner and more apart, with such an exquisite charm, (in my fancy, at least,) that I even think I enter too soon (for the trees do not extend far,) on the noble prospect, divested of the partial veil of the branches."

The country lying on the west side of the Malvern hills, is remarkable for the large plantations of apple and pear trees, and the consequent productions of cider and perry, particularly the latter, which is, in general, rich and of fine taste.

However, it may be proper to observe that, there is, in most places, a manifest superiority in the quality of the fruit, and, consequently, of the liquor produced on the low grounds, over that which grows on the elevated parts. This difference originates from the nature of the soil, which, on the low grounds, is a strong clay, and the banks, a light earth, mixed with gravel, which, in some places, is incumbent on lime-stone.

It is well known that the fruit, produced on the low grounds, affords the liquor, in general, rich and pleasant; but on the latter is more pale and acid.

FOREST OF MALVERN.

This forest belonged to the king, and was, formerly, so much overgrown with wood as to be
called, by the monk of Malmsbury, a wilderness:
it extended, in length, from the river Teme, in the
north, to Cors forest, in the south, and from the
river Severn, on the east, to the top of Malvern
hill, on the west, where there is still to be seen the
remains of a trench, drawn on the narrow ridge of
this steep hill, to divide the possessions of the
Bishop of Hereford from the chace, and to limit
the two counties, made upon the great controversy
that happened between that bishop and the Earl of
Gloucester, soon after this forest had been given
to him.

This Gilbert de Clare, Earl of Gloucester, commonly called the Red Knight, married Joan
d'Acres, the king's daughter, and thereupon was
given to him, by her father, this forest of Malvern,
together with the forest of Cors adjoining to it, to
hold of the honour of Gloucester. These forests,
thus falling from the king to a subject altered

their names, and the first was called a chase. Leland saith, " the chase of Malverne is bigger than either Wire or Feckingham, and occupieth a great part of Malverne hills. Great Malverne and Little also is set in the chace of Malverne. Malverne chace (as I here say) is, in length, in some places, twenty miles; but Malverne chace doeth not occupy all Malverne hills." The second forest also altered its name to that of a Lawn, by which name it now goes; though we find, in Dugdale's Baronage, that, upon Gilbert the second's marriage with Maude, daughter of John de Burgh, among other lands, was assigned to her, for her dowry, the chace of Cors, the castle and manor of Hanlegh, and chace of Malverne; but she having no children by him, his sisters became his heirs; and Elianore, the eldest, who married Hugh le Despencer, the younger, brought Malverne, with other large possessions, into that family: and from them, after the third generation, it came, by an heir general, to Richard Beauchamp, Earl of Warwick, in the time of Henry V. who had issue Henry, Duke of Warwick, and Ann, married to Richard Nevil, Earl of Warwick and Salisbury, who, upon the death of her brother Henry, became his sole heir, and leaving two daughters by Nevil, their whole estate was divided between them: of whom one was matched to Edward, Prince of Wales; and after he was murthered at Tewkesbury, she became the wife of Richard, Duke of

Gloucester, after King of England, as was shewed in the great west window of Malvern church, which proves that Malvern chace, in the partition of Warwick's lands, fell to King Richard III. The other sister and coheir was married to his brother George, Duke of Clarence, and God not suffering any issue to spring from King Richard's loins, this ample inheritance descended to Edward Plantagenet, the duke's son and heir, the unfortunate and only remaining branch of that family, upon whose attainder, in Henry the VIIth's time, it returned to the crown, from whence it came, together with the castle and manor of Hanlegh, the parks of Blackmore, Hanley and Cliffey, all lying in the bosom of the chace, with the market town of Upton-upon-Severn, from which time this chace remained in the crown till about the year 1630; when King Charles I. granted one third-part of the forest or chace of Malvern to Sir Robert Heath, then his Majesty's Attorney General, and Sir Cornelius Vermuyden, and the other two to the commoners, the dividing of which caused several riots and disorders. An information against Francis, Lord Bishop of Hereford, Sir Thomas Russel, Knight, Sir William Russel, Baronet, and John Horniold, Esq. and other commoners, was exhibited in the Exchequer, in Hilary term 1630—1, by Sir R. Heath; whereupon a decree was made by consent of the parties for the disafforestation of the same, and by his Majesty's letters patent, dated

May 12, 7th of his reign, it was declared to be
d'safforested ; but the said decree proving doubtful
in some things, a bill of review was exhibited by
the commoners, which being brought before the
king's council, it was by them ordered, that all
controversies should cease, that no part should be
enclosed but the king's, and that learned council
in the law, should meet in the beginning of Michaelmas term then following, to settle all differ-
ences ; in which term, by the barons of the exchequer, it was declared, adjudged, and decreed,
that only the king's part should be enclosed, and
that the other two-thirds to be for ever left open
and free for the commoners to take their common
of pasture, and common of estovers therein, as
before they had been accustomed : and that no
mean lords of manors, or other freeholders, should
enclose any part of the same, or fell any woods or
trees growing thereon, whereby the commons
might be hindered of their estovers ; and, amongst
other things, it was then decreed, that no new
cottage should be erected on the third part allotted
to his majesty, or any new tenement, whereunto
there should not be laid and continued twenty
acres at the least, nor any new cottage erected on
any part of the said two other parts to be left to
the commoners, but such only as should be war-
ranted by the laws and statues for the maintenance
and provision of the poor, and that the king's
part, wherever set out, should contribute to the

charge of church and poor, in the several parishes where they shall lie. This decree, made November 19, 8 Charles I. was afterwards ratified and confirmed by an Act of Parliament, 16 Charles II. most of the king's third part being then, by mean conveyances, come into the hands of Sir Nicholas Strode, of the Inner Temple, Knight, and the rest, in Herefordshire, being then in the hands of John Birche and William Thackwell, Gentlemen.

Since that period, however, there have been several trials respecting the right of common, all of which were terminated, so as ultimately to establish that privilege (with very few exceptions) equally among thirteen parishes, which are situated upon the confines of the ancient chace, until that part of the common, which was in the parish of Hanley, began to be enclosed.

The lord of the lordship of Hanley was the chief lord of this chace, and of all the royalties of it, and appointed the constable of the castle of Hanley, the parker of Blackmore, the steward, the bailiff, the master of the game, four foresters, and a ranger, to hold, once in the year, a lord day and a court baron: every three weeks, to determine all manner of pleas and trespasses, debts, or detainer, which exceeded not the value of forty shillings. To this court, besides the homage and customary tenants thereof, were free suitors, the Abbot of Westminster, the Abbot of Pershore, the Prior of Much Malverne, the Prior of Little Malvern, the

Lord Clifford for the lordship of Stoke-upon-Severn, the Lord of Madredsfeyld, the Lord of Bromesbarrow, and the Lord of Byrtes Morton.

The Bishop of Worcester had lands within this forest, for, in the 8th of Richard I. John de Constantiis, then bishop, had liberty granted him to assert, in his own wood, in the forest of Malvern, near to the mill of Wenland, three hundred acres of land, for the use of the church of St. Mary Wigorn, to hold to him and his successors for ever, and to do herewith what they would, free from all exactions of the foresters. These lands of the bishoprick were, it seems, encroached upon by the trench made by the Earl of Gloucester, on the top of Malvern hill before mentioned, which, by the mediation of Robert Burnell, Bishop of Bath and Wells, and others, was thus ended, that the earl and his countess should pay, yearly, to the bishop and his successors, a brace of bucks and a brace of does, out of his chace of Malvern, at his palace of Kemsey: and, in the vacancy of the see, the same to be paid to the prior and convent of Worcester, demanding them, by their attorney, at the castle of Hanley, which agreement was afterwards confirmed by King Edward I. at Norham, 19th year of his reign. These privileges were granted to the Bishops of Worcester; but we do not find that ever they were free suitors to this court.

No sheriff, escheator, or any foreign officer whatsoever, had any power to intermeddle within the said lordship: but the bailiff of Hanley was to execute and serve all precepts, and to return the same at his jeopardy: and, as for the peace, no warrant from the justices to be obeyed or executed there by any foreign officer, for as much as the constables of the said lordship of Hanley were to sue and arrest the parties, named in the said warrants, and the said parties to commit to ward.

The foresters only had authority to arrest every felon, for felony and murder, found within the said chace, and they were to bring him before the chief forester, who held of the chief lord in fee by a certain rent of an axe and an horn; and he had power to sit in judgment on the said felonies and murders, as also to execute the office of a coroner: and if the persons tried were found guilty, by the verdict of twelve men, thereupon charged and sworn, of the four next townships, adjoining unto the place where the said felony and murder was done, his head was to be struck off with the forester's axe, at a place called Sewet Oaks, within the said chace, where they always sat in judgment on such persons, and the body was to be carried unto the height of Malvern hill, unto a place called Baldeyate, and there to be hanged on a gallows, and so to remain, unless license were granted by the chief forester to take it down; which power of judgment extended from a certain place called Charmey's Pool, upon the south part, unto a certain place called Gowelfyate, upon the north part, and in breadth, from a way called the Roadway, unto the height of Malvern hill. Beneath the said Roadway, as far as the franchise of Hanley extended, the power and authority of sitting on judgment on felony and murder, and also of executing the office of a coroner, belonged to the constable of the castle of Hanley; and the person accused was to be brought before the steward at Hanley, and there interdicted, and if found guilty, he was to be executed at a certain place called Ryddegreen, within the said franchise aud liberty of Hanley. There were also certain verdurers, viewers, and riders, which, by their tenure and holding of land, had power to ride and perambulate the ground, soil, and townships, of every lord, from the aforesaid Charmey's pool unto Powyk bridge and Braunceford bridge, to oversee the highways and water courses, and to take care that the wood edges adjoining to the chace be lawfully made for the preservation of the deer. Also for the hombling of the dogs, the said viewers and riders were to have the oversight and the correction thereof, twice every seven years, and such manner of dogs as were found unlawful, that is to say, as could not be drawn through a certain sterop of eighteen inches and a barley corn in length and breadth compass, the farther joints of the two middle claws were to be cut clean away, and the master and owner of the dogs were to be amerced 3s. 1d.

To add one thing more. As many as were free suitors unto the aforesaid lordship of Hanley were to be arbiters, and had power to reform the homage, and the twelve men, at every law day, and other courts, in all such matters as were done by them wrongfully and unlawfully to any of them and their tenants, dwelling in the said chaço: and the said homage and jury of twelve men were to be ordered and reformed by the said free suitors, according to law and reason. Lastly, if need required, the said free suitors were to be of counsayle at the said law day, and other courts with the aforesaid homage, and they and their tenants, dwelling within the chace, were to have the same freedome and liberties with the tenants and inhabitants of the lordship of Hanley. See documents relative to the law of forests, in an Appendix to the History of Malvern, in Dr. Nash's Worcestershire.

CHAPTER XI.

NOBLEMEN & GENTLEMEN'S SEATS

IN THE

Vicinity of Malvern.

MADRESFIELD,

The elegant modernized seat of the Right Hon. Earl Beauchamp, of Powick, is situate to the right of the Worcester road, from Malvern. The luxuriant woods of lofty oaks and spreading elm and beach, which surround this charming mansion, are in full view from the village of Malvern, stretching over to the banks of the Severn; but the house is entirely hid, except from the summit of the hills.

In a right line, the distance is perhaps not two miles; but by the Worcester road to Newland Green, and thence to the house, may be nearly three. Passing Newland Chapel, to the right, a level road brings the stranger to a handsome modern park gate, with lodges of cut-stone, from whence a well-gravelled winding road, thickly skirted with trees, leads him to the small chapel of Madresfield, now in the grounds. This rustic scene of mortality, though close to the road, is so completely embosomed in trees as to shew nothing but

its humble turret and spire peeping forth, until
it is approached, when it appears in all the solemn
silence adapted to such a scene. Though very
small, it has double ailes, quite in the Gothic
style, and is extremely neat in the inside, but
without destroying its air of antiquity; and altogether presents a very picturesque appearance.
A fine extent of lawns and rising plantations are
now seen through the trees to the left, as they have
judiciously been cleared of their underwood for
that effect; some well-formed and quite inartificial
pieces of water also appear; and, at different
breaks, the house, with its venerable moat, are
some times caught; when, at once, by a sudden
sweep, the tourist sees an extensive lawn, with
the mansion on his left. It has been said, that
this is a true representation of an ancient baronial
castle; but the fact is simply, that it is an old baronial castle, "but unfortunately too much modernized," says Mr. Laird, in his Beauties of Worcestershire, "in some parts of the outside;" a fault,
however, which the present noble proprietor seems
to have, in some measure, corrected. At the same
time he confesses that, in those parts where the
mansion has gained in comfort, convenience and
elegance, it has unavoidably parted with a portion
of its ancient grandeur. Still, however, the very
first glance brings back the days of old to the imagination; the moat still sleeps along the walls,
whose grey foundations spring from the water:

the bridge which crosses to the gate also, has an air of much antiquity, and though the excursions of fancy may, at first sight, have been a little checked by unbattlemented walls and square modern windows; yet the gateway, with its flat gothic arch, its grated doors, its spandrelled roof, and solemn silence, soon restore that illusion which destroys the recollection of intervening centuries, and peoples the gloom with iron-clad knights, stiff bodiced dames, sprightly pages, milk white palfreys, the twanging horn, and the minstrel's tinkling melody.

This impression is still kept up in crossing the interior court, which is irregularly grand, and surrounded by the most antique part of the house. We now pass through a vestibule, and enter the

Hall.

This is a lofty, ancient apartment, well preserved, or rather restored; for we believe the house suffered much in 1646, when it was a garrison for the king, being taken from the Lygons, who were then on the Parliament side, and kept against several attacks, until it surrendered along with Worcester.

The lofty, ancient roof is in good preservation, and a fine effect is produced, by the glow of the modern painted glass, in its richly tinted windows, which throw a most striking light upon some very large paintings from the Shakespeare gallery, whose subjects are well adapted to the scene around. Some elegant candelabra are also here displayed, and a solemn gallery, dimly lighted from windows of orange and purple glass, and ornamented with some antique and highly valuable marble slabs, lead us to the

Breakfast Room,

Which is rather low, as are indeed most of the ancient apartments in the mansion, but is elegantly fitted up in a most domestic style, with a handsome bow recess, and some very superb cabinets. From hence the

Saloon,

Which is highly deserving of notice, for the elegant profusion of its painted glass, producing the mellow tone of evening, even in the glare of day, leads us to two

Drawing Rooms,

Superb in the extreme, without, at the same time, being rendered unfit for social intercourse, as is too much the case with many apartments of laboured magnificence. Here are elegant marble slabs, which are interesting, not only to the mere hunter after fine furniture, but even to the naturalist Here also are some very curious cabinets of highly gilt brass and tortoise-shell from the *Garde meuble* of Louis XVI. and here is even the one which stood in his own private chamber, not only before the revolution, but for some time after its commencement. The ideas, excited by this specimen

of magnificence and memorial of departed, in-
sulted royalty, are of a nature that will not admit
of discription, but must naturally strike every
feeling heart with a conception of their force and
extent. We now enter the

Dining Parlour,

Which is rich in the extreme, though so *elegant* as
even to seem plain amidst its glow of decoration;
its walls are crimson, with white pannels, and ornaments interspersed with classical medallions, in
chiaro scuro.

Over the chimney piece is a very handsome
flower piece, in the style of Van Huysum. The
candelabra are classically elegant; and the general
effect of the apartment is well preserved, and even
heightened by the judicious light, which is admitted
only from one window. This apartment leads into
the *Orangery,* which, indeed, seems to form a part
of it; and the effect produced, when its doors are
thrown open, by the gleams of tinted light from
its painted glass, crossing the simple rays from the
dining room window, is rich and bizarre in the extreme, whilst the perfume arising from its glowing
exotics, adds to the general impression. The
windows of the orangery open at once to the
grounds, which, seen through their variegated
shades, have a most picturesque effect. A steep
staircase, which seems constructed in one of the
ancient *towers,* being too broad for a turret, leads
into the

Winter Drawing Room,

An apartment where there seems to have been a sedulous attention paid, lest comfort should be sacrificed to show, yet elegance has not been neglected.

This room is hung with great taste, and its walls are, in some measure, covered with a profusion of rich miniatures, commencing with Holbeins, several of which are evidently originals, exhibiting a general collection of portraits, foreigners as well as natives, both male and female, from the reigns of Henry VIII. to Charles the II. One of them, in particular, is highly curious, being but the size of a common miniature, and containing seventy heads, all of which are portraits. Books, music, &c. complete the furniture of this room, which opens to the

Long Gallery.

This is the ancient gallery of the old mansion, and is preserved quite in its antique state, but rendered sufficiently comfortable and commodious for domestic purposes; it seems to be now the general mansion room of the family. Its furniture is in a good style, and it is ornamented with a profusion of pictures, books, busts, china, &c. and is, in short, quite a cabinet of curiosities. From its windows are some very fine views of the grounds and of distant scenery; and from it opens the

King's Room,

As it is called—a plain simple bedchamber, in

which the family tradition says that King Charles
II. slept, the night before the battle of Worcester.*
From this we go to a

State Bed Room,

Containing an elegant bed, whose quilt and furniture, of flowered damask, embroidered in coloured silks, were worked by Queen Anne and the
Duchess of Marlborough. We now descend the

Staircase,

Which is light and airy, and has a good Dutch
painting of a shipwreck. Upon the whole, the
variety of curious, as well as elegant furniture, collected here by the taste of the present
noble owner, renders it a place well worthy examination. "This, however," continues Mr.
Laird, "is not allowed, in general, from the inconvenience it would be attended with, to its noble
owner, through its near approximation to a watering place." The grounds are very extensive, but

---

" * The house at the corner of the north end of New-street, on the east
side, is said to have been the king's quarters, whilst at Worcester. The
tradition, is handed down in strong and direct terms, by the oldest
inhabitants of the city, and by the relatives of the proprietor and pos-
sessors of that house, at that time, whose names were Durant. The
room in which the king slept faces the corn market. Over the entrance
of the house is the inscription, " Love God and honour the King." All
this, however, does not contradict the story of King Charles having slept at
Madresfield, on the night which preceded the battle."—*Green's Worcester.*
With submission to Mr. Green, I conceive it is more likely the king slept
nearer the scene of action, the night preceding the battle : it is said,
he also slept at the White Ladies ; but I hope to throw a gleam of light
on this circumstance, in a projected history of Worcester.   I. C.

rather flat, except two small eminences, which, being judiciously planted, have a very good effect from the house, from whence the lowness of its situation does not preclude it from a fine view of the Malvern hills, which are just at that distance, that softens all deformities, without removing beauties, beyond the reach of examination.

MRS. WAKEMAN's,*

Near the church of Little Malvern, is the remains of a gothic building, to which is attached a round tower : this is the property and residence of Mrs. Wakeman, situate on the spot where the ancient monastry once stood. Near the front of this house, is a fine piece of water, and its situation commands various beautiful prospects : the declivity of the adjoining glen, clothed with bold impending wood, and the hill receding above, affords a scene highly romantic, to which the church of Little Malvern, covered with ivy, and peering above the house, gives considerable effect. To the eastward lies an expanse of fertile meadows, variegated with trees, rendering this place one of the most romantic situations near Malvern.

BROMSBEROW PLACE

Is situate near the southern extremity of the Malvern hills, at a distance of about eight miles from

* Mrs. Wakeman was the Miss Williams mentioned in page 102, as late of Little Malvern.

the Well-house. It was, formerly, the residence of Col. Walter Yate, and, afterwards, became the property of H. W. Yate, Esq. It is now occupied by John Biddulph, Esq. This is a handsome spacious building, containing many excellent apartments, some of which are furnished in a style of great taste and elegance. A gravel walk, through a shrubbery, on the confines of a beautiful lawn, leads to the gardens, the walls of which are concealed from the mansion by the form of the intervening ground, so as not to interrupt the prospect, nor break the line of beauty.

The views, from hence, are highly beautiful, and, to the southward, very extensive, being terminated by the distant hills of Gloucestershire. Some small protuberances, enriched with plantation, seen over a varied ground, adorn the western prospect; and the Malvern hills, clothed with hanging woods, contribute to render this scene highly interesting. At this are some remarkably fine elms.

HOPE END

Is situate in a retired valley, on the west side of the parish of Colwal, in the county of Hereford, and distant about three miles from the Holy Well. It was, of late, the seat of Sir Henry Vane Tempest, Bart. but now of E. M. Barrett, Esq. The house is, in part, a modern structure, somewhat large and commodious: some of the apartments are highly finished. This seat is nearly surrounded with eminences, and therefore does not command any distant prospect, except to the southward; but this defect is compensated, by the various and beautiful scenery, which immediately surrounds this secluded residence. In the front of the house, are some fine pieces of water; and, on the banks, are placed, a variety of shrubs and evergreens, which, in conjunction with the water, are highly ornamental. The deer park, which is a small, but pleasant tract, lies on the ascent of the contiguous eminences, whose projecting parts and bending declivities display much beauty.

Much of this park, and its profusion of wood, is to be seen from the house. In the park is an ash of a remarkable growth, said to be, probably, the largest in Great Britain.

OLD COLWAL,

In the parish of Colwal, is a pretty residence, the carriage road being only two, the foot road four miles from the Holy Well. It is the property of Mrs. Bridges, the relict of Richard Bridges, Esq. The house is pleasantly situated at the eastern foot of an eminence which abounds with wood, interspersed with cultivated fields and pastures. The plantations of fir adjacent, display a solemn grandeur over the scene. Springs of water arise at a small distance from the house, affording a plentiful supply for use or ornament. From hence you may view the Herefordshire beacon, terminated by the Malvern hills, which are about two miles distant.

BRAND LODGE,

About two miles distant from the Malvern Wells, is a neat villa, late the residence of Col. Roberts, but now the property of Mr. Bright: it is, at present, occupied by the Hon. Mr. Cocks, the brother of Lord Somers. Brand Lodge stands on the western declivity of a pleasant part of the Malvern hills, on a plain elevated about 500 feet from the level. From this romantic spot is a fine view of the camp, which is about half a mile distant; and there is also a very extensive prospect to the westward. This situation is not affected with that greater degree of cold peculiar to elevated situations, being happily sheltered from the east and north winds; from the former, by the Malvern hills, and from the latter, by woods that lie at an agreeable distance. The front of this house is white, and shaded by a range of evergreens, which give it a picturesque effect.

HANLEY CASTLE,

In Hanley parish, is the property, and late in the possession of Thomas Hornyold, Esq. it is about five miles from the Holy Well: the castle, formerly, belonged to the Beauchamps, Earls of Warwick. Henry Beauchamp, Duke of Warwick, was born 1424, and died at Hanley Castle. With him ended the name of Beauchamp, of which

family there had been six earls and one duke.: the
name has since been revived in other families.
This seat was lately in the occupation of Mrs.
Hall, who kept a ladies school : it is well entitled
to peculiar notice, on account of its beauty and
grandeur. The way to it lies across the chace
leading to the Severn. About a quarter of a mile
from Hanley Castle, is the parsonage of Hanley,
the residence of Mr. Tuberville ; its situation is
picturesque.*

THE BARTONS

Is about a mile from Brand Lodge, two and a half
from the Holy Wells, and about a quarter of a
mile out of the Ledbury road. It is the residence
of Mrs. Griffiths and her sister, and was lately in
the occupation of Mr. Lambert.

BLACKMORE PARK,

Late in the occupation of the elder Mr. Hornyold,

---

* Hanley Castle once belonged to the Lechmeres. Its once venerable
castle stood near the Severn, and must have been a place of some importance, as the residence of the Nevilles, Dukes of Warwick, and afterwards
of the Despencers. It is described as having been surrounded by a deep
moat, forming an immense quadrangle, with a lofty keep. It seems,
however, to have been much delapidated even in the reign of Henry VIII.,
for Leland says, " Hamley is from Upton a mile in dextra ripa Sabrinae,
a mile above Upton and a flint shatta from Severne ; it is an uplandisch
toune ; the castello standith in a parke at the west end of the toune. Sir
John Savage and his father, and his grauntfather, lay much about Hamley and Theoksbury, as keepers of Hamley. The Arles of Glouster were
owners of this castelle, and lay much there. Mr. Cometon alone defaced
it in his time, being keeper after Savage."

is situate about two miles from the Wells, and about three from Hanley Castle. It is the seat of Thomas Hornyold, Esq. whose family is connected, by marriage, with the Russels, of Strensham, the Lygons, and, in short, with all the ancient stocks of the vicinity.

The present elegant house is quite a modern building, in a dry and pleasant situation, and, though comparitively low, with respect to the surrounding scenery, yet possessing extensive prospects on all sides. It would have certainly appeared to greater advantage, as a picturesque object, if the profusion of timber, in the park, had been planted with a little less attention to regularity, particularly as there are some large pieces of water, in its immediate vicinity, which afford good objects for the planter of landscape, but lose all their effect when combined with lines laid down by the rule and square.

WOODFIELD,

In this neighbourhood, was part of the lands of the dissolved monastery of Malvern, as appears by a confirmation of Philip and Mary, of a purchase made by Henry Fayrefield, of that manor, now preserved in a Manuscript, in the British Museum, (Ayscough's Catalogue, 2251-6) and is the more curious, as, in that reign, violent steps had been taken to restore the various church lands to their original purposes.

BIRTS MORTON

May also be mentioned here, as it is within the
range of a morning's ride. It was long the property of a very ancient family of Cornish origin,
the Nanfans; and it is even said that one of the
branch, settled in this county, was instrumental
in the first political rise of Cardinal Wolsey, his
father having been esquire of the body to Henry
VII. and of course about the court. The manor
house is very ancient, and was moated round, but
is now only a memorial of ancient times, the rooms
being all wainscoted and carved with armorial
bearings. In the church, are many curious monuments of different families of consequence in the
county; also one of the late rear Admiral William
Caldwall. In the churh-yard, is a raised monument of the Earl of Bellamont, who died in 1766,
and, by his own express order, was buried here,
in a deep grave, half filled with stones.

CASTLE MORTON,

Lies between Birts Morton and Little Malvern,
but is in Longdon parish; and the hall, which is
near the chapel-yard of Morton, was the foundation of the keep of the ancient castle. Nothing,
indeed, is now to be seen : but the "Murcurius
Rusticus," which was published during the civil
wars, tells a curious story of a party of the parlia-
mentarian army, collected from Gloucester and
its neighbourhood, having come here, in 1643, to

plunder the house of a Mr. Rowland Bartlett, so well beloved in this district for his hospitality, and for his general benevolence and philanthropy, that if these marauders, who amounted to 150, had not taken the opportunity of his friends being at a fair, their force would have been too weak to accomplish their purpose. These rascals carried away a gold watch, and all the plate, money, linen, and all they could find : among other things, valuable both for its rarity and sight, a cock eagle stone, for which thirty pieces had been offered by a *physician*, and refused: but such was their dastardly feeling, that they scattered about the store of sweet meats, not daring to eat them for fear of poison.

EASTNOR CASTLE.

At Eastnor, in the S. E. of the county of Hereford, distant about five miles from the Holy Wells, is Castleditch, and near this Eastnor Castle, the magnificent seat of Lord Somers, erecting, and partly finished from the designs of Robert Smirke, F. R. S. and R. A., architect of Covent Garden theatre, &c. &c. The ancient seat of his Lordship, which was pulled down to make room for the present elevation, was, at least the greatest part of it, an ancient building, drawings of which are in the possession of the family;—to which was added several elegant apartments, built of free stone, on a modern plan, and situate on a fine lawn, having a rivulet flowing on each side. It was a small plain building of white stone, with a portico in front, and semi-circular wings.

The approach to Eastnor Castle is perhaps the finest in England, being through an access of three miles of road composed of fine woody country, where the juniper-tree, the oak, and other trees, form an umbrageous shelter over the domains of their lordly owner, and ever and anon we perceive the noble domain frowning in majestic pride at every opening. The castle is erected nearly on the site of the old family mansion, and exhibits a fine specimen of an elevation of proud baronial dignity; it possesses all the exterior of the ancient castle, but it combines also all the convenience of modern and elegant comfort. Its front spreads from a broad terrace; at each end are seen circular bastions or towers, surmounted with battlements, and its centre rises and crowns the *tout ensemble* of every thing that chivalry can wish for, or romantic feeling produce. The intended grand entrance is not yet raised; but it is presumed, from the appearance of the foundation, the bases of the gothic intercolumniations, &c. that the portico will have an appearance at once venerable, grand, and imposing. Here the projecting declivities of the Malvern hills, and other eminences with which it is environed, being ornamented with a profusion of wood, produce a sublime effect. The park which surrounds it, is extensive and well stocked with deer, and, before the castle is a fine piece of water.

The Dining Room,

A beautiful specimen of the artist's taste, presents a plain but elegantly simple cieling, of oak, in square compartments, ornamented at the ribs, and corners with gold, presenting a chaste and novel effect; the doors are of massive oak, with brass knobs and gothic pannels, as is also the wainscot, chair high, above which the walls are hung with a rich paper of crimson embossed figure; the curtain, of purple velvet and gold bullion, spreads over the whole extent of gothic windows in front, and the chairs of ebony, ivory, and scarlet leather, are in unison with the character of the place; the sideboard recess, at the end of the room, is formed of the gothic, arched with fine oak, with ornaments of gold from their springing and centres; and over the chimney is a portrait of the present Lord, by Harrison, possessing considerable merit;—this is the most finished apartment in the house, and exhibits a fair specimen of what the whole may be expected to realize. The drawing, and other rooms, are of splendid dimensions;—the library is 66 feet by 60, and conveniences of dressing-rooms, chambers, &c. possess all the advantages which may be expected from such an architect as Mr. Smirke.

The following is a list of most of the pictures at

present in Eastnor Castle, not a few of which are excellent; but as they are only hung *pro tempore*, we shall not designate the apartments which enclose them ;—they are as follow :

Lord Chancellor Somers, by Kneller.—Mrs. Cocks, heiress of Castleridge.—Col. Cocks, by Mather Brown.—Mrs. Cocks, first settler of Castleridge.—Richard Cocks, husband of the above, who purchased Castleridge.—The Hon. Major Edward Cocks, eldest son of Lord Somers *, by Bigg.—Charles Cocks, Esq. brother of Richard, proprietor of Dumbleton, Gloucester. —Hon. Mrs. Reginald Cocks.—The late Lord Somers, by Mather Brown.—Sir Richard Cocks, Baron of Dumbleton.—Elizabeth, mother of the present Lord Somers, by Sir J. Reynolds. —Lord Jekyll.—John Cocks, Esq. of Castleridge.—Ditto, nephew of Lord Somers.—A Noble Venetian.—A Holy Family. —Virgin and Child, and St. John.—David, with the head of Goliah.—Empedocles, leaping into Mount Ætna, by Salvator Rosa.—A Resurrection.—Two Historical, said to be by Polemberg.—Poultry.—Crucifixion, by Salvator Rosa.—Archbishop Tillotson, by Kneller.—The Poulterer, by old Mieris.— Virgin and Child, by Carlo Dolce.—A Marriage of St. Catherine.—The Philosopher.—The present Lord Somers, with a lock of his brother's hair, who was drowned bathing, a whole length, by Romney.— A Portrait of the Chancellor Somers, and one of the Duke of Shrewsbury.—James Cocks, Esq.—Lord Chancellor Somers.—Rev. Thomas Cocks, of Castleridge.—Mrs. Cocks, of ditto.—Greenwich Hospital.— Sampson and Dalilah.—Thomas Cocks, Esq.—Hobbes, the Metaphysician.—Henry VIII.—Mrs. Cocks, of Castleridge.— Rubens' Wife.—Miss Freeman.—Perseus and Andromeda, by Cipriani.—The Queen of Bohemia.—Lord Clarendon.—Composition, still life.—The Family of Charles I.—Girl at a Fruit

* Who fell at Burgos, vide inscription on the obelisk.

Stall, presumed by Schalkin.—A Musical Party.—Lady Bartley, mother of Lady Cave.—Lady and Child.—Christ in the Garden.—Chancellor Somers.—Lady Cave.—Two separate whole length Portraits of ancestors of Lord Somers, brother of Richard, Ambassadors to the Czar of Muscovy, in the reign of James I., in eastern costume.—Virgin and Child.—Sir Edward Winnington.—Alderman Nash, the founder of Nash's hospital, Worcester.—Phæton.—A Triumph of Neptune. — John Cocks, Esq. of Castleditch.—Tarquin and Lucretius. —Booth, the actor.—Christ crowned with Thorns.—Dr. Nash, the father of Lady Somers.—Mrs. Nash, the mother of ditto.— Louis XIV.—Butler, the poet.—Henry VII., Mrs. Booth, &c.

Lady Somers's dressing room is decorated with many prints and drawings, of the latter are several by amateurs, relations and friends of her ladyship, particularly ladies, rivalling works by the regular professor : Lady Somers has also a number of interesting relics of her father, the late Dr. Nash, the historian of Worcestershire, drawings and prints illustrative of his works, a curious brass dish, apparently intended for the use of the communion service, at the bottom of which is embossed the subject of the "Two Spies." She has also in her possession the common place book of Butler the poet, also a sort of dictionary, compiled by him, relics highly interesting and worthy the attention of those who are allowed the honour of visiting the interior of Eastnor Castle.

The grounds about Eastnor Castle are assuming a character in unison with the building; already has the lake been rendered more picturesque; the broad terrace is dressed with green house plants; the sward skirts the walks 'turned to pleasure grounds; while glens are forming, as the distances from the castle increase, melting in scenes of uncultivated nature, where art can do nothing to add to their natural beauty. From the castle and the surrounding country is seen the obelisk, erected by the present Lord Somers, about six years ago; it is commemorative of the virtues and talents of his family, and rises ninety feet from the plynth, on each side of which are the following inscriptions, written by its noble erector:

WEST SIDE.

To the memory of John Lord Somers, Baron of Evesham, Lord High Chancellor of England, in the reign of William III. and President of the Council in that of Queen Anne,—To the uniform ability, and integrity of his public conduct, posterity has done justice, by acknowledging, in the most ample manner, the wisdom of his counsels, and continually appealing, both in, and out of Parliament, to the opinion of Lord Somers, as the standard of political rectitude. His spirited defence of the seven bishops in a court of justice, and his able speech in Parliament, proving the abdication of King James, are well known. The nation, it is generally admitted, is indebted to him above any other statesman, for the union between England and Scotland, and the establishment of the Protestant succession. When his political enemies of the day impeached him before his Peers, the House of Commons did not appear at the bar of the House of Lords, or attempt to prove a criminal act against him. He was loyal and faithful to the Sovereign whom he served, a sincere and useful friend to his country, and to his family he bequeathed what they ought to value above earthly possessions or dignities—a great and good example; in gratitude for which, and in general admiration of his character, this Obelisk is erected by his heir and representative, John Somers, Lord Somers, Baron of Evesham.

EAST SIDE.

LORD CHANCELLOR SOMERS, died a bachelor, and had no brothers—his only sisters were Mary and Elizabeth Somers; Mary, the elder, was the wife of Charles Cocks, Esq. of Worcester, nephew of Thomas Cocks, Esq. of Castleditch; and Elizabeth, the younger, of the Right Honorable Sir Joseph Jekyll, Knight, Master of the Rolls. Lady Jekyll left no issue, consequently, in the descendants of her sister Mary, must be traced the heir and representative of Lord Chancellor Somers: she had only two children, who eventually left issue Margaret, Countess of Hardwicke, and John Cocks, Esq., who, by his wife and cousin, Mary Cocks, heiress of Castleditch, had many children. The eldest son and heir, Charles, was created Lord Somers in 1784, and was succeeded in 1806 by his eldest son, who erects this Obelisk, A. D. 1812.

SOUTH SIDE.

Inscribed to the memory of James Cocks, Ensign in the Guards; he was the only surviving issue of James Cocks, Esq., eldest nephew of Lord Chancellor Somers, and of Ann, sister of the last Lord Berkeley, of Stratton,—possessed of an ample patrimony, he preferred honor to security, and before he had attained the age of twenty, fighting for his country, fell in battle at St. Cas, on the coast of France, A. D. 1758 *.

NORTH SIDE.

Inscribed to the memory of the Honorable EDWARD CHARLES COCKS, eldest son of John Somers, Lord Somers, and Margaret Lady Somers, his wife. With strong inducements to apply himself to the safer duties of civil life, the energies of his mind

* He was the first to land upon, and the last to quit, the enemy's coast.

determined him on a military career. Having chosen a profession, he devoted himself to it with successful ardour and perseverance; at the age of 26 he fell, respected, beloved, and regretted. His great Commander, the Marquis of Wellington, thus officially announced his death to the Secretary of State, Earl Bathurst:—" At three in the morning of the 8th (October, 1812,) we had the misfortune to lose the Honorable Major Cocks, of the 79th, who was Field Officer of the trenches, and was killed in the act of rallying the troops, who had been driven in. I have frequently had occasion to draw your Lordship's attention to the conduct of Major Cocks, and in one instance very recently, in the attack of the hornworks of the castle of Burgos, and I consider his loss as one of the greatest importance to this army and his Majesty's service." Lord Wellington had successively recommended him to the brevet rank of Major, and Lieutenant-Colonel in the army ; the former, in acknowledgment of previous good conduct, and the latter, as a reward for his gallant acts in the siege which proved fatal to him. Both recommendations were confirmed by authority ; but that to be Lieutenant-Colonel, not till five days after he had bravely fallen before Burgos.

A father who loved, and thought highly of his son, feels himself justified in inscribing these truths to his memory ; and bound to add, that he acted on public and religious principles, and that he was dutiful to his parents, an affectionate brother, a sincere friend and benevolent man.

THE CHURCH AT EASTNOR

Is, with regard to its exterior, an object of picturesque effect, peeping from among the trees; its interior is dry, comfortable, and clean, and in perfect character with the scene around it; but it is distinguished by the splendour of many elegant monuments, and we never remember to have seen a church of so small an extent embellished with so many tributes of vain but elegant regret:—here lie many individuals of the Cocks' family, for the ground is literally paved with the names of his Lordship's ancestors. Among those monuments entitled to notice and admiration, is one to the memory of Joseph Cocks, Esq. who died in 1775, at the age of 42; it is executed by Scheemaker and Stuart, and exhibits the bust of the deceased, with other sculptures. Another, by Scheemaker, is erected to the memory of Mrs. Mary Cocks; it displays a figure of Hope, with a rich urn, and a boy with an inverted torch. There is also a monument to the memory of Mrs. Elizabeth Cocks, on one side of which is the pelican, the symbol of maternal affection; on the other side, a female, bowing with resignation to the will of God. This design is by Westmacott, and is highly creditable to his talents; it possesses all the classical simplicity of the veteran Flaxman. There are two other monuments, by Scheemaker—one to the memory of the Rev. Joseph Cocks, the other, commemorative of the virtues and talents of Edward Charles Cocks, brother to the present Lord Somers, who was unfortunately drowned at the early age of 14, while at school at Westminster.

" Unfortunately for his friends, not for himself, for he was innocent and good, his faults and frailties trivial;—to him, therefore, to be taken out of the world, must be happiness, through the merits of Jesus Christ, of whose blessed sacrament he was a partaker the day before his death. To his elder brother, who erected this monument, he was all that could be wished."

At the bottom of a long inscription, is the cap of Westminster, and a few volumes, one of which is open, with the beautiful words from Milton's Lycidas, inscribed on a leaf:—

"Where were ye, nymphs, when the remorseless deep
Clos'd o'er the head of your lov'd Lycidas."

This sculpture is the expression of an idea full of tender sentiment, as is also that of the lock of his brother's hair, represented in the hand of the present Lord Somers, in his whole length portrait, by Romney, in the castle.

Imperfect as is this account of Eastnor Castle, it is the only one in print.

Eastnor Castle is open to the public every Tuesday, from 11 to 5 o'clock.

THE RHYDD

Is five miles from the Holy Well, and now the residence of Anthony Lechmere, Esq. banker, of Worcester, than whom, no one is more revered as a neighbour, respected as a gentleman, or valued as a skilful agriculturist. The lands round about his dwelling are employed by him in grazing to a great extent. This seat, standing on a rising ground, is a fine object from both sides of the river, which is here seen, skirted with fine wood, and trees raising their bushy heads above the steep cliffs which form the Severn's bank, near which they rise like a bold barrier from the inundations of the river, which forms a pleasing curve under the cliffs, from whence an extensive view stretches over Worcester, to Perry Wood, and towards Staffordshire.

SEVERN

Is a little to the left of the above, and is the comfortable residence of Mr. Terrett, whose house you arrive at through the Rhydd-green, an open unwooded space of considerable extent, very distinguishable from the hills. Near this place is also another house called the RHYDD, the residence of Mrs. Allen, whose grounds command a fine view of the Severn; and almost contiguous to this estate is

DRIPSHILL,

The rural and picturesque abode of William Chambers, Esq.: the place was long the residence of Sir Charles Trubshaw Withers, to whom the city of Worcester are obliged for planning the Sansom Walks. Over these residences, at a distance of 13 miles, the woods, plantations, white rotunda and gothic church of Croome, the seat of the Earl of Coventry, arrest the eye, and will amply gratify the spectator's nearer survey.

Excursions from Great Malvern, down the River Wye,

Are often made by the visitants from this charming place—their best order of rout is as follows:

1st Day.—Arrive at the Swan Inn, at Ross, which is 21¼ miles, where boats are provided with provisions.

2d Day.—Embark, view Goodrich Castle, &c. arrive at the Beaufort Arms Inn, Monmouth, require 8 hours.

3d Day.—Continue down the river, view Tintern Abbey, &c. &c. &c. to the Beaufort Arms Inn, Chepstow, require 9 and 10 hours.

4th Day.—View Chepstow Castle, Piercefield Walks—this will require 2 hours; they are only to be seen Tuesdays and Fridays—ascend Wind Cliff —see Ragland Castle—sleep at Monmouth.

5th Day.—View the church at Ledbury, and the paintings at Upper Hall, the property of John Marton, Esq. M.P. for Overbury, inhabited by John Kerney, Esq.—return to Great Malvern.

The HEREFORD MAIL COACH sets out from the White Horse Cellar, Piccadilly, London, at half past eight in the morning, arrives at the Angel Inn, at Oxford, (54 miles) at four in the afternoon; sets off from thence at four the next morning, and arrives at the Star and Garter, Worcester, at twelve at noon (57 miles); sets out from Worcester at half past two P. M. and arrives at the Crown, Great Malvern, at three in the afternoon, and at the Malvern Wells, (121 miles from London,) at half past three; reaches Hereford at six in the evening, 22 miles from Malvern Wells, and 143 from London. It goes from Hereford to Worcester every Tuesday, Thursday and Saturday mornings, at half past six, and returns the same days through Malvern. There is a stage coach which sets out an hour earlier, and goes to Worcester every Sunday, Wednesday, and Friday, and returns the same day; and various others, whose hours of departure and return are continually changing.

MALVERN BOTANICAL NOTICES

Of a few rare specimens which are found in great perfection, in the compass of a morning's walk round the hills:

Great wild climber, *clematis vitalba*, a most exuberant parasitical plant, twisting round every thing in its way, and even hauling down the fences—a troublesome hedge weed—the cottony hairs of this shrub are said to be manufactured for some purposes in France, and have been recommended here for the stuffing of chair bottoms.

Spreading bell flower, *campanula patula*, *Linn.* July, along the hedges and sides of the roads.

Snow drop, *galanthus nivalis*, a very pretty specimen in February and April, but too early for visitants, grows at the foot of Malvern hills.

Meadow saffron, *colchicum autumnal*, *Linn.* or autumnal colchicum, found in the pastures and low meadows, in October, between Madresfield and Blackmore Park, &c.; its root has long been in great esteem, as a specific for the dropsy.

White stone-crop, *seedum album*, *Linn.* whilst sauntering amongst the rocks round St. Anne's

Well, June and July, many handsome specimens of this may be found.

Wood calamint, *melissa calamintha,* is plentiful in thickets and amongst hedge rows, in the very fullest time of the season.

White climbing fumitory, *fumaria clavicularia, Linn.* is found, July, in great quantities, in the rough stony places, by the sides of the hills, particularly on the eastern declivity, and about Great Malvern town.

Besides these, the *digitalis,* fox-glove, grows about Malvern, the specimens of which are beautifully luxurious.

CHAPTER XII.

MISCELLANEOUS INFORMATION.

Some account of those persons whose literary efforts are connected with the History of Malvern, Poetical Tributes, &c. &c.

SIR REGINALD BRAY,

Who superintended the renovation of the old Malvern Church; St. George's Chapel, at Windsor; and Henry VIIth's Chapel, at Westminster Abbey, of which he has the credit of laying the first stone, was also a patron of the fine arts. He was born in the parish of St. John's, Worcester, about the year 1424: he was a great statesman and soldier—-and was intrusted with the plan of raising Henry VIIth to the throne. Knighthood was conferred on him by Henry, for his valour at the battle of Bosworth' Fields, and he was appointed constable of Oakenham Castle, in Rutlandshire, and Chief Justice, with Lord Fitzwalter, of the forests south of Trent, &c. He died in 1502, and was buried in his own chapel, at Windsor, where his coffin was discovered in 1740. Hollingshed says

" He was a verie father of his countrie, and for his high wisdome and singular love to justice, well worthie to bear that title. If anie thing had been donne amisse contrarie to law and equitie, he would, after an humble sorte, plainlie blame

the Kinge, and give him good advertisement that he should
not only reform the same, but also be more circumspect in
anie like case."

His portrait, in Jesus chapel, is in tolerable perfection.*

JOHN ALCOCK,

Bishop of Worcester, 1476, was born at Beverley, Yorkshire, and educated at Cambridge; he
was Dean of St. Stephen's, Westminster, Keeper
of the Great Seal, President of Wales, Master
of the Rolls, and Chancellor of England. About
the year 1481 he re-built the church of Little
Malvern, a chapel at Beverley, and a chantry
for the souls of his parents, &c. &c. He was
a considerable writer and an excellent architect;
and lies buried in the chapel or chantry which he
founded in 1484, on the south side of Trinity
Church, at Kingston-upon-Hull. Alcock had the
honour of christening the high and mightiest
Prince Arthur.

THOMAS ABINGTON, or HABINGTON,

Who wrote an account of the painted glass, &c.
at Malvern, was born at Thorp, near Chertsea, in
Surrey, August 23, 1560, admitted a Commoner of
Lincoln, Coll. Oxon, and afterwards sent to the
universities of Rheims and Paris. He was confined
six years in the tower, for combining to release

* It is said, we know not upon what authority, by the editor of the
"Beauties of England and Wales," article Worcestershire, that Sir
Reginald was born at Malvern.

Mary, Queen of Scots, but being godson to Queen Elizabeth, was pardoned. He afterwards narrowly escaped with his life, for being concerned in the celebrated gunpowder-plot, with an injunction, it is said, of never quitting Worcestershire. It was during this seclusion that he set himself to collect the antiquities of the county of Worcester, which he left in manuscript. He wrote also an account of the cathedrals, and of the Bishops of Worcester, printed in 1717, and re-published in 1723. He died, October 8, at Henlip, 1647, aged 87.

DR. HOPKINS.

Dr. William Hopkins, the historian of Malvern, whom we have mentioned in a note at page 110, as having B. D. only against his name in *Green's Worcester*, in the list of Prebendaries, was a native of Evesham, and born August 28, 1647. He was the son of a clergyman, and was entered of Trinity College, Oxford, in 1660, and in 1671 attended Mr. Henry Coventry, who was appointed ambassador to Sweden, as his chaplain. Dr. Hickes, in his *Septentrional Grammar*, and Bishop Gibson, in his continuation of *Camden's Brittannia*, article Worcestershire, owe much assistance to his learned communications. In 1675 he was made prebend of the Cathedral of Worcester, in 1698 master of St. Oswald's Chapel, and died without issue May 18, 1700: it is not said if, or when he took the degree of D.D.

DR. WILLIAM THOMAS,

Author of the Antiquities of the Priory of Great Malvern, &c. was born 1670. He was grandson of Bishop Thomas, and only son of John Thomas, and Mary, the daughter of Mr. Bagnall, of Worcester. He was educated at Westminster school, from thence elected to Trin. Coll. Cam. June 25, 1688, took his Master's degree in 1695, and soon after went into orders. In 1718 he took the degree of Dr. and had the living of Exal, Warwickshire, given him through the interest of Lord Somers, to whom he was distantly related. In 1700 he travelled to France, and married the daughter of George Carter, of Brill, in the county of Bucks, by whom he had a numerous family. In 1721 he came to Worcester for their education, and in 1723 was presented to the rectory of St. Nicholas, by Dr. Hough, to whom he dedicated *Antiquitates Prioratus Majoris Malverne*, 1725; his edition of *Dugdale's Warwickshire*, in 1730, and his *Survey of Worcester Cathedral*, with an account of the bishops to A. D. 1660, in the year 1736. To Dugdale he made many valuable additions: he died July 26, 1738, aged 68, and is buried in Worcester Cathedral.

JOHN WALL, M. D.

To whom the public are principally indebted for the virtues of the Malvern waters, was born at Powick, in the county of Worcester, 1708; he was the son of Mr. John Wall, mayor of Worcester in 1703, and was educated at the Grammar School of Leigh Sinton and that of the Cathedral of the city in which he was born, elected a Scholar of Worcester, Coll. Oxon, in June 1726, and Fellow of Merton 1735; soon after which he took the degree of Bachelor of Physic, and removed to his native city. In 1740 he married Catherine, youngest daughter of Martin Sandys, of the city of Worcester, barrister at law, and united to the first Lord Sandys. He took the degree of Doctor of Physic in 1759, and continued in the practice of his profession until his death, which occurred after a lingering illness at Bath, June 27, 1776, and was buried in the Abbey church, where a plain stone on one of the pillars enumerates, in concise terms, his eminent abilities and goodness of heart. To the exertions of Dr. Wall, the city infirmary owes much of his usefulness. The establishment of the porcelaine manufactory of the city also originated with him; and he found time, during the continued and arduous pursuit of his profession, to cultivate the art of painting; many of his productions are in the possession of private individuals, one of which, a large historical painting, he presented to Merton College, Oxford; he also made the design for the window at Hartlebury. As productions of art, they are upon a large scale, and do not yield in point of merit to many cotemporary productions. Lord Lyttleton expressed an opinion, that if Dr. Wall had not been one of the best physicians, be would have been one of the best painters of the age. He wrote experiments and observations on the Malvern waters, &c. &c.

To Dr. Wall, on his publishing his Experiments and Observations on the Malvern Waters.

Hail, thou whose every act bespeaks
   A heart humane and kind,
Whose soul with secret pleasure seeks
   The welfare of mankind.

Hence prompt to choose the generous theme,
   Which might new health bestow ;
To paint the clear, the healing stream
   Where Malvern waters flow :

For this, by various arts, you sought
   Their virtues to explore ;
For this, with kindest skill, you taught
   Their salutary power.

Here shall the sighing wretch oppress'd
   With pain of stubborn kind,
At once of all his sufferings eas'd,
   Leave all his fears behind.

Here, lepers of a frightful hue
   Discharge their livid spots ;
There, wither'd limbs again renew,
   And cast their scaly coats.

To health and vigour, by degrees,
   The scrophulous and lame
Are rais'd, whose obstinate disease
   No human art could tame.

Here, from the brink of darkness drawn,
  Restor'd to cheerful light,
The wretch looks up and hails the dawn
  Who mourn'd his fading sight.

Oh, Malvern, never envy thou
  The springs enroll'd by fame,
Since Wall's ingenious pen has now
  Immortaliz'd thy name.

Henceforth shall rapturous poets sing
  Of Helicon no more;
The waters of thy purer spring
  Can boast superior pow'r.

We, too, of inspiration tell,
  Since bards who drink shall feel,
The streams from Malvern's holy well
  Can both inspire and heal.

Worcester, May, 1755.   Hydropota.

MARTIN WALL, M. D.

An eminent physician, and reader in chemistry in Oxford, is the son of the late Dr. John Wall, mentioned above, and was born in Worcester.

Dr. Martin Wall was bred at New College, Oxford, where he proceeded M. A. July 2, 1771—M. B. June 9, 1773—and M. D. April 9, 1777; he has published " The Medical Tracts" of Dr. John Wall, his father, collected 1780.—" Malvern Waters," being a republication of cases formerly collected by John Wall, M. D. and since illustrated with notes, by his son, 1806. He is also the author of some curious papers in the transactions of the Manchester Literary Society, &c. &c.

DR. TREADAWAY RUSSEL NASH,

The late historian of Worcestershire, and consequently Malvern, published his book in 1781-4 : he was also the editor of an edition of "Hudibras," 1795.   Dr. Nash was of Worcester Coll. Oxford, M. A. 1746, and B. and D. D. 1758: he died at his seat, at Bevere, near Worcester, January 26, 1811, in his 86th year : his daughter married the present Lord Somers. We hope, in a projected work, to be entitled " *The Worthies of Worcester*," to lay many interesting particulars of Dr. Nash and his cotemporaries before our readers, which have never been before the public.

DR. JOHNSTONE JUN.

And not Dr. John*son*, as we have it in p. 116, was a physician of Worcester, and a Member of the Royal Medical Society of Edinburgh; he was the eldest son of Dr. James Johnstone, M. D. of Worcester, and of Hannah, daughter of Mr. Henry Crane, of Kidderminster, at which place the subject of this sketch was educated, and at Dr. Atworth's academy there. He graduated at Edinburgh, in September, 1773, when he had barely completed his 20th year. His treatise on the *Angina Maligna* was republished in 1779, in an English translation, with additions. In 1774 he was chosen a physician of the Worcester Infirmary, and died in August, 1783, in the 30th year of his age, of the gaol fever—a victim to his humanity. His history of *The Cure and Symptoms of a malignant sore Throat and Fever*, which in 1750 raged in Worcester, is held in high esteem.

DR. MACKENZIE.

Vide p. 115, was also a physician at Worcester, and the first person to whom the Bishop of Worcester communicated the design of an infirmary at Worcester : he was author of *The History of Health*, and a volume of devout meditations.

THE REV. J. BARRETT,

We believe, was curate of Colwall; he wrote a description of Malvern and its environs, comprising an account of the efficacy of the Malvern waters, &c. 1796, of which there is a later edition.

Mr. Barrett's work possesses considerable merit; it has been quoted by many authors who have written on Malvern, but it is at present out of print :—we should be obliged to any of our readers who would transmit any account of the Rev. J. Barrett to our booksellers.

We refer the mineralogical reader to the works of KIDD, FAREY's answer to Dr. GIBLY, in the *Philosophical Magazine*, BAKEWELL, JAMESON, HORNER, and TOWNSHEND, all of whom have, in their works, mentioned circumstances relative to the state of the Malvern hills.

LORD SOMERS.

John Somers Cocks, Lord Somers, Baron of Evesham, Chief Steward of the city of Hereford, and Recorder of Gloucester, was born May 6, 1760, being the eldest son of Charles, the late lord, by his first wife, Elizabeth, sister of Lord Elliot: the present peer was member of Parliament for Ryegate; and in 1806 succeeded to the family honours, by the death of his father. The late lord was a friend to Mr. Pitt, and a supporter of his administration, but the son has generally been on the side of opposition. He married Margaret, daughter and only child of the Rev. Dr. Nash, the historian of Worcester. His lordship had three sons and one daughter : one son, the Hon. Major Cocks, was killed in the service of his country, in 1812. His lordship is the author of the following works :

"A Dialogue on Patriotism," 8vo. 1791.—"A short Treatise on the dreadful Tendency of Levelling Principles," 8vo. 1793.—"Speech in the House of Lords, in favour of the Catholic Question," 8vo. 1812.—"A Reply to the Bishop of Gloucester's Protestant Letter, on the subject of that Speech," 8vo. 1813 ;—and a "Defence of the Constitution against the Innovating and Levelling

Attempts of the Friends of Annual Parliaments and Universal Suffrage," 1817.

The erection by Lord Somers, of his Castle at Eastnor, will ever remain a monument of his taste and liberality, while his kindness and hospitality within it revive in us all the poetical visions of the best character of the feudal times.

DR. LUKE BOOKER, L. L. D.

Author of the very pleasing poem of " *Malvern*," is Vicar of Dudley, Worcestershire, and Rector of Tedstone, Delemere, Herefordshire, of which county he is also a Magistrate: he is a native of Nottingham, where his father was a schoolmaster, who, by four wives, had thirteen children, to four of whom he gave the names of the four Evangelists. Dr. B. was for many years minister of St. Edmund's, a chapel-of ease in Dudley; and, on leaving it in 1806, to enter upon the rectory of Tedstone, Delamere, was presented by his congregation with a valuable piece of plate. In 1812 he returned to his former parish, on being presented by Lord Dudley and Ward to the living of Dudley. Dr. B. has been visited with his share of affliction, and the bitter tears of a father, a husband, and a brother, have been shed by him with real but unavailing regret. His literary productions are, "Malvern," and " The Highlanders," poems.—" Miscellaneous" ditto.—" The Hop Garden," a poem.—"A Discourse on the Duty and Advantage of inocu-

lating Children with the Cow-pox."—"Poems,"
inscribed to Lord Dudley and Ward, having a
reference to his seat at Himley.—"Calista, or a Picture of Modern Life."—"Tobias," a poem.—"Il-
lustrations of the Litany."—"An Address to Parliament, on the Necessity of enlarging the Accommodations in Parish Churches."—"The Temple of
Truth," &c., with upwards of eight Sermons, Ad-
dresses, &c. &c. Dr. Booker has given two volumes cf Discourses on particular subjects, in aid
of building a new parish church at Dudley, the
old edifice being incompetent, from its ruined
state and size, of accommodating a tenth part of
the inhabitants.

Extract from Dr. Booker's "Malvern."

—First—as 'tis fit—thy village, MALVERN! claims
Description's powers; and she, with ready zeal,
Unfurls her canvass for the pleasing task.
Its sloping site (from western gales secured)
Morn's virgin blush beholds, what time the sun,
Darkness dispelling with his orient light,
Summons the lark to quit his mossy bed,
And sing his matins, quivering in the air.
Its scattered mansions—some like rural cots,
Whited and deck'd with woodbine or with rose;
While some, more spacious, raise their storied fronts
Discried afar:—all neat, in traveller's breast
Mild admiration kindle, and excite
Desire to sojourn, or to spend his days
Where nature looks so lovely.—Here no damps,
In swampy marsh engendered, ever rise

Baneful to health : no poisonous breezes blow ;
No smoke ascending from unnumbered fires
(As in the crowded city oft is seen)
Blackens the atmosphere with murky cloud,
Or vestment of inhabitant defiles.
Not his these noisome ills—whose roseate cheek
(Fanned by the purest breath of favouring heaven)
Bespeaks of years a long and happy train.
Beauty no dread has here of felon gnat *,
Despoiler of her lips nectareous dew,
In sleep's soft arms while lies she, fancied bliss
In dreams enjoying, at night's stillest hour
(Where gales impure less gifted climes infect)
Unseen the plunderer enters, where no eye
Obtrudes forbidden, and with lulling hum
Of wings transparent, on the ruby spoil
Alights exulting :—then away he flies,
Insidious ingrate ! poisoning the source
From whence his sweets he drew.—So ruins, oft,
The viler felon, man, some artless maid,
And leaves her, pitiless, to grief a prey,—
To cureless shame and ever dark despair !

THE REV. HENRY CARD,

Vicar of Great Malvern, was born at Egham, in Surrey, 1779 : he was first placed in a private school at Woodforde, and afterwards with Dr.

---

* However trifling a circumstance it may seem, (the total absence of gnats, by which damp and foul situations are generally infested) furnishes, perhaps, as just a criterion of the purity of the atmosphere of this place as other circumstances apparently of more consequence. A respectable gentleman, who had regularly visited Malvern every summer, for more than 20 years, assured the author that he there never saw or heard of an insect of this kind.

Thompson, of Kensington, where his abilities as a reciter in the plays acted at the academy are well remembered. At his thirteenth year he removed from Kensington to Westminster, where he remained four years; in his seventeenth year he entered his name at Pembroke, Coll. Oxon, 1797; he took his Bachelor's degree in 1800. His first literary efforts that appeared in print were the characters of Bonaparte, of Marquis Cornwallis, and Lord Hawkesbury; the two first appeared in the *Herald*, the latter in the *Traveller*. He then wrote a tragedy, called " The Florentines," and in 1803 came out his " History of the Revolutions of Russia;"—about 1804, he produced " Historical Outlines of the Rise and Establishment of the Papal Power;"—in 1807, " The Reign of Charlemagne," considered chiefly with a view to religion, laws, literature, &c.—" Beaufort, or a Picture of High Life," a novel, 1811.—"Literary Recreations," 1809.—" A Letter upon the Subject of Tythes."—" A Letter concerning the Objections made by the Antipœde Baptists to Infant Baptism,"—and " An Essay on the Holy Eucharist." These are the avowed works of the Rev. author; but, we are informed, from pretty good authority, that he is a frequent contributor to a Review of high reputation, and to other literary journals: he is also the author of a comedy entitled " The Son in Law," an elegant production, which issued from the Lee Priory Prees. The letter signed " An Old Westminster," in the *Courier*, and addressed to Sir Francis Burdett, and which at the time it appeared was ascribed to the pen of Mr. Canning by the opposition prints, was written by Mr. Card. Thus, of his literary talents, the public have long passed a favourable judgment. His " Essay on the Eucharist" is out of print ; and it is said to have been so much admired by the late Dr. Vincent, that he spoke of it as the most masterly refutation of the Hoadleyan scheme ever put before the public. To Mr. Card's exertions in the interest of Great Malvern, our pages bear witness ; but we beg leave to add, that when he took possession of the living of Malvern, he found the Sunday school in arrears, and the greatest collection ever yet made for it amounted to no more than 33*l.* In one appeal to the feelings of the visitants, he was enabled to increase the school to nearly 100 children ; and, on the settling of the accounts, there remained a balance in hand of 30*l.* By his second sermon, there was collected at the doors the sum of 56*l.* which, with other donations, will enable him to admit into the school *every poor man's child in the parish.*

JOSEPH COTTLE,

Many years a bookseller, at Bristol, is the author of a poem called " Malvern Hills," 1798 ;—he also wrote " Poems," 1802.—" Alfred," an epic, 1816. —" A New Version of the Psalms of David," 1805.—" The Fall of Cambria," 1811.—" The Mes-

siah," 1816.—and the last edition of "Chatterton's
Works," 1803, was published by Mr. Cottle, in
conjunction with Mr. Southey, P. L., for the exclusive benefit of Chatterton's sister, the late Mrs.
Newton, from the profits of which she received
near 300*l.*:—the notes and essays are wholly by
Cottle.

Extract from " Cottle's Malvern."

" As up I climb, the freshness of the morn
Smells grateful, though no object meets my view.
Through the dark mists, which now with coming day
Struggle for mastery, the giant hill
Casts not a shade. Now back I turn to mark
The winding path, but all is grey and void ;
On every side thick clouds ; the spacious world
Lives but in memory! whilst forth I roam
A wandering, unlov'd, solitary thing.
Now on the Beacon's tow'ring head I stand,
The radient sun just peeps o'er yonder hill
In silent grandeur, whilst the neighbouring land,
Like ocean, drinks the splendour of the morn,
One mass of glory. Now the last faint star
Withdraws its timid ray, and slow the moon
Sinks shadowy in the western hemisphere.
Beneath my feet, down the dark mountain's side,
The clouds are troubled, now dissolve they fast :
A fairy vision! whilst the early lark,
Up through their bosom mounts most merrily."

E. COOPER

Of Magdalen Coll. published, in 1759, "A Poem
on Malvern Spaw," &c.: he was a schoolmaster, of
Chaddesley Corbett, Worcestershire.

ALEXANDER WILSON PHILIP, M. D. F. R. S.

Author of " An Analysis of the Malvern Waters,"
1806, including corrections on " Experiments on
the Malvern Waters," by Dr. John Wall, and
edited by his son, Dr. Martin Wall, of Oxon, is a
native of Scotland : he received his education at
Edinburgh and in London, and at the former place
was admitted a Member of the College of Physicians. He has published " An Inquiry into the
remote Causes of Urinary Gravel," 1792.—" An
Experimental Essay on the Manner in which Opi-
um acts on the living Body," 1796.—" A Treatise
on Febrile Diseases," 4 vols. 1804.—" An Essay on
the Nature of Fever," 1807.—" A Paper on Pulmi-
nary Consumption," in the " Medica Chirurgical
Transactions of London," 1816.—Two papers in
the "Philosophical Journal" of 1815 ;—1st, " On
the Principle on which the Action of the Heart depends, and its relation to the Nervous System ;"—
2d, " On the Principle on which the Action of the
Blood Vessels depend, and their Relation to that
System."—One paper in the same transactions for
1817, " On the Influence of Galvanism in restoring
the due Action of the Lungs."—Also, " An Experimental Enquiry into the Laws of the vital Functions, with some Observations on the Nature and
Treatment of internal Diseases," 8vo. 1817 ; and
various other papers in different periodical journals connected with medicine.

POETICAL TRIBUTES

TO THE

BEAUTY OF MALVERN.

" While Malvern, king of hills, fair Severn overlooks,
And how the fertil fields of Hereford do lye,
And from his many heads, with many an amorous eye
Beholds his goodly sight, how towards the pleasant rise,
Abounding in excess, the vale of Eusham lies," &c.

AGAIN,

" Which manly Malvern seest from furthest off the sheere,
On the Wigornean waste where northward looking neare,
On Corswood casts his eye, and on his home-born chace,
Then constantly beholds, with an unusual pace,
Team with her tribute come unto the Cambrian Queene."
DRAYTON's *Polyalbion*, 1613, *Song 7, vol. 2, p. 785.*

" Health opes the healing power her chosen fount,
In the rich veins of Malvern's ample mount,
From whose tall ridge the noon tide wanderer views
Pomona's purple realm in April pride,
Its blaze of bloom expanding wide,
And waving groves array'd in Flora's fairest hues."
Ode, by T. WARTON, *on his Majesty's Birth Day,* 1790.

———————— " such as decks
The vale of Severn, nature's garden wide,
By the blue steeps of distant Malvern wall'd,
Solemnly vast." DYER's *Fleece,* 1757.

SONNET.

" I shall behold far off thy tow'ring crest,
  Proud mountain! from thy heights as slow I stray,
  Down through the distant vale my homeward way,
I shall behold, upon thy rugged breast,
The parting sun set smiling: me the while
  Escap'd the crowd, thoughts full of heaviness
  May visit, as life's bitter losses press
Hard on my bosom: but I shall " beguile
The thing I am," and think, that (e'en as thou
  Dost lift in the pale beam thy forehead high,
  Proud mountain! whilst the scatter'd vapours fly
Unheeded round thy breast,) so, with calm brow,
  The shades of sorrow I may meet, and wear
  The smile unchang'd of peace, tho' press'd by care!"

W. LISLE BOWLE.

" Through Ledbury, at decline of day,
The wheels that bore us, roll'd away,
To cross the Malvern Hills. 'Twas night;
Alternate met the weary sight
Each steep, dark, undulating brow,
And Worc'ster's gloomy vale below.
Gloomy no more, when eastward sprung
The light that gladdens heart and tongue;
When morn glanc'd o'er the shepherd's bed,
And cast her tints of lovely red
Wide o'er the vast expanding scene,
And mix'd her hues with mountain green;
Then gazing from a height so fair,
Through miles of unpolluted air,
Where cultivation triumphs wide,
O'er boundless views on every side,
Thick planted towns, where toils ne'er cease,
And far spread silent village peace;

As each succeeding pleasure came,
The heart acknowledg'd MALVERN's fame.

Oft glancing thence to Cambria still,
Thou yet wert seen, my fav'rite hill,
Delightful Pen-y-vale! Nor shall
Great Malvern's high imperious call
Wean me from thee, or turn aside
My earliest charm, my heart's strong pride.

Boast Malvern, that thy springs revive
The drooping patient, scarce alive;
Where, as he gathers strength to toil,
Not e'en thy heights his spirit foil,
But nerve him on to bless, t' inhale,
And triumph in the morning-gale;
Or noon's transcendant glories give
The vig'rous touch that bids him live.
Perhaps, e'en now, he stops to breathe,
Surveying the expanse beneath;
Now climbs again, where keen winds blow,
And holds his beaver to his brow;
Skims o'er Worc'ster's spires away,
Where sprung the blush of rising day."

BLOOMFIELD.

*The following Lines were written by a Lady at Malvern Wells,
in 1801, and were first, and the only time, printed in a
" Guide to the Watering Places, for 1810."*

Where Malvern rears her sky capp'd head,
And smiling health has fixed her court;
Where purest streams their blessings shed,
And balmy zephyrs laughing sport.

I often wander forth at eve
To view the soft retreat of day;
The tranquil shades my mind relieve,
As night unfolds her cloak of grey.

Then, where no footsteps mark the hill,
Or sounds obtrusive strike the ear,
Save the low murmur of the rill
That fills Hygea's fountain near.

I woo thee, Hope! sweet child of Heaven,
And press thee fondly to my breast;—
For, ah! to thee, the power is given
To soothe e'en misery to rest.

Oh! never more my bosom leave,
Too long the prey of fell despair;
Still with delusive tales—deceive—
Still smiling chace away my care.

Bid drooping fancy live anew;
Her pencil guide with fairy art;
Tint her soft scenes with golden hue,
And let the sunshine reach my heart.

E. C. S.

THE HEREFORDSHIRE BEACON.

BY 'G. H. TOULMIN, ESQ.

I.

When armed hate, with gore defiled,
Vindictive roam'd his mountains wild;
Or, ambush'd in the dusky wood,
As the gaunt wolf terrific stood, —
'Gainst foeman rear'd the bloody knife!
When *Albion* bled by native strife!
Rampart sublime! thy bale-fire high
Blazed as a meteor of the sky.

II.

From hills remote, to meet the war,
Barbaric roll'd the Scythian car;
With stern delight the chieftains red,
From *caves* the painted Britons led;
When near they view'd the hostile field,
Clang'd were the spear and bossy shield—
Foremost thy steep ascent to gain,
As erst in contests fierce, the leaders of the plain!

III.

On thy bleak summit, altar crown'd,
Within the circle's magic bound—
With mystic spells, the Druid priest,
Prepared the rituals of the feast;
Pour'd the libation to the power,
Who ruled supreme in battle's hour:
Whilst fix'd he pray'd the *Gods* to gain,
Quaff'd was the *Mead* from skulls of warriors slain.

IV.

Rampart sublime, of iron war!
The Roman eagle from afar
Cower'd as he ken'd thy crested pride!
Whose mighty strength the host defied!
Freedom thy birth exulting view'd,
From thee she saw her foes subdued!
Time has in vain the mound essay'd,
Where fled from tyrant power her last retreat she made!

V.

Bulwark of sacred *Freedom*, hail!
No more thy soil fierce bands assail—
No more is heard wild war's alarms—
The banner'd shout, the clang of arms!

But peaceful on thy hallow'd ground,
The shepherd feeds his flocks around !
Freedom again resumes her throne,
And makes fair *Albion's* land her blest abode alone !

VI.

Oh ! *Liberty,* Heaven's best award,
Its blessings *thus,* 'tis thine to guard !
Aloft thy ensign wide unfurl'd,
Waves o'er the zone that girds the world!
With sun-burnt face thy front is seen,
Keen the fix'd eye,—with dauntless mien—
Albion's brave sons, thy throne defend,
And nations *saved* by thee, in adoration bend!

Written at Worcester, Sept. 1815.

APPENDIX.

APPENDIX,

The Sunday School at Great Malvern

Owes its foundation to the liberality and philanthropy of the Hon. Lady Lyttelton *, who has for
many years exerted herself, and continues to
watch over the morals of the lower orders of society
round Malvern, in the welfare of which place she
has always felt much interested. The school is
held, until the new school house is dry enough

---

* The Right Hon. Apphia Baroness Lyttelton is the second daughter of
Broome Witts, Esq. late of Chipping Norton, Receiver General of the
county of Oxford, and born April 27, 1743. She was first married to
Colonel Joseph Peach, second in command in the East Indies, who
died at Monghair. On her return to England she purchased the Leasowes, in the parish of Hales-Owen, once the property of William Shenstone, Esq. where she lived in retirement until her marriage, June 26,
1772, with the late Thomas Lord Lyttelton, only son of the celebrated
George Lord Lyttelton, who ever expressed the highest respect and ten-
derest affection for his daughter-in-law, who became the solace of his
latter days, and incessantly watched by his pillow during his last illness.
The letters presumed to have passed between the great Lord Lyttelton
and the present Lady Lyttelton, and published under the title of " The
Correspondents," 2 vols. 1776, are *certainly* fictitious. We have, in
page 90, erroneously styled her Ladyship " The Dowager Lady L."

for the reception of the children, in a room over a house of public resort, called the *Unicorn*, which is also appropriated to the meeting of a friendly society: and as early as the year 1814 we find her Ladyship indefatigably exerting herself to gain the gift of a spot of ground on which she might, at her own expence, erect premises more suitable to the occasion. It was first in idea to erect the building, adjoining to the *Crown* inn stables, close to the road. She applied for the grant of a piece of land to Mr. Foley, in 1814, who suggested that the approbation of the Rev. Dr. Graves, then Vicar of Great Malvern, should first be granted. With the consent of both parties, she ultimately (April 11, 1815,) gained permission to build the present edifice on part of the glebe*. The circumstances of, and in what manner the money was procured by lady L. for the payment of building the school, is interesting.—When her Ladyship married Col. Peach, he presented her with a valuable set of filagree dressing plate, and she determined (for her Ladyship is not a woman of large property) to dedicate at one time or other the value of the plate to some charitable purpose, and a more convenient opportunity never presented itself than at Malvern, to honor the memory of the donor by so worthy

---

* Which was given up by the vicar for the time being, who received, in lieu of it, the ground by the Crown stables, alluded to above.

an application of his gift, particularly as her Ladyship has arrived at a time of life which makes death more than usually uncertain. We shall be somewhat particular in our account of this school, in order that, if its prerogative should at any time be broken into, a reference to our work may enable some person to recover its right and proper title, and for this purpose we insert the following communications from a deed preparing for the purpose, well aware that the funds for many a useful institution, particularly those dedicated to schools, have been perverted from the uses of the donors, and persisted in, for want of any ready reference with regard to their original destination :—

" Sir,   " Pickham Grove, July 3, 1817.

" As I obtained the favor of a grant of land, Aug. 7, 1814, from Edward Foley, Esq. lord of the manor of Great Malvern, through the application and at the particular request of the Rev. Morgan Graves, D. D. late Vicar of Malvern, on which to erect a building for a Sunday school, with a snitable outlet, and it being now completed, I request you will prepare a deed that may be duly executed and enrolled, thus to enable me legally to give the school-house, by a separate distinct deed, to the parish of Great Malvern for ever in trust. The undermentioned gentlemen I wish you to request to do me the honor to accept such trust, for the security of the building and premises, and that it may never be converted to any other use than a school, nor any other school than a Sunday school, and the number of children never to exceed 90. The trust to take also the sole direction and guard of any fund that may hereafter be formed for the repair of the structure out of the interest of it ; and, finally, the trust to confirm the appointment of a master or mistress in case of a vacancy, by death. Whenever a change might be found requisite by a local Committee, such local Committee to be authorized by the Trustees, to direct and superintend the business and progress of the school, and enforce all the appointed rules for the management of it, written on boards and fixed in the school-room.

" A. LYTTELTON.

" To W. Wall, Esq.

INTENDED TRUSTEES.

" Edward Foley, Esq.	Rev. F. E. Witts.
Earl Harcourt.	Captain John Witts.
Earl Beauchamp.	Wm. Wall, Esq.
Rev. Henry Card.	John Surman, Esq.
Anthony Lechmere, Esq.	And the Churchwardens for the
Admiral West.	time being."

Intended Business of the Local Committee, authorized by the Trustees for the Management of the Sunday School at Great Malvern.

The Committee to meet once a year in the school-room, in the month of August, after the sermon has been preached for the benefit of the charity, at which time the accounts to be audited, and an examination of the state of the school business in general; and, in particular, as to the religious improvement of the children, eighty in number; ten additional may be admitted as preparatory scholars, should the Rev. H. Card judge it proper, in order to keep up the full number of eighty*.

* It is presumed this will tend much to encourage the ten extra children in application and correct conduct, as it holds up to them, in the event of their behaving well, the gift of clothes, &c. which the select eighty will be entitled to.

Lady Lyttelton, as President during her life, to have the privilege of appointing the master and mistress;—after her death, the privilege to devolve on the Committee, by vote, to be confirmed by the Trustees. In the like manner an appointment of a necessitous widow or spinster, of suitable age, to live rent free in the cottage part of the school-house, to keep it clean and aired, &c. the master and mistress not being intended *ever* to reside in it, lest it might occasion embarrassment, should their removal become requisite, or otherwise unfit; the kitchen and dark sleeping-room adjoining being the only apartments. The small east room on the ground-floor, appointed and locked up, for transacting the affairs of the school. The long room adjoining, appropriated for the children to dine in;—each child to bring its dinner, living either near or distant, and *this rule* to be made a condition of *admittance into the school,* for which suitable tables are provided, and seats, in which seats their new garments are always to be locked up. This room *never* to be *converted* into one for teaching, the extra expence of building it being designed to induce *regularity* and *decency,* which are considered by the donor *essential parts of education,* and most important to be enforced in the lower orders of youth of each sex.

The Committee will exact of the master and mistress, *invariably,* mild behaviour to the children, and strict attention to every rule on the boards hung up in the school-room.

Every subscriber to the school of one guinea, or a donation of five guineas, to be of the Local Committee if agreeable to them.

Her Ladyship has also determined, that the exterior of the school-house shall be finished with a gothic architrave, or in some way completed so as to make it in *accord* with the church adjoining ;—and, after her death (for the humility of her Ladyship will not allow it to be done during her life), her armorial bearings to be erected on the outside, and at a conspicuous part of the elevation, with the following inscriptions :—

" Every devoted thing is most holy unto the Lord."

Leviticus.

and

" But Jesus said, suffer little children to come unto me, and forbid them not."   *St. Matthew.*

And here we cannot help admiring, in the above clauses, the care with which her Ladyship has guarded her infant institution from imposition or irregularity; at the same time, she has exerted herself to prevent any nuisance resulting from it annoying others.

In consonance with her Ladyship's idea of setting her house in order, before the time comes when she shall be no more seen, and stimulated by that propensity which has ever actuated her Ladyship, in the wish to be of service to her fellow-travellers through this life, Lady Lyttelton has conferred a lasting benefit on Malvern by founding the following institution :—

A School for Ancient Industry for spinning of Wool, Flax, Hemp, Knitting, &c. &c.

It being judged expedient that there should be an institution of a school of *real* industry, for females in the poorer classes of this parish, an unexpensive building is erecting near her Ladyship's cottage, Pickham Grove, in which is a room 35 feet by 14, suitable for the work to be carried on by 30 children, taught to card and spin wool, flax, and hemp, knitting and every sort of *common needle work*,—such as making and mending coarse garments, jackets, and linen for their parents and themselves, to be able thus to be comfortably and cheaply clothed (as in times past) in apparel suitable to their condition in life. And, to preserve to society an useful *hardy* peasantry, it is intended to encourage field work *; and, that it may not be the means (as certainly it has been when under no restraints) of corrupting young persons' morals, one of the matrons of the school will always attend and work with them in the fields. Reading will be regularly attended to, and religious duties enforced, and the scholars encouraged by an exact account of their respective earnings.

The Lord of the Manor, Edward Foley, Esq. has generously given some timber for the building, and unites with the Rev. Henry Card, and the se-

* Such is the present eager efforts after light and *genteel* work by the peasantry of Great Malvern, that the farmers find great difficulty in procuring weeders, &c.

veral land and freeholders, in granting leave for
the enclosing of the school-room on the waste land;
and many of them, who could make it convenient,
are liberally aiding the work by drawing materials
to the spot—a very important assistance, as well as
a most pleasing proof of the unanimity and zeal
for the benefit of the poor, so creditable to the
parish, that it cannot be doubted that the visitors
of Malvern, under the pressure of the times, will
be induced to contribute, by small subscriptions,
to a fund for an unexpensive erection, and to purchase raw materials, cheap implements, benches,
&c. for the school business.

The suggestor of the plan feels it incumbent on her to give a proof of the conviction of its utility, by a subscription of	£10	10	0
Hon. Mrs. T. Yorke......................................	1	1	0
Fennes Trotman, Esq....................................	1	0	0
Mrs. Law, Lady of the Bishop of Chester............	1	0	0
Lord Beauchamp	10	10	0

Subscriptions will be received by the landlords of
the several hotels, and at the library, &c. &c.

Long may her Ladyship live to continue her benevolent exertions, so advantageous to the community at large, at a time when the necessity of all
ranks "*falling into their own level*," appears the only
means capable of saving the country and working
our own *real* happiness; and, when it pleases the
divine Disposer of events to call her Ladyship to
himself, she will leave behind her the name of a

benefactress to human nature—a more proud appellation than that claimed by the visionary levelling reformer, who increases the evils with which his country is visited, by unnerving the arm of exertion, and by rendering every one dissatisfied with his situation. To such men the efforts of her Ladyship will be treated as chimerical and delusive ; but let them visit Malvern, and they will acknowledge their capability, if they shut not their eyes wilfully against conviction.

BISHOP ALCOCK's LETTER.—See page 104, note.

Littere direct ; a domino episcopo Priori et conventui Minoris Malvernie.

" Right well beloved bretheryn, I grete you well. And as it is notory knowen through all my diocyse, to the grete displeasure of Godd, disworshipp of the church, and slaunder to the religion of the blessed Patrone thereof Saynt Bennet, and many other innumerable blessed confessors of the same, the mysly-vying and dissolute governnance of the bretheryn that hath byn inhabite yn the place of Littel Malverne, beying of my fundacion and patronage; the rules of that holy religion not observed ne kept, but rather the seide bretheryn yn all their demeanounce hath byn vagabunde and lyved lyck laymen, to the pernicious example of all Christen men, and therefore it is a grete presumpcion, that the grete ruyne of the church, and place, the decay of lyvehood, and the grete poverty that the seid place hath be now late yn, was that Godd withdrew his grace and benyfytes, and for the mysgyding thereof was not pleased ; and for as moche as now by his grace and mercy I have bylded your church, your place of your legyng is sufficient repaireid, and as I suppose, a grete part of the dette of the seyde place be content : and for that cause, and by the cause ye shuld the better understande your religion, ye have byn this ii yeres yn worshippfull and holy e places of your religion, supposing that ye be now sufficiently instructe yn the same, I am now content, that everych of you that was ther before now late, when I take the rule thereof into myne hands, except Dan John Wittesham, which by the law may not be thear, resort to the said place of Lyttel Malverne, and thear to abyde and lyve after your holy profession, exhortyng you in the name of our Christ Jesu, the blessed patrone of your religion, and virtute obediencie, et sub pena excommunicationis, that fro henceforth ye kepe your religion with the hoale observaunce and discipline rules thereof, the service of God, nocte dieque, devoutely be said and song; your chapytre, cloyster, fraytor, and dormytor, be kept according, with all dewe obedience nnto your Sovereynes, and that none of the bretheryn go into the towne or the fields without an urgent cause, license asked, and obteigned of the prior; and yet that he that shall be so lycenced have a felow with him; and also, I desire, and will and pray you, for my recompence gostly to have every day a masse at our Lady aulter seyde by oon of the bretheryn for me, videlicit, qualibet die Dominica de Trinitate: die Lune, de Angelis; die Martis, salus populi, die Mercurii, de requiem; de Jovis, de corpore Christi; die veneris, de Sancta Cruce; et die Sabati, de Sancta Maria, cum Evangelio, Stobant juxta crucem, cum collect. Secret et post com. de sancto Johanne Evangelista; ac in qualibet die, post vesperas, cantetur Antiphona, oh Maria, et Johannes, cum versibus, et collectis; and also I will that in every masse be said the collect Rege quis, &c. with the secret et post cum et post mortem meam, in qualibet missa oratio, deus qui inter apostolicos, &c. which articulls, and everych of them above writen, be kept and observed, under the peyne before written, we will and charge you; and yf ye su so doe, ye shall fynde me good Lord to you, and to your place, and ye shall have Godd's blessing and myne, and yf ye do the contrary, I shall see the reformacion thereof to your grevous punyshment; in example of all other. Whereof I wol be right sory, as God knoweth, which ynforce you to be his trew servants, and to doe your dewtye, and ever have you in his blessed kepyng. Written at Bewdeley, in hast, the xxii day of October, anno Domini 1482.

"JOHN ALCOCK, Worcester.

"To the prior and bretheryn of the priory of Little Malvern."—See *Thomas's Survey*."

Since the former part of this work went to press, I have been fortunate enough to gain a sight of the book alluded to in a note at page 31, vol. 2, in which are the following words:—"It is certain that neither Henry VII, his Queen, nor Prince Arthur, were buried here; although there are inscriptions both to Elizabeth and the Prince (see p. 42 of our work). 'Tis very probable that Prince Arthur, making his general residence near the castle of Ludlow, nigh this place, might design it for his burial-place, but being taken off in his youth, and in his father's life-time, his corpse was carried to the Cathedral of Worcester." The author then proceeds to give a description of Prince Arthur's tomb at Worcester from this MS. Vide p. 31 of "*A Journey through England*, in Familiar Letters from a Gentleman here to his Friend abroad; the third edition, with large additions.

"London: printed for J. Pemberton, at the Buck and Sun, against St. Dunstan's church, in Fleet-street, MDCCXXXII."

In page 2, article Entymology of Malvern, add—"We are informed by Mr. Baxter, that Jones, in his *Brecknockshire*, vol. 1, p. 26, makes Moel-y-yarn, which is pure Welch, signify the high court, or seat of judgment."

DESCRIPTION OF MALVERN, 1757,

IN A LETTER FROM BENJAMIN STILLINGFLEET, ESQ. TO MRS. MONTAGUE.

MADAM, *Great Malvern, July* 18, 1757.

At length the hopes of having the honour of a letter from you, and the impatience to be informed of your health, have prevailed over my aversion to writing, which is sometimes so great that I can hardly expect that my friends will forgive me. I have been at Malvern about twelve days, where, with difficulty, I have got a lodging, the place is so full, nor do I wonder at it, there being some instances of very extraordinary cures, in cases looked on as desperate, even by Dr. Wall, who first brought these waters into vogue. I do not doubt but that the air and exercise, which at present is absolutely necessary here, the well being about two miles from the town, contribute very much towards restoring the health of the patients. The road is very fine, and made on purpose for the convenience of the drinkers; it is on the side of a hill, which I am told is found, by exact measuration, in some parts to be half a mile perpendicularly high, above a wide plain that lies at the bottom; towards the well the road ascends considerably, so that I imagine the end of it is not much more than half way up to the top. A gentleman in the neighbourhood* has, at his own expence, made a walk above the well; this walk runs on a level for about 600 yards, winding with the breaks of the hill, and makes the noblest terrace I ever saw, the plain over which you look being bounded by some very fine hills, and on it lying on one side Worcester, on the other Gloucester. The hill is fed on by sheep; here and there some cattle graze; over head, I see my favourite bird, the kite, sailing; and all the while I tread on porphyry, the consciousness, you may guess, adds not a little to my satisfaction, when I consider that princes are proud to have a few pillars of this material. I have now done with the well, and must come to the town, which is the chief place for the reception of strangers; this lies high on the side of the hill, and still on porphyry; the church, which stands a little lower than some parts of the town, was a priory, and is one of the finest and largest parish churches I know of. If you will excuse me, I will transcribe, for the perusal of Mrs. Montague, an epitaph

* Mr. Berkeley, of Spetchley.

on a tomb-stone there, written in Monkish rhyme: it appears
that the person buried under it, was a mathematician, whose
name I do not remember to have heard of; and yet, consider-
ing the age he lived in, in all probability it must be found
in *Vossius* or *Wolfius*. We will, with your leave, Madam,
go a little lower, and here we find very delightful dry meadows, and corn fields, with now and then a spring, which
issues out of the side of the hill, a circumstance I forgot to
mention, in giving an account of the well road: not far below the church, is a spring of the same nature with that at
Tunbridge, which has also done great cures; it is weaker
than that, but it is also purer, and may be drunk with great
safety to some constitutions.

A gentleman whom I went to visit at Ledbury t'other day,
told me he received very great benefit by it about 30 years
ago. I wish this place was nearer to London, for it seems to
be exactly adapted to do you good. There cannot be plea-
santer roads for a wheel carriage than all about this place.
There is a subscription going forwards for building a large
lodging-house near the well; at present there is only one old
house in the town, turned entirely to that purpose, which
contains about fifteen persons, and one large room in it, where
once a week there is a sort of public breakfast and dinner.
We have had one public tea drinking and card playing in the
afternoon, by particular invitation; to-day it will begin on
another footing, and is to be weekly*. Thus I have given you
the best account I could of this place, which, to you, who
are not quite out of the noise of the great world, may appear
of very little importance, &c. &c.

I am, &c. &c.
BENJ. STILLINGFLEET.

* "We hear that a Meeting of the Friendly Society, annually held at
the Crown Inn, in Great Malvern, will this year be held on Wednesday,
July 17, 1754."—*Worcester Journal*, 1754. Our information, then, that
the Crown was opened so lately as 1796, is of course incorrect, See p. 92.

MALVERN HILLS,

A NEW SONG, BY JOSEPH BIRD.

From a Broadside Ballad, printed and sold by J. Grundy,
Friar's-street, Worcester.

Tune—" *Robin Hood's Hill.*"

On *Malvern's* gay summit, so rural and sweet,
Where young Men and Maidens for Pleasure do meet,
You view at your Leisure those murmuring Rills,
That gently are gliding from sweet Malvern Hills.

A Prospect commanding so distant to View,
Those Prospects you have will for ever seem new ;
The Serpentine River our Pleasures do fill,
Which we view from the Summit of gay Malvern Hill.

Ascending this Hill, you may view with Delight,
Old *Gloucester's* fam'd City, and *Cheltenham* in Sight ;
No Prospect is equal, I'll own with it still,
To those we behold upon *Malvern's* high Hill.

The different Counties display'd to your sight,
A prospect of *Worcester*, that place of Delight ;
While gazing Abroad you may view *Over's* Mill,
From off the gay Summit of sweet *Malvern's* Hill.

A prospective View of *North Wales* it displays,
The fair Town of *Radnor*, if strictly you gaze,
Fresh Prospects anew in our Minds 'twill instil,
If you view all around from sweet *Malvern Hill.*

On a clear Summer's Day, when the Sky quite serene,
The Shipping in *King's-road* is plain to be seen,
You *Upton* and *Tewkesbury* may view at your will,
While gazing from off *Malvern's* lofty high Hill.

To the Eastward we view *Bosworth's* gay plain,
Renowned by Battle, where King *Richard* was slain ;
The Flying Fish, too, we behold on *Broadway Hill,*
From off the Ascent of noble *Malvern Hill.*

Thus Prospects anew on this Hill to be found,
You see at your Leisure while viewing around,
The Waters much fam'd by Physicians of Skill,
That's found underneath *Malvern's* lofty high Hill.

For the above letter and song we are obliged to Lady Somers, who extracted them from Dr. Nash's unpublished notes.

Memorandums relative to the first and more recent Notices of Malvern.

FROM THE WORCESTER JOURNAL, 1745.

Whereas there is something regarding the rectory of Birch Morton, otherwise Birt's, or Brute's Morton, in the county of Worcester, which wants very much to be regulated : (a noble design appearing to me to be in a manner lost, or very much perverted,) a meeting of such of the nobility, gentlemen and clergy (now in the county of Worcester,) as have most at heart their king and country's welfare, on Tuesday next, the 11th of February inst. at 11 o'clock in the forenoon, at the 'Talbot, in Sidbury, is humbly desired by

MEDER EDWARDS*,
Rector of Birch Morton.

This meeting is, with all humility, desired by me, who, at the same time, beg pardon for my presumption, in order to a right representation to the king, (and parliament, if there be

---

* " Died 1770,'in the Fleet Prison, where he was confined for contempt of the Court of Chancery, Meder Edwards, Rector of Birt's Morton."

occasion,) of some things essential to my country's welfare, and necessary for the preservation of its borders, upon its true original right and just footing : I have hitherto taken all regular methods for the settling of this affair, which my circumstances will admit, and which I with a good conscience can, without the effect wished.

AUGUST, 1754.—" 'Experiments and Observations on the Malvern Waters,' published without a name. The profits of the work to be appropriated to the augmentation of a sum, raised by subscription, to make the springs commodious."

OCTOBER 7, 1756.—"We hear that, pursuant to the advertisement inserted in this paper, several noblemen and gentlemen, in this county, (Worcester,) met yesterday, and subscribed considerable sums, in order to make the springs at Malvern more commodious and extensively beneficial. This good example, we hope, will be followed by the neighbouring counties of Gloucester and Hereford ; for, as the source of these excellent waters are contiguous to the confines of each, they must, when put in order, be of particular service to them, as well as of general advantage to the public."

An advertisement was inserted in the same paper, for November 18, saying, that several contributors met at Worcester, when a committee was chosen, and Dr. Wall and Mr. Dandridge nominated as receivers, and a meeting appointed, to consider on the best way of employing the money.

JUNE, 1757.—"At ten o'clock every Wednesday, during the season, will be a public breakfast, at 1s. 6d. each person, at Dugard's Assembly Room, in Great Malvern, after which ' The Shepherd's Lottery' will be played here.

" N. B. Music will be in waiting, in order to perform, if the company should be disposed for a dance."

" ☞ Thursday being judged an inconvenient day, occasioned the alteration as above." The charge at Dugard's for diet and lodging, in 1759, was 15s. per week, exclusive of tea, sugar, fire and candles: hot rolls, tea and chocolate 1s. 6d. each person : public breakfast and balls on Wednesday : card assembly on Monday.

1760.—" An annual venison feast established at the Crown, Great Malvern."

JULY 16, 1761.—"Last week Lord Walpole, Sir Edward Blount, and Wm. Warburton, Esq. on different days, complimented the company at Malvern with a breakfast, at the new house at the wells, which gave general satisfaction."

OCTOBER 16, 1761.—"A great storm at Malvern."

APRIL 5, 1768.—" Dugard advertises a large and convenient house at Great Malvern, and that this summer is the second season." This is followed by a paragraph mentioning that there was a numerous appearance of gentlemen and ladies of distinction, mentioning names, at the concert, ordinary and ball, at Dugard's assembly rooms, who were pleased to express their highest satisfaction. "The pureness of the air of Malvern, the convenience of the walks, and variety of fine rides, cannot fail of recommending this place to persons of taste and delicacy, who ask nothing from the waters."

JULY 13, 1769.—"The great house opened near Malvern Wells, and seats erecting in different parts of the hills."

1773.—" A new bath built at Malvern."

LINES,

Wrote on a pane of glass at Malvern Wells, May, 1776.

" Ye nymphs, oppress'd by Wor'ster's stagnant air,
To Malvern's high aerial walks repair,
Where springs, and gales, their mutual aid dispense,
To purge the blood, and quicken every sense ;
Here the pale face its former tints resumes,
And every charm with fresher beauty blooms ;
Haste, then, ye nymphs, and range awhile at large,
So shall ye save for paint an annual charge."

NOVEMBER 16, 1789.—"Mr. Berwick sent me (Dr. Nash) a ring ousel, shot at Malvern ; about that season, or somewhat sooner, they appear in considerable numbers about the foot of the hill, to feed upon the berries of the mountain ash and haws."

August, 1815.—" Some silver pennies of King Edward the IId's time were discovered lately in one of the Malvern hills—they are almost as large as sixpences.

" The neighbourhood of Malvern was lately visited by a storm of hail, thunder and lightning of extraordinary violence—the average size of the hail-stones was that of a walnut, and, in some places, they lay several inches deep."

December 24, 1810.—"There were gooseberries in Mr. Essington's garden (of the Hotel) that measured an inch and a half long, and an inch round ; and six apple trees were in full blossom, in the same garden, in the Christmas of 1815."

DR. BEAL.

Doctor John Beal, vide p. 145 of our work, was an English divine, and a very early and useful member of the Royal Society, having been elected a Fellow in January, 1663. Dr. Beal was born of a good family in Herefordshire, in 1603, and was educated successively at Worcester School, Eton College and King's College, Cambridge, after which he spent some time on his travels abroad. About 1636 he was very useful in promoting the apple orchards in his native county, and was author of a small tract on that subject, entitled " Herefordshire Orchards, a Pattern for England." He resided chiefly at Hereford till 1660, when he became rector of Yeovil, in Somersetshire, where he resided till his death, which happened in 1683, at 80 years of age. Dr. Beal was made D. D and King's Chaplain in 1665: several of his papers were printed in the Philosophical Transactions, and elsewhere. He was a man of excellent parts, extensive learning, and great public spirit.—*Vol.* 1. *p.* 415, *note, Philos. Trans. abridged.*

Extract from his Account of some Sanative Waters in Herefordshire :

"There are two springs in Herefordshire, whereof one is within about a bolt or bow shot of the top of the near adjoining hill of Malvern, and has had a long and old fame for healing the eyes:

when he was for some years molested with tetters on the back of one, and sometimes of both his hands, notwithstanding all endeavours of his friends and skilful physicians, he was speedily healed by a neighbouring spring of far less fame. Moreover, this spring healed very old ulcers on the legs of a poor fellow, after other applications had been useless ; and by many trials upon his hands and the tetters, Dr. B. was persuaded that in long draughts and lasting dry frosts these waters were more effectually and speedily healing than at other times."—No. 20, p. 358 Philos. Trans.

The following Communication, politely transmitted to us, we regret to say, came too late for insertion in its proper place.

TRADITION RELATIVE TO BRANSIL CASTLE.

" Bransil Castle was at one time the property of Mr. Reed, of New Court, Herefordshire, and by him left to his sister, whose son, the late Mr. Sheldon, of the same place, and of Abberton, in Worcestershire, enjoyed it in right of his mother: Mr. Reed was descended from Lord Beauchamp, of Powick, and claimed the title, but died before he could deliver in his claim *. The estate was afterwards purchased by Sir Charles Cocks, father of the present Lord Somers. There is a tradition, that the ghost of the late Lord Beauchamp, who died in Italy, could never rest until his bones were delivered to the right heir of Bransil Castle, and accordingly they were sent from Italy, enclosed in a small box, and are said to be now in the possession of Mrs. Sheldon, of Abberton. The tradition further states, that the old castle of Bransil was moated round, and in that moat a black crow, *presumed to be* an infernal spirit, sat to guard a chest of money, till discovered by the right owner. This chest could never be moved without the mover being in possession of the bones of Lord Beauchamp."

* After the death of Mr. Read, the title of Beauchamp was in abeyance:—he had two sisters, one married to Mr. Lygon, who died without issue ; the other married the father of the late Mr. Sheldon, alluded to above, and who, it is supposed, might have obtained the title.

Translation of the lines on Dr. Wulcher, vide page 50.
See Worcester Journal, Sept. 1778.

" Here lies Dr. Walcher pent up in this cavern,
First a monk of Loraine, and then prior of Malvern ;
His learning extended to all the beau arts,
His virtues were gentle and won all our hearts.
The loss of such worth caused a general mourning,
The poor miss his alms, and the clergy his learning.
October the first he departed this life,
One thousand one hun-der-ed thirty and five,
And 'tis hop'd all his friends, who are piously given,
Will pray most devoutly—his soul is in heaven."

ADDITIONAL SUBSCRIPTIONS

TO THE CHURCH OF GREAT MALVERN.
See page 71.

	£.	s.	d.
Winchcomb Hartley	20	0	0
Sir Henry Carr	5	0	0
Lady Carr, second subscription	5	0	0
Sir Thomas Winnington	5	0	0
Mr. Chase A. Holl	31	10	0
Mr. Bray	1	0	0
Rev. Mr. Hampden	5	0	0
	£72	10	0

To the Sunday School of Little Malvern.—See page 182.

	£.	s.	d.
June. Countess Harcourt, fourth subscription	3	0	0
Col. Watson, Wisbeach, Cambridgeshire	1	0	0
Mrs. Grainger, second subscription	1	0	0
Bishop of Chester, (passing through)	0	10	6
The Hon. Miss Trefusis	1	1	0
Carried over	£6	11	6

Brought over £6	11	6
Earl Harcourt... 2	0	0
Mr. George Wolf...................................... 1	1	0
The Hon. Mr. Bouverie............................ 1	0	0
Mr. and Mrs. Wigram, fourth subscription 5	0	0
Mr. Reddell... 2	2	6
Lord Colchester..................................... 2	0	0
Sundry separate small subscriptions.......... 0	15	6
£20	10	0

On Wednesday, July 7, 1817, several ladies visited the above school, and examined the children in the different branches of their education, in which they found them much improved since last summer, and expressed themselves delighted with the regularity and decency of their conduct, and above all, with their improvement in religious instruction, for which they highly complimented Mr. Phillips, through whose exertions this desirable end has been accomplished.

To the new road.—See page 191.

To the new road.—See page 191.

Sir Robert Wigram...................................... £10 10 0

And here we beg to offer our acknowledgments to Mr. Phillips for the correct information with which he has supplied us during the progress of our work,—we have borne testimony of his zeal for the interests of Malvern, and he is entitled to our sincere thanks for his voluntary services, and for contributing several items to this production.

INDEX.

** The Editor will feel obliged to any Gentleman for corrections or additions relative to the *History of Malvern,* addressed to Mr. Walcott, Bookseller, Worcester.

FINIS.

Printed by T. HOLL and SONS, Worcester.

SD - #0031 - 070323 - C0 - 229/152/16 - PB - 9781331993919 - Gloss Lamination